SEARCHING
FOR THE
LOST TOMBS
OF
EGYPT

SEARCHING
FOR THE
LOST TOMBS
OF
EGYPT

CHRIS NAUNTON

For my Dad, and in memory of my Mum

Frontispiece: One of the colossal statues of Akhenaten discovered at Karnak and now on display in the Luxor Museum.

Searching for the Lost Tombs of Egypt © 2018
Thames & Hudson Ltd, London

Text © 2018 Chris Naunton

First published in 2018 in the United States of America by Thames & Hudson Inc., 500 Fifth Avenue, New York, New York 10110

www.thamesandhudsonusa.com

Library of Congress Control Number 2018932306

ISBN 978-0-500-05199-3

Printed and bound in Slovenia by DZS-Grafik d.o.o.

CONTENTS

INTRODUCTION

THE LIVING, THE DEAD, TOMBS AND REDISCOVERY

The tombs, mummies and spectacular grave-goods that have emerged from the sands of Egypt have come to define what Egyptology means to most people. This is a story about ancient Egypt, and what happened when people in that part of the world, thousands of years ago, died. It's about their belief in an afterlife, and how they buried their dead. It's well known that for the wealthiest and most important members of that society, and particularly for the man at the top – pharaoh himself – funerary preparations were very extensive, and at times this meant constructing elaborate, beautifully decorated and cleverly secured tombs to receive the remains of the dead.

Almost as captivating as the ancient ruins themselves are the stories of their rediscovery – the exploits of a huge cast of explorers, archaeologists, robbers and others who have sought out these tombs, motivated variously by the desire to understand the ancient past, to uncover works of art for people to look at in museums, or just to make a fast buck by discovering rare and beautiful treasures.

In particular, this is the story of a series of tombs that belonged to some of the most famous individuals in the ancient world: Imhotep, Nefertiti, Alexander the Great, Cleopatra and others. Their names have survived in the texts, in hieroglyphs and other scripts and languages, left on the walls of temples and the tombs of their contemporaries, on papyri and other artefacts, and in the historical accounts composed by classical and later writers. The possibility of rediscovering the last resting places of these ancient celebrities, and perhaps even their mortal remains, has inspired many an archaeologist or historian to set out on an expedition to the ruin-rich deserts of Egypt. This is the story of those archaeologists' quests, and an examination of the possibility that some of the tombs in question might yet be found.

Obsessed with death?

The ancient Egyptians have acquired a reputation for being obsessed with death, but it's probably undeserved, and as much about the kinds of archaeological evidence that have survived – and how they have been interpreted – as an accurate reflection of past preoccupations.

Western interest in Egypt's ancient past began to accelerate in the 19th century, following Napoleon's invasion of the country in 1798. At that time many ancient monuments were half buried in drift sand, or overtaken by more modern buildings that had sprung up in and around them, but they were nonetheless very visible. The team of scholars and scientists who accompanied the Napoleonic expedition produced a detailed record of its ancient monuments, a series of volumes published as the *Description de l'Égypte* between 1809 and 1829. Antiquities had already begun to leave the country by this point; by the time the British Museum opened in 1753, around 150 of the objects in its collection were Egyptian. As interest in acquiring such objects among the elite and those collecting on behalf of museums began to grow, excavations uncovered new sites and monuments. Among the most famous of the early Western excavators was Giovanni Battista Belzoni, an Italian who, following a career as a circus strongman, came to work for the British Consul General in Egypt, Henry Salt. Belzoni was among the first to begin digging and made some spectacular early discoveries, including the tomb of Sety I in the Valley of the Kings, and was also the first in modern times to enter the second pyramid, of Pharaoh Khafre, at Giza.

Cemeteries, and the tombs within them, tended to yield antiquities of the most spectacular kind and quantity, and so naturally attracted the most attention. It was immediately clear that the ancient Egyptians believed strongly in an afterlife, and were very concerned to ensure that they got there, through a complex system of beliefs and rituals that, crucially for modern collectors, involved material possessions. The passage of the deceased from this world to the next was conceived as a journey, and the list of provisions with which the dead could be equipped seems to have been almost infinite, and was for most probably only limited by their financial wherewithal and that of their relatives. But most fundamentally of all, a place needed to be found to bury the body – for those who could afford it, an elaborate tomb.

The earliest burials in Egypt, during the Predynastic Period, were little more than shallow pits, covered with a mound of sand, into which the body of the deceased, wrapped in goatskins or mats, was placed along with various possessions – typically pottery vessels, ivory or bone combs, slate palettes and sometimes ceramic figurines. Over time, tombs began to take on a more formal, rectangular shape, the number of items placed alongside the body increased, and the finest examples came to be lined with mudbrick, and occasionally divided into two chambers. The tombs of the kings of the 1st Dynasty are found at Abydos, in Middle Egypt. These were square, brick-lined cuttings in the desert floor, in which a central chamber of wood was constructed. This chamber was surrounded on three sides by storage magazines. It is unclear what lay above these tombs, although a low mound seems likely, and the location of each tomb was marked by two stone stelae bearing the name of the deceased king.

The highest-status burials became larger and more elaborate over time. The number of chambers and provision of funerary equipment increased, and superstructures evolved into straight large rectangular structures, built of mudbrick, sometimes reaching 10 m (33 ft) in height. These superstructures are known as 'mastabas' (an Arabic word for the kind of wooden bench typically found in or outside Egyptian houses), and while many are simply filled with rubble, they sometimes housed chambers – in addition to any subterranean compartments – containing burial equipment, and often incorporated chapels on the exterior in which the bereaved could place offerings to the deceased.

At the beginning of the 3rd Dynasty, a crucial step was taken in the development of royal funerary architecture: the subterranean tomb of the first king of the line, Djoser, was surmounted by a square-based platform, on top of which a sequence of further platforms of diminishing size was placed, creating a stepped structure. This was the 'Step Pyramid', the first example of the triangular building that defines ancient Egypt more than any other. The structure was also revolutionary in being the first monumental structure built of stone anywhere in the world. The Step Pyramid was part of a wider complex of buildings within a vast enclosure, providing not only for the burial of the king but also the maintenance of his cult beyond the end of his life, sustaining his spirit in the afterlife. His successors were to innovate and experiment almost constantly with this type of monument, as their chief architects and builders strove to create larger and more perfect 'true' pyramids, culminating eventually in the reign of the 4th Dynasty king Khufu with the largest pyramid of all, the Great Pyramid at Giza.

Non-royal individuals at this time continued to be buried in mastaba tombs, pyramids being reserved for royalty, and these eventually came to be lined and built in stone and elaborately decorated with reliefs. In addition, during the 4th Dynasty, some tombs began to be cut directly into the rock in the hills and cliffsides at the edge of the Nile Valley.

Pyramids continued to be the default form of burial for pharaohs throughout the Old Kingdom (the 4th, 5th and 6th Dynasties). There seems then to have been something of a hiatus during the succeeding 7th to 11th Dynasties, but the practice was revived in the 11th Dynasty, under Mentuhotep II Nebhepetre, and continued into the 13th.

At least some of the 16th and 17th Dynasty rulers, who were buried at Thebes, seem to have been buried in tombs marked with pyramid superstructures, but at a certain point early in the 18th Dynasty an important change occurred, one that is a defining feature of the New Kingdom. From the reign of Hatshepsut at the latest, the pharaoh came to be buried in a new necropolis hidden away in the high desert wadis to the west of Thebes, which in modern times has come to be known as the Valley of the Kings – perhaps the most famous cemetery anywhere in the world. Here, successive pharaohs cut their tombs deep into the bedrock, with often numerous chambers being built around one or more lengthy passageways, many of the surfaces of which were lavishly decorated with esoteric scenes of the king on his journey to the afterlife. Some had been left open since antiquity, but many more were uncovered by archaeologists, particularly in the 19th and early 20th centuries, culminating in the ultimate archaeological discovery: that of the undisturbed tomb of Tutankhamun by Howard Carter in November 1922.

That Tutankhamun's tomb, and all the fabulous treasures he was buried with, had lain intact since he was buried was exactly how the Egyptians would have wanted it. Unlike earlier funerary monuments – particularly royal tombs surmounted by that most monumental of markers, the pyramid – the tombs of the Valley of the Kings were intended to be invisible once sealed. They lay far away from civilization, in a place that was otherwise entirely barren and unoccupied. They couldn't be seen, and were difficult to get to; anyone who wasn't a part of the official necropolis administration discovered in such an unlikely place would have found themselves with a bit of explaining to do. But part of the reason Carter's discovery was such a sensation was that Tutankhamun's tomb was exceptional in its unviolated condition. Although the ancients' efforts to protect the tombs of the deceased was a significant factor in the evolution of tomb

The southern end of the antechamber in the tomb of Tutankhamun,
shortly after the discovery.

design, they seem ultimately to have been wasted in the majority of cases – practically every tomb that archaeologists have found in recent times was first entered by robbers (ancient or modern).

But what if, in a few select cases, the ancients succeeded in keeping the tombs of their most revered citizens from the robbers? Does this explain why some are still lost, and if so, might it finally be archaeologists rather than plunderers who will be first to the prize?

Provision for the afterlife

As the conventions of tomb architecture developed, so did the canon of funerary rites designed to aid the deceased on their passage to the afterlife. The body itself, before being laid to rest in the tomb, would be prepared for its everlasting survival. It was purified, embalmed, adorned with jewels and amulets to ward off evil spirits and wrapped in linen bandages – the process known as mummification. As part of the purification process, certain internal organs were removed and preserved separately, including the stomach, lungs, liver and intestines. These were then typically stored in a set of four containers, which we now call 'canopic jars', following an early misunderstanding that associated them with the worship of the Greek god Canopus. The mummy was placed inside a wooden coffin, or perhaps a set of nesting coffins. For the wealthiest, these would then be placed within a stone sarcophagus.

During the funeral, a complex set of rituals ensuring the rejuvenation and revivification of the deceased would be performed on the mummy by a priest, and the individual would be buried with all manner of furniture and other items they may have used in this life and would need again in the next, including food and drink, oils, unguents and incense, all contained within a bewildering variety of jars and vessels of various kinds. The deceased would even be provided with a crew of helpers, in the form of figurines called *shabtis* (an Egyptian word meaning something like 'answerer'), which would symbolically perform tasks on behalf of the deceased in the next world. For those who could afford a full set, there would be one shabti for every day of the year, and a sort of supervisor for every ten – over four hundred in total. These shabtis would help the deceased maintain their homestead in the Netherworld, conceived as a

A group of shabtis from a Third Intermediate Period tomb. One foreman oversees each group of ten workers.

boundless field of reeds called Aaru, a pastoral idyll apparently representing the most beautiful aspects of the landscape that surrounded them.

Many such items, particularly coffins, and in many cases the walls of the tombs themselves, were elaborately decorated. Inscriptions would provide the name and titles of the deceased, and sometimes a little information about their accomplishments in life or their close relatives. Other elements of the decoration, both textual and pictorial, described aspects of the journey the deceased would make from this life to the next. The Egyptians seem to have believed that by articulating these things through the texts and images created by the sculptors and painters, they would be made real. All of this investment in providing things for the deceased – items made of the finest materials, and shaped by the most highly skilled craftsmen – ultimately performed a function. In part this involved the memorialization of the deceased, keeping their memory alive for the loved ones who were left behind. But more important was the resurrection of the individual, and their eternal survival, in the afterlife. It was thus not death as such that the Egyptians were preoccupied with,

but life, specifically the next life, which they conceived as being more or less an idealized form of this world.

The association in modern times of ancient Egypt with mummies – all decaying flesh and evil intent – speaks more to a contemporary, gory fascination with dead bodies, and while this was inspired by the mummies recovered from Egypt, the Egyptians would never have thought of them like this, but as rejuvenated individuals in the prime of life. A scene from the tomb decoration of an individual named Harwa, who lived in Thebes in the 7th century BC, illustrates this perfectly. Harwa is depicted in the company of the jackal-headed god Anubis, the overseer of the mummification process, who takes Harwa's hand as he leads him onwards. Here, Harwa is shown as an old man, with a sagging belly and breasts, symbolizing his long and successful (well-fed) life. This scene is followed by decoration in the next part of the tomb relating to the rituals performed on the mummy in order to prepare the body of the deceased for its journey into the afterlife, and beyond this point the scene of Harwa and Anubis is repeated, but now Harwa is shown rejuvenated: his belly and breasts are gone, and he has the slim figure of an athletic youth. *This* is how the Egyptians imagined themselves in death – not as terrifying monsters, staggering around inside their tomb looking for someone to strangle.

So it is true that the Egyptians invested a great deal of wealth and effort in equipping their dead for the next life. But there is more to it than that. The dead were generally buried not in the fertile Nile Valley, where everybody lived and worked, but in the surrounding desert, where the dry, lifeless conditions are perfect for the preservation of material of all kinds, particularly organic material such as wood, which would quickly perish in the wetter conditions close to the river and life of all kinds. And so it was in the cemeteries that the travellers, explorers, collectors and archaeologists who came to take an interest in the ancient remains found an extraordinary wealth of exotic and beautiful works of art. As interest grew and enthusiasts realized that there was more to be discovered with a little excavation, it must have seemed as though there was apparently

Left Jackal-headed Anubis takes the hand of the deceased, Harwa, and leads him on his journey to the afterlife. TT 37.

an infinite abundance of such treasures simply waiting to be carried off, just beneath the sand. It boggles the mind now to think just how much material there was within such easy reach at the beginning of the 19th century. To begin with, such excavations were practically a free-for-all. While permits were issued in some cases, vast quantities of material were removed from the ground without them, sometimes by those interested in keeping it for themselves but also by those who realized they could make a very good living uncovering things for sale to others. For decades, very few – if any – records were made of these excavations. There was no recognition yet of what could be learned not only from the objects themselves, but from where they were found – their archaeological context. In any case, for all the wealth and variety of new material being discovered, so much was either made specifically for the rituals of death and burial, or at least found in and around tombs and cemeteries, that it must have seemed as though the Egyptians were preoccupied or even obsessed with death.

Settlements and the evidence for the real lives of the Egyptians

While this mythologized version of ancient Egypt continued to take hold in Hollywood and the popular imagination, from the second half of the 19th century onwards archaeologists began to seek *information* about the past, rather than beautiful objects alone. And as archaeological endeavour and techniques advanced, it became apparent that towns and cities, not just remote cemeteries, had survived; it would be possible to recover the material evidence of ancient ways of life, complementing the Egyptians' presentation of daily life in funerary art.

But urban sites presented a much greater challenge to early excavators. Domestic buildings were typically made of mudbrick, which has not survived as well as other materials, such as the stone used to build temples and tombs. This is not only because it is naturally less durable, but also because much ancient mudbrick was removed in the 19th century by excavators who failed to recognize its value. Much was lost, for example, in the clearance of ancient temples such as that in the centre of Luxor. An ancient town had grown up in and around the stonework, but centuries of urban development were irretrievably lost in a single stroke as the authorities hurried to reveal the New Kingdom temple. The problem was exacerbated by local farmers, who saw an entirely different value in the ancient bricks – they were very useful as fertilizer for the crops. Furthermore, as settlements tended to be based along the banks of the Nile, where inhabitants benefited from the annual flood that irrigated and fertilized the land, many have disappeared as the river has moved, gradually swallowing up the ancient remains.

Even when they survive, mudbrick houses tend to present a greater challenge to excavators than tombs. They are often part of settlements that were occupied for decades and centuries, and have typically been adapted and rebuilt periodically. That many of Egypt's modern towns and cities lie on top of ancient settlements is a fascinating testament to the continuity of life in this part of the world, but has made it harder for us to access this kind of ancient material. But even in the case of more accessible sites, archaeologists have had considerable challenges to face in disentangling one set of walls from another, and from other debris and detritus accumulated in between. Archaeological material within them might also at first glance seem less promising than the kind of treasures found in the richer cemetery sites: the most commonly recovered object class is the humble potsherd. But these fragments have proved to be of critical value, as over time archaeologists came to amass a vast database of knowledge about their forms and materials, which could be used to establish the age of the original artefact, and, therefore, date the context in which it was found.

Ancient Egyptian settlements can sometimes look like featureless expanses of mud, and must have seemed less immediately rewarding research projects, particularly in the early days of archaeology. But such sites, and the work of investigating them, has been crucial in enhancing our understanding of ordinary people's lives in the ancient past. This approach was exemplified by Sir Flinders Petrie, who is sometimes referred to as the 'Father of Archaeology'. His first excavation in Egypt, in 1884, explored the important site of Tanis in the Delta (to which we will return in Chapter 5). The site was already well known for its temple, and a scatter of associated monumental sculptures, but Petrie was more interested in the city that lay around it. Petrie not only recognized the value of settlement sites like this, but also invented new techniques to recover the new kinds of material they yielded, and had the energy and perseverance to gather, document, analyse and publish vast quantities of it, opening an entirely new window onto ancient Egypt in the process. In the 21st century the focus is shifting again: tombs provided a flavour of ancient Egypt in microcosm; towns and cities revealed a much broader perspective; and now, with a great deal of help from specialists in other fields, such as geology, we are beginning to improve our understanding of the natural environment in ancient times, and how it affected people's lives.

Many scholars have since made their careers out of 'settlement archaeology', but this is not to say funerary archaeology – the search for and study of tombs and burial equipment – has ceased. It continues to yield new discoveries and useful information about the ancient past. And although settlement archaeologists can sometimes be heard to complain that 'we don't need any more tombs!', many Egyptologists continue to be lured to cemetery sites by the greater promise of spectacular discoveries. We don't *need* any more tombs, of course. And I can understand why some archaeologists are much more interested in other kinds of archaeology in Egypt. But it is true that tombs have played an enormous part in helping us to understand what Egypt was like in ancient times, through the intricately detailed scenes of humans engaged in all manner of day-to-day activities – hunting, fishing, farming, craft production and leisure activities – and engaging with a vivid menagerie of animals, birds, fish and insects against the backdrop of various aspects of Egypt's built and natural environments. Tombs provide us with some of the most awe-inspiring works of art, architecture and technology, and some of the most compelling stories of discovery, in our field.

Reconstructing the pharaonic era

The combination of funerary and settlement archaeology and study of the ancient literary sources has enabled Egyptologists to put the flesh on the bones of the chronological framework of pharaonic Egypt, a civilization that endured for three thousand years. The classic view of Dynastic Egyptian history sees this great civilization as having been through a series of peaks and troughs. The age of pyramid-building, which began with the great technological leap that enabled the construction of the Step Pyramid – credited to Imhotep – is known now as the Old Kingdom (2550–2150 BC), and corresponds to the 4th, 5th and 6th dynasties. This was followed by the first of the three Intermediate periods. The second great flourishing of Egyptian civilization is called the Middle Kingdom (2020–1750 BC) and corresponds to the 11th and 12th Dynasties. This was followed by a Second Intermediate Period (1640–1532 BC), the last dynasty of which was the 17th, and which was followed by the New Kingdom (1539–1069 BC), which therefore began with the 18th. The end of the former, and establishment of the latter, did not happen in a single instant, but rather unfolded in various ways over a longer period of time.

The Old, Middle and New Kingdoms are conceived as periods of great achievement – when Egypt was powerful, made great leaps forward in art, architecture and technology, and expanded the frontiers of its territory – and the Intermediate Periods as periods of supposed decline – when it was weaker, sometimes divided and its accomplishments more modest by comparison. This is an extremely reductive and over-simplistic narrative, which masks a much subtler picture of constant change of all kinds. Nonetheless, this framework, created by historians over the last two centuries (contrary to the system of dynasties, which was an ancient idea), is useful to an extent.

The system of 'dynasties' was set down in its final form by Manetho, an Egyptian priest and historian living under the Ptolemaic rulers who wanted a Greek-language version of Egypt's long history. His grouping of kings into dynasties seems to have derived from an earlier system in use by the ancients at least as far back as the 19th Dynasty. The 'Turin Kinglist', or 'Turin Canon', is a list of royal names, in historical sequence, written on a fragmentary papyrus believed to have been written during the reign of Ramesses II, third ruler of the 19th Dynasty. This extraordinary document was acquired in Luxor by Italian antiquities collector Bernardino Drovetti in 1820 and sold to the Egyptian Museum in Turin in 1824. The earliest names in the sequence are those of gods and mythical rulers, but in the third column, known historical kings are recorded in chronological sequence, and separated by headers into dynasties that broadly correspond to those set down by Manetho. In addition to the names of the kings, the number of years each reigned for is given.

The Egyptians dated the historical events they recorded in scenes and inscriptions according to when during the reign of the present pharaoh they occurred. They used a solar calendar, dividing their year into three seasons – Akhet, the time during which the inundation would deposit water on the land, Peret, when the waters would recede and crops would grow, and Shemu, when the crops would be harvested – of four 30-day months, each season lasting 120 days in total. A further 'five days upon the year' were added to bring the total in the year to 365. When they needed to ascribe a date to a particular event, the formula would include the day, given a number from 1 to 30, the month, numbered 1 to 4, the season, in 'Year X' of the reigning king. The first three elements related to the solar calendar and were unaffected by the reign of the king, whereas the last would be re-set with the change from one pharaoh to the next; were a king to die on the first day of the first month of Akhet, the next day would still be the second day of the first month of Akhet, but in the 'Year 1' of the new king. Such dates are invaluable to Egyptologists in establishing the chronological placement of such events, but they are also our main means of establishing the length of the reign of each king. The Egyptians recorded neither the circumstances of the death of pharaoh, nor the date at which it happened. The 'highest regnal date' is therefore the best guide to the point at which any given pharaoh died, i.e. an inscription of year twenty in the reign of such and such a pharaoh shows that he must have reigned into his twentieth year (as the first day of pharaoh's reign would be dated 'Year 1'). Of course such dates are subject to change when new evidence is uncovered: if an inscription dating to the thirtieth year of the same pharaoh were to be uncovered, the length of his reign as recorded in the textbooks would have to be extended by ten years.

There is an additional significance to this: although we have a pretty good idea of the sequence of kings, thanks to Manetho and other king-lists, and the archaeological evidence, we do not often know exactly when their reigns began and ended. The earliest fixed point in Egyptian history is agreed to be 690 BC – the date of accession of Taharqa of the 25th Dynasty, whose reign ended in his twenty-seventh year, which we know, thanks to Assyrian sources that can be correlated with our calendar, fell in 664 BC. But this is relatively late in ancient Egyptian history, a full twenty-five dynasties after the first pharaohs. Highest regnal dates provide our best source of information on the dates of the earlier kings; by adding up the highest dates for all the known kings prior to Taharqa in sequence, and counting backwards from 690 BC, we eventually arrive at a date of approximately 3000 BC for the accession of the first king of the 1st Dynasty, Narmer. Certain points in Egyptian history can be fixed by other synchronisms, like that which allows us to date the end of Taharqa's reign, but events can otherwise not be dated with certainty; for this reason Egyptologists often prefer to use the regnal dates provided by the Egyptians themselves, as these at least provide a date that is reliable within the framework of the reign of the king in question.

When Jean-François Champollion's decipherment of hieroglyphs allowed ancient Egyptian texts to be read for the first time, he and generations of archaeologists, philologists and scholars of various kinds began to gather evidence of the kings of Egypt. The royal names that have been found on countless objects and monuments have allowed us to put the flesh onto the bones of Manetho's lists of kings and dynasties, constructing a reasonably sound chronology defined by the succession of pharaohs. In general, Manetho's lists seem to correspond well with the primary evidence, although, as we will see, some of his names do not match any found elsewhere, while we have also recovered the names of kings of whom Manetho appears to have had no knowledge.

The names given by Manetho are Greek forms of the names given to each king at birth (known to Egyptologists as the 'nomen'). These are the names most familiar to us, such as Ramesses, Amenhotep and Tutankhamun. Each king also had a series of other names referring to various aspects of the kingship, which from the Middle Kingdom comprised the nomen and four other names (the 'fivefold titulary'). This tradition persisted into Roman times. The four additional names included the 'Horus name', typically written inside a rectangular enclosure representing a palace surmounted by a Horus falcon; the 'two ladies' name, following an image of two goddesses, the vulture, Nekhbet of Upper Egypt and serpent, Wadjet of Lower Egypt; the Horus of Gold name; and finally, that which appears most commonly along with the nomen, the 'prenomen', also known as the 'throne' or 'coronation' name, which generally followed the sedge plant and bee hieroglyphs that, with the addition of two 't' signs, is read as *nesu bity*, which we translate as 'the King of Upper and Lower Egypt' – the principal title of the pharaoh.

The use of the words 'upper' and 'lower' here is a reference to the Nile, which runs from Central Africa to the south of Egypt northwards, eventually reaching the Mediterranean. The boundary between Upper and Lower Egypt lay just south of the head of the Delta, the point at which the Nile splits into several different branches; the capital city of Memphis, which lay at the junction of the two lands, was the southernmost of the Lower Egyptian administrative districts. Upper Egypt was the territory to the south of this point (the Nile Valley), and Lower Egypt the lands in the north (the capital city of Memphis and the Delta). The Egyptians considered their country to have been formed by the union of these two lands, and the idea that they were held or bound together is a recurring motif of kingship throughout Egyptian history, most notably in the epithet, 'the Lord of the Two Lands', which was one of the most frequently cited in the titulary of the king. When referring to modern locations, the term 'Middle Egypt' is sometimes used to describe sites along the Nile Valley between the Faiyum Oasis and the province of Assiut, but its boundaries are not clear, and the territory in any case fell within what the ancients considered to be Upper Egypt.

The nomen was not necessarily unique: for example, there were four kings named Tuthmosis and four named Amenhotep in the 18th Dynasty, and eleven named Ramesses across the 19th and 20th Dynasties. Each can be distinguished from the others by their prenomen, which was unique. Thus, Djeserkare Amenhotep I can be distinguished from Aakheperure Amenhotep II, Nebmaatre Amenhotep III and so on. During later periods, things become more confused as both birth and coronation names recur. This has made reconstructing the history of the Third Intermediate Period in particular very tricky. In general, pharaohs are referred to by their birth name, followed where necessary by an ordinal number – Ramesses I, Ramesses II and so on – but their prenomina are sometimes called upon to avoid confusion. Egyptologists tend to use the Egyptian forms where possible, but the Greek forms have also made their way into modern literature: one might variously read that the Great Pyramid was built by Cheops or by Khufu. These are one and the same pharaoh, with the name given in the Greek and Egyptian forms respectively. In some cases, the

Greek forms are so much better established that sticking dogmatically to the Egyptian can be confusing: the 21st Dynasty pharaoh Psusennes is much better known by this, the Greek form of his name, and is almost never referred to as Pasebkhaenniut.

According to Manetho, each king came to the throne following the death of his predecessor. But this leaves no room for those periods when other evidence tells us there was more than one reigning king – one ruling in one location, and another ruling elsewhere, or kings ruling simultaneously as co-regents, as was the case with the woman-king Hatshepsut and her nephew Tuthmosis III. Nonetheless, Manetho's lists provide something of a starting point for our search for tombs: while the places where many of the known kings of Egypt were lain to rest have been identified, a number remain to be found.

Vanished celebrities

Unashamedly, this book isn't about the lives of the ordinary people in ancient Egypt. It's about famous pharaohs and other ancient celebrities, their achievements, the spectacular wealth they may have accrued and been buried with, and the sometimes legendary circumstances in which they were buried – and how those circumstances might have contributed to the difficulties archaeologists have faced in finding them, despite their best efforts.

Imhotep, whose name is best known as that of the principal antagonist in the Hollywood films *The Mummy* (1932 and 1999), is perhaps one of the most significant figures in human history. An official of unusually high status at the court of his king, Djoser, of the 3rd Dynasty, we attribute the design and construction of the Step Pyramid to him. Not only was this the first pyramid in Egypt, it was the first monumental building to be built of stone anywhere in the world. This was no easy feat: erecting a building of stone on this scale – approximately 125 m (410 ft) along the base and 62 m (200 ft) in height – without it collapsing under its own weight required a thorough understanding of the forces and stresses involved, and mastery of design that would distribute the load evenly, resulting in a stable structure. It was a huge leap forward for humankind. Imhotep was remembered for millennia after his death, and even came to be worshipped as a god. As a high-ranking court official, he must have been buried in a substantial tomb, and many centuries after his death, his devotees seem to have identified North Saqqara as the place of his burial, but despite many years of excavations in the area, the tomb has never been securely identified.

Amenhotep I was the second pharaoh of the 18th Dynasty, at the very beginning of the New Kingdom. This great era was characterized by the expansion of the Egyptian empire, and some of the pharaonic period's finest achievements in art and grandest architectural feats. It is in part defined by the adoption of a new means of burying the royal dead, in a remote valley away from civilization, which we now call the Valley of the Kings. Amenhotep's tomb has never been found, yet official records of tomb inspections suggest it was still intact almost four centuries after his death. It cannot have remained so, however, as his mummy was eventually found, along with those of numerous other New Kingdom pharaohs, in the 'royal cache' tomb, TT 320. Archaeologists have long sought the tomb itself, but to no avail.

Akhenaten is one of the great characters of the ancient world. From the beginning of his reign he began a revolution in religion, art and politics, banning the worship of traditional gods in favour of one alone, the sun disc called the Aten. He also adapted centuries-old religious iconography to show not just this one god, but Akhenaten himself, often with his wife, Nefertiti, and their daughters, emphasizing his role and that of his family in the new religion. He smashed the rigid conventions governing the depiction of pharaoh, showing himself in a radically new way with exaggerated features that blur the lines between the male and female forms, suggesting to many modern observers that he may have suffered some terrible illness (see frontispiece and p. vi). Finally, he founded a new capital city at the site we now call Tell el-Amarna, and moved the entire administration there with him. Despite such comprehensive and wide-ranging change, Akhenaten's revolution lasted only a few years beyond the end of his reign, by which time there seems to have been something of a crisis of succession. At some point a boy named Tutankhamun, apparently the only male heir, came to the throne, but died only a few years later without children, thus ending the royal line. A number of individuals are known to have come to the throne after, and even during the last years of, Akhenaten's reign, including possibly Nefertiti, whose image is famous throughout the world thanks to the discovery of a strikingly realistic-looking bust depicting her as a beautiful and confident woman at Amarna in 1912 and now in Berlin. Perhaps owing in part to the brevity of the reign of these individuals, and to the attitude of the authorities in the period after the restoration of the old ways, we seem to be missing much of the evidence of their burials, including at least some of their tombs. Might they still lie undiscovered, as Tutankhamun's did for three and a half millennia?

The bust of Nefertiti discovered by a German expedition to Amarna in 1912 and now in the Ägyptisches Museum, Berlin.

Herihor was an army general of the 21st Dynasty whose influence in Upper Egypt came to rival that of the pharaoh in the north, to the point that he eventually began to adopt some of the trappings of kingship and even enclosed his name inside a cartouche, the name-ring usually reserved for royalty. He reigned at a time when many of the tombs of the pharaohs of the preceding New Kingdom were stripped of their finery and the mummies reburied to guard against their desecration by robbers. Herihor's immediate successors and predecessors seem eventually to have been reburied themselves, but conspicuously almost no trace of any tomb or other evidence for the burial of Herihor survives, leading many to speculate that it still awaits discovery – and may even contain riches to rival Tutankhamun's.

The Third Intermediate and Late Periods, comprising the 21st to 30th Dynasties, are far less well documented than, for example, the New

Kingdom that preceded them. The country was fragmented for much of the period leading to a profusion of ephemeral kings, which archaeologists have struggled to reconcile with kinglists such as Manetho's. But a crucial leap forward was made just before the outbreak of the Second World War, when French archaeologist Pierre Montet discovered a cemetery of the 21st and 22nd Dynasty kings, several of whose burials were intact and preserved some of the most spectacular – if relatively little known – treasures from ancient Egypt (see pp. ix–xi). But gaps remain in the record of the tombs of these lines of kings and also their successors, including all of the tombs of the 26th Dynasty, a time of great achievements in art and of a unified and powerful Egypt, which must surely have been impressively provisioned.

Alexander the Great is rightly remembered as one of the greatest conquerors of any period, the vastness of his territory ensuring that his story has a relevance across Europe, North Africa and Asia. But of all the countries he visited, he was buried neither in his homeland, Macedonia, nor the city of his death, Babylon, but in Egypt. The country, the religion of its people and the might of the monuments erected to their gods had a powerful effect on Alexander. His burial there may have had more to do with the machinations of one of his generals, Ptolemy, following his death, but whatever the reason a powerful myth binding Alexander as a god himself to Egypt sprang up following his death and formed an important part of the basis for the establishment of a new Hellenistic Egyptian kingdom under Ptolemy and his successors. Though his tomb was revered for centuries, and was even visited by many of the great Roman emperors and classical authors, very little archaeological evidence for it has survived.

At the end of the Dynasty founded by Ptolemy, Egypt was ruled by another of the most famous figures in the ancient world: Cleopatra. The story of her life, relationships with first Julius Caesar and then Mark Antony, and the part she played in the Roman Empire, is well known the world over, thanks to the classical sources, but later also to Shakespeare, and then Hollywood. The classical texts provide fairly detailed information about the circumstances of her death and burial, including descriptions of the mausoleum in which she was buried, and yet this, too, is one of the tombs that eludes us. Could it be that its remains have already begun to come to the surface, having been submerged off the coast of Alexandria for centuries, or was Cleopatra in fact buried elsewhere in secret at a location that might yet be revealed by archaeologists still looking for her last resting place today?

There is a certain mystery here – why haven't we found these tombs yet? What's going on? Could the thousands of votive offerings to Imhotep discovered at Saqqara have been left at the location of his tomb? What connection do the anonymous mummies found in KV 35 have to the undiscovered burials of the Amarna royals? And what are the chances that a sarcophagus of the last native Egyptian pharaoh, Nectanebo II, once actually held the remains of Alexander the Great in Egypt's capital city of Memphis?

Ancient names and faces

It is possible to build a case to suggest where each one of these tombs might be. And in some cases, we might already have some of the evidence. As we have seen, the burial of any ancient Egyptian, no matter their status, comprised three essential parts: place (the tomb), equipment (the provisions that would aid the deceased in the afterlife) and body. In the vast majority of cases where we have any evidence of an individual's burial at all, we only have one of these three: we have found thousands of tombs of various kinds, but usually they have been found empty, subjected to robberies in ancient times; other evidence from the same interment might crop up elsewhere, the items having appeared in secondary contexts such as caches, or cropped up without provenance on the antiquities market (in those cases the items were probably discovered in or around the relevant tomb but illicitly, by plunderers, before any archaeologists got there). Thousands, if not millions, of items that would have accompanied burials have been recovered, but cannot be connected to any particular tomb.

In ancient Egypt, we can recognize an alignment with our modern preoccupation with celebrity. The Egyptians placed great importance on setting down the name of the individual at death – believed to ensure a person's continued existence in the afterlife – and the relative abundance of such inscriptions has allowed us to identify the owners of thousands of tombs and items of burial equipment, including major historical figures like Ramesses the Great. The Egyptians' genius for preserving the bodies of the dead through mummification has also meant that human remains have survived incredibly well, allowing us to look at the very faces of the same people whose names we know from the inscriptions accompanying their burial.

What more human qualities can there be than a person's name and their face? Thanks to the Egyptians' skills and funerary practices, which focused on the survival of these elements of a person, and the archaeologists who have meticulously uncovered and recorded them, we can *know* the people of ancient Egypt in a way that is rare in archaeology.

Of course, this abundance of archaeological and textual material raises expectations. We are spoilt in Egyptology in being able to connect so many things to individual people, because hieroglyphs tell us their names; no circumstantial evidence – no amount of high-tech gadgetry, geophysics, magnetometry or ground-penetrating radar – will ever be enough to prove beyond a shadow of a doubt that a particular tomb belonged to such-and-such a person; only when the name of the owner can be read can the identification be made with certainty. And as we shall see, some of our missing tombs might not be undiscovered, so much as unidentified.

Undisturbed tombs…

Perhaps the most exciting prospect when hunting out an ancient tomb is the possibility that it might be *intact*. Howard Carter's discovery of the tomb of Tutankhamun in 1922 was so thrilling in large part because the marvellous objects the young king had been buried with were still in place. Over three thousand years had passed between the sealing of the tomb by the priests of the necropolis and the moment when Carter broke through that same seal, looked beyond and saw 'wonderful things', and yet nothing had moved. I imagine that those intervening millennia simply disappeared for those who were lucky enough to see the tomb in the moments after it was first opened. Like a *Mary Celeste* for ancient Egypt, it must have seemed as though the priests had left only a few minutes before. There's something magical about stepping into a centuries-old scene, every object still precisely in its place – it forces you to consider the actions of those who left them behind, which somehow brings you closer to the Egyptians themselves. In this way, even the 'houses of the dead' can seem to bristle with life.

Though I have never been fortunate enough to be a part of such a discovery, an experience I had in 2006, while working for the Italian Archaeological Mission to Luxor, directed by Dr Francesco Tiradritti, came close. During the previous year, Professor Lorelei Corcoran of the University of Memphis, Tennessee, and I had spent a season together documenting decorated fragments from the walls of the tomb of Pabasa, a high official buried at al-Asasif, not too far, as the crow flies, from the Valley of the Kings.[1] By this time, however, Professor Corcoran's time was taken up with her university's mission, directed by Otto Schaden, which earlier that year had announced the first discovery of a new tomb in the Valley since Carter's great moment in 1922. The new tomb was designated KV 63.

The Theban necropolis is probably the richest of the many ancient cemeteries in Egypt and comprises hundreds of tombs, with more being discovered each year as excavations continue to uncover new material. Here and elsewhere, numbering systems have been introduced in modern times to aid the identification of the tombs, which is particularly useful when the name of the owner is unknown. In Thebes, tombs of non-royal individuals are given a number preceded by the letters 'TT', which stand for 'Theban tomb'. Confusingly, the letters are occasionally changed to reflect more precise locations within the necropolis: for example, TT 320, which, famously, was found to contain the mummies of many of the pharaohs of the New Kingdom, is sometimes referred to as DB 320 because of its location in the area of Deir el-Bahri. Tombs in the Valley of the Kings are numbered according to a separate system, in which the prefix is 'KV' for 'Kings' Valley'. In this case, the system was introduced by the British Egyptologist John Gardner Wilkinson in 1821. He listed twenty-one tombs that were known to him, and tombs discovered subsequently were given numbers following this original list. Hence the numbering sequence, at least from KV 22 onwards, reflects the sequence in which the tombs were found. The tomb of Tutankhamun was the sixty-second to be discovered, and is thus KV 62. And so Otto Schaden's discovery, being the first in the valley since Carter's, is called KV 63. The tombs in a separate branch of the Valley of the Kings are sometimes referred to by a 'WV' ('Western Valley') number, but the numbers are the same as those in the main Valley, hence KV 23 is also WV 23. Tombs in the so-called 'Valley of the Queens' are also given separate 'QV' ('Queens' Valley') numbers, and there are further tombs including many now lost or only recently identified that have not yet been given numbers in any of the main sequences.

Schaden's discovery turned out not to be a tomb in the sense that we might usually mean, in that it was never used to bury anybody; rather, it was an undisturbed cache of embalming equipment, perhaps associated with the burial of Tutankhamun (see Chapter 3). To the Egyptians, the materials used in the preparation of the body, such as jars containing embalming oils or the salts used to purify the body, were themselves considered sacred, even if they were not to be buried with the deceased, and could not therefore be discarded carelessly. Instead, they were often given a burial of their own, referred to now as an 'embalming cache'. The best known of these is a deposit bearing the name of Tutankhamun found in 1907 in a shallow pit in the Valley of the Kings. This was initially mistaken for the remains of the tomb of Tutankhamun, and the pit given a tomb number, KV 54. It was only fifteen years later, when Carter discovered

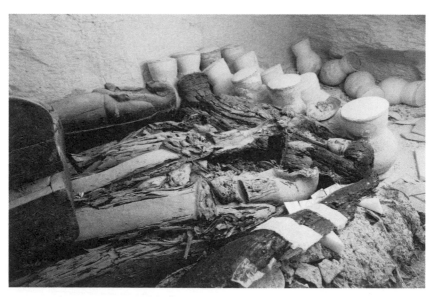

The jumble of coffins and jars as found by Otto Schaden in KV 63.

the real tomb of Tutankhamun in another part of the Valley, that it was shown conclusively that KV 54 was not a tomb as such, but a cache.

I was invited with the rest of the Italian team to visit KV 63 before the objects were removed for cataloguing and conservation – my first encounter with a tomb left essentially intact since it was sealed. It may only have been a cache, but it was still quite a sight. The material – mostly a series of coffins of varying sizes, and some large jars – was obviously ancient, and from its disposition – everything somewhat piled up, without the care and attention we now accord anything this fragile and ancient – obviously still *in place*, exactly where it had been left, probably in the late 18th Dynasty. This was the first time I became aware that objects like this, far from being inanimate, could be very much the opposite, when their position conveys something of the actions of the last person to have handled them. I stood with the others at the bottom of the shaft, a few metres away from the material itself, and gawped, rooted to the spot. Professor Corcoran, arriving last, seemed amused: 'you know, you can go a little closer'. I wasn't conscious of having stood back, but I obviously had, too nervous, reverent even, to get any closer. It was like meeting an ancient past I had until then known only from a distance – from books, or objects I had seen in museums, behind glass – for the first time, and I was overcome. I went into the tomb a little blasé, thinking that I was more interested in other, less sensationalist aspects of Egyptology than a new tomb in the Valley of the Kings. But I came away with a different perspective, an altered understanding of why archaeology, ancient history and ancient things can be so compelling. I feel immensely privileged to have had that experience, and I hope some of that excitement, the thrill of connecting with the ancient past, might come across in the pages that follow.

Modern mavericks

Many of the discoveries of the past were made at a time when archaeology in Egypt was, by modern standards, often as much a treasure hunt as a serious academic pursuit. Egyptology in the 21st century is a rigorous scientific discipline, practised by highly trained and talented individuals in controlled conditions. But that is not to say that there are not also a few mavericks. The great discoveries discussed in this book were made by extraordinary individuals, possessors of the kind of dedication, focus and expertise that does not come easily to most – and also, perhaps, a degree of eccentricity. This book is also intended as a celebration of those qualities, long may Egyptology continue to benefit from them all.

I have also tried, in writing this book, to convey some sense of the archaeological process, of discoveries unfolding. In the days when it was still not unusual for excavation projects to uncover very substantial monuments almost as a matter of routine, there seems to have been a greater sense of excitement and anticipation ahead of each new season, which I fear has been now lost to some extent. Archaeology is now revealed in much greater detail than in the past – to the great benefit of science – but perhaps to the detriment of the excitement felt by the non-specialist public. Bryan Emery's end-of-season reports from Saqqara might seem ill-considered and unscientific now ('Although our excavations are as yet only in their early stages…I think that in all probability…we shall find the tomb of Imhotep.'[2]), there's no question that his readers would have felt a great sense of excitement ahead of the next year's work.

At the heart of this book is the excitement of the possibility of discovering such things. The stories gathered here, of sensational discoveries that were made in the past and research missions still ongoing, will, I hope, get the reader excited by the possibility that there might be such extraordinary surprises yet to come.

CHAPTER 1

IMHOTEP

The man who became a god

We begin our search with a non-royal, but certainly not an ordinary man. Imhotep is one of the world's first known inventors, credited as the architect of King Djoser's Step Pyramid at Saqqara, the first monumental building made of stone anywhere in the world. Centuries after his death, from the New Kingdom onwards, Imhotep was remembered as a polymath, and associated in particular with writing and healing. Ultimately his name would come to be better known than that of all but very few pharaohs; although from the earliest times the cult of the deceased pharaoh was maintained by the placement of offerings at the chapel or other cult building(s) associated with the tomb, in reality the practice probably ceased in the case of most pharaohs within perhaps a few generations at most. Imhotep's cult, by contrast, seems to have gained momentum over time; while there is no extant mention of his name in any text from the period following his death until the reign of Amenhotep III of the 18th Dynasty, it seems that by this time libation offerings were commonly made to him, indicating his status as a demigod. By the 26th Dynasty, this status was clearly established, with the construction of a chapel devoted to his cult at Saqqara. The historian Manetho, writing during the Ptolemaic Period (see pp. 19–21), noted that Imhotep was 'the inventor of the art of building with hewn stone' and also that he was associated with Asklepius, the Greek god of medicine, and 'devoted attention to writing', aligning him with the Egyptian gods Ptah and Thoth.[1] In more modern times, he has lent his name to the villain played by Boris Karloff in Hollywood's *The Mummy* (1932). This Imhotep was revived in the public imagination with the 1999 re-make starring Brendan Fraser and Rachel Weisz.

One of the greatest figures in the emerging discipline of Egyptian archaeology, the British excavator W. B. Emery, dedicated the last years of his life to the search for Imhotep's tomb, focusing his efforts at North Saqqara, close to the Step Pyramid. He uncovered a mass of evidence of the veneration of Imhotep and other deities associated with him in Ptolemaic and Roman times, concentrated on a cluster of tombs of the 3rd Dynasty. He seems to have come agonizingly close to locating the tomb of this great figure, and yet the clinching evidence eluded him, and he died before he could make what would unquestionably have been his greatest discovery.

Who was Imhotep?

Imhotep was undoubtedly the most successful non-pharaoh in achieving what all Egyptians wished for: to 'cause his name to live' – *sankh renef*, to use their phrase – in perpetuity. In other words, to ensure that he would be remembered, along with his achievements, for eternity, sustaining his existence in the afterlife. In fact, the memory of him took on a life of its own many centuries after his death. So how do we distinguish between the man and the legend?

We will begin with what we know of the man. His name and titles are preserved on the base of a statue, now in the museum at Saqqara, of which only the feet remain.[2] It probably depicted the king under whom Imhotep served: Netjerikhet, better known as Djoser, first ruler of the 3rd Dynasty. On this statue, Imhotep is given the titles 'Seal-bearer of the King of Lower Egypt, Foremost one under the King of Upper Egypt, Ruler of the Great Mansion [i.e. the palace], the Noble, and Chief Priest of Heliopolis',[3] a repertoire that provides an indication of his rank and influence both at the court of the king and within the temple administration. This alone would be enough to show that Imhotep was among the most important men in the country, if not the most important after the king himself, but an intriguing phrase to the right of this text might indicate that he had even higher status vis-à-vis the king. It reads *bity sensen* or *bity senwy*, a very literal translation of which would be 'the King of Lower Egypt, the two brothers'. This title appears to be unique to Imhotep, and is very difficult to interpret, but it has been suggested that it should be understood to indicate that he was the childhood companion, confidant, twin or even 'alter ego' of the king.[4] In any case, the implication is that Imhotep was in some way the equal of the king, an extraordinary situation without parallel in ancient Egypt.

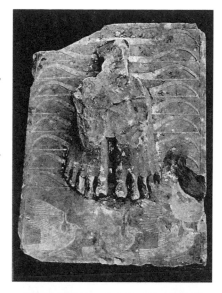

The statue base bearing his titles was found in close proximity to the Step Pyramid complex, and is among the admittedly scarce evidence firmly linking Imhotep to this pioneering monument.[5] A group of seal impressions found in the mortar of the walls in the subterranean galleries of the pyramid and a group of stone vessels, also

Statue JE 49889, which bears the name and titles of Imhotep on the base.

discovered in the subterranean part of the pyramid complex, similarly preserve some of the titles given on the statue, although not Imhotep's name.[6] Finally, his name appears on the northern enclosure wall of the mortuary complex of Djoser's successor, Sekhemkhet, suggesting that his skills had been put to use in the following reign as well.[7]

The temple devoted to the cult of Imhotep at Saqqara seems to have been established no later than the 26th Dynasty, by which time his image as a god was firmly established: he was generally shown seated, wearing a long apron and tight-fitting cap, and with a papyrus scroll unrolled on his lap. The cap evokes the spirit of Ptah, patron god of artisans and architects, said to be Imhotep's divine father. Imhotep, along with Ptah and Apis, would become the pre-eminent deity in the region of the capital city of Memphis, which lay at the head of the Delta, at the point where the Nile splits into multiple branches, and the junction between Upper and Lower Egypt. Apis, a manifestation of Ptah, was believed to be the son of the cow-goddess Hathor and the falcon-headed Horus. As Horus was the mythical king of Egypt, of whom each pharaoh was thought to be the living manifestation, Apis evoked some of the qualities of strength associated with pharaoh, who was often shown in human form but with a bull's tail. Apis was believed to be manifest on Earth as a living bull of black-coloured hide, bearing a particular set of markings that would allow its identification by the priesthood. These bulls were worshipped at Saqqara, and upon the death of each animal an elaborate burial would be prepared, and the deceased bull lain, from the New Kingdom onwards, in a series of purpose-built catacombs known today as the Serapeum (after the Greek combination of Apis with Osiris, who was known as Serapis; see p. 206).

In addition to his familial connection with Ptah, and thus his living form as the Apis bull, Imhotep was aligned with Asklepius, the Greek god of medicine. By the 30th Dynasty, an Asklepieion (a temple dedicated to Asklepius and to his powers of healing) was built at Saqqara, at which Asklepius took the form of Imhotep. Is it possible that the temple may have been formed of, or at least built close to the location of, Imhotep's tomb? A series of inscriptions at Saqqara dating to this period show that people were making pilgrimages from all around – 'from the towns and nomes' – to pray and to make offerings to the god so that he could cure their ills.[8]

Imhotep's worship would continue into Roman times, and his name even survived into Arabic texts of the 10th century AD.[9]

Although Imhotep's fame today rests largely on his legend having grown long after his death, it seems likely that, given the position he held in the royal court and in the graces of his king, he would have been lain to rest in a very substantial tomb. It is probable also that this would have been located in close proximity to the Step Pyramid, tomb of his king, Djoser, at Saqqara; Egyptian nobles often chose burial sites near to their pharaoh, even in these early days of the pharaonic era. However, despite extensive investigations at Saqqara by archaeologists for almost two centuries, and numerous tombs of the right kind and the right period

The Step Pyramid of Djoser, Saqqara.

having been uncovered, Imhotep's has yet to be found – or yet to be *identified*, perhaps.

The earliest monumental tombs

The Step Pyramid was a revolutionary leap forward in architecture and building, and apparently unique in its time. It seems to have set in train an astonishing sequence of similar leaps and innovations, culminating in the building of the first true pyramids, the crowning achievement among which was the Great Pyramid of Khufu at Giza, built approximately half a century after Djoser's pioneering monument.

The construction of private tombs had also become quite sophisticated by Imhotep's time, and because we have investigated so many, we can build a reasonable picture of the kind of monument Imhotep may have had for himself. During the 1st Dynasty, the largest private tombs came to be marked at ground level by mastabas built of mudbrick, encasing a core of rubble and overlying the burial compartments below ground. A man named Merka who served under Pharaoh Qa'a, the last king of the 1st Dynasty, was buried in a particularly elaborate monument[10] that established a series of features that would become typical of later tombs of high-ranking private individuals. He had his image, name and titles inscribed on a stela embedded in a niche at the southern end of the east side of the mastaba, and in an extensive building at the north end of the monument a pair of feet was found, representing the earliest evidence of a cult figure in a private tomb in Egypt. This combination of ritual emplacements – niches – at the northern and southern ends of the tomb became standard in private tombs of the 2nd Dynasty. By this period, the underground parts of these tombs had also become quite complex, and were typically entered via a staircase cut into the top of the mastaba.

By the 3rd Dynasty, mastabas for private individuals had come to be constructed on a massive scale, and the largest and most elaborate of the Saqqara monuments also display several innovations in the ritual parts of the tomb. The tomb of the confidant of the king and chief of scribes, Hesyra,[11] provides the best example. It includes a number of new features that would become a standard part of Egyptian tomb design, exemplifying the sense of experimentation and creativity that characterizes the work of the designers and architects of the time. These innovations included the first attested false door, a decorative feature that was intended to allow the deceased passageway between the earthly and spiritual realms, and a full list of offerings, increasing the provision made symbolically to the deceased in the afterlife. In addition, a narrow corridor within the centre of the mastaba was lined down one side with niches incorporating wooden panels with raised relief images of the deceased, including hieroglyphic inscriptions allowing us to identify him by name; many of these tombs lack such inscriptions, and so remain anonymous.

The location of Imhotep's tomb: Saqqara

Saqqara is clearly the prime candidate for the location of the tomb of Imhotep. It had been, along with Abydos, the most important cemetery in the country since the Two Lands had been unified at the beginning of the 1st Dynasty, and it was of course the cemetery that Imhotep's king, Djoser, chose as his burial place. While Abydos had been the burial place of the pharaohs of the 1st Dynasty and some of the 2nd, and would remain an important site throughout Egyptian history, Saqqara was the cemetery attached to the capital city of Memphis. The funerary monuments

Bryan Emery's excavations at North Saqqara. View looking northwest, towards the pyramids of Abusir.

of the courtiers of the time would have been very visible from the city, which lay below the desert plateau in the Nile Valley, the Step Pyramid being the grandest statement of all, a reminder to pharaoh's subjects and any visitors to the capital of the king's might. Saqqara is also home to a number of huge mastaba tombs of the time of Imhotep, the owners of quite a number of which have yet to be identified.

Saqqara is a very large and very rich archaeological site, and was in use throughout Egyptian history, not just in the early days of the pharaonic era. The Step Pyramid itself lies in the centre of the necropolis, and the large mastabas of the first three dynasties lie to the north. The history of exploration and discovery at North Saqqara is long, and certainly not yet finished. Many different archaeologists and institutions have carried out separate campaigns in the area over the decades since it was first recognized as a site of considerable interest, and so reconstructing a plan of this part of the cemetery is no easy feat. No standardized maps or numbering systems are in place, and creating a comprehensive map of the monuments even just in this part of Saqqara is a considerable undertaking, such is the size of the area and richness of the archaeology beneath the ground. Complicating the picture is the variety of archaeological material, which is not confined to a single historic period; rather, the archaic tombs were overlain and cut into by other monuments. Thirdly, although this incredibly important archaeological space has been the subject of numerous investigations carried out by leading experts over the course of a century, it has still not yet been comprehensively explored.

W. B. Emery and the 'Quest for Imhotep'

One man, perhaps more than any other, made it his quest to discover the tomb of Imhotep. An invitation to take over the Egyptian Antiquities Service excavations brought Emery to Saqqara in 1935, and his genius for discovery brought him immediate rewards: in his first season, he decided to investigate the fill of a mastaba that had previously been thought to be solid.[12] It turned out to conceal no fewer than forty-five intact chambers, containing the funerary goods the deceased would take with them to the afterlife, precisely as they had been left. In the years leading up to the Second World War, Emery would uncover numerous mastabas of the 1st, 2nd and 3rd Dynasties, often with spectacular results, including, uniquely, the intact skeleton of a 1st Dynasty noble,[13] and a mastaba designated 3038, which incorporated a stepped mudbrick structure overlying the burial chamber that he interpreted as being perhaps a precursor to the Step Pyramid itself.

Bryan Emery during his final years at North Saqqara.

His work at Saqqara was interrupted by the war, and the diplomatic work he would become involved with as a result. He managed one season of excavation in 1945–46, during which he discovered one tomb, but for financial reasons he had to suspend operations to take up a post at the British Embassy in Cairo. It wasn't until 1951, when he was appointed Edwards Professor of Egyptology at University College London, that he was again in a position to resume his work at Saqqara, this time as Field Director of the Egypt Exploration Society (EES), under the auspices of which the excavations would be undertaken. Four seasons passed, during which the excavation of a sequence of 1st Dynasty monuments was completed, but work was again interrupted, this time by the Suez Crisis and the pressing need to transfer all archaeological efforts to Nubia, in the far south of Egypt and into Sudan, where masses of archaeological sites stood to be lost to the lake created by the High Dam at Aswan. Emery served as perhaps the single most influential archaeologist involved in the associated UNESCO rescue campaign.

In October 1964, Emery returned to Saqqara for the final six campaigns of his life, and it was then that he became fully occupied with the hunt for Imhotep. He concentrated his excavations on the area at the extreme west of the Archaic necropolis at North Saqqara – where Cecil Firth, inspector of antiquities at Saqqara, had excavated in the early 20th century – intrigued by the Ptolemaic and Roman pottery that he observed covering the adjacent area. He thought these later deposits probably indicated that this had become a place of pilgrimage. At the end of his 1956 season, Emery had decided to investigate further, opening two test trenches in the flat area to the north of several tombs discovered by Firth. His nose for discovery again brought success: the excavations revealed brickwork of the 3rd Dynasty, two sacrificial bull burials, lidded jars containing mummified ibises and a mass of Ptolemaic pottery, deposited as part of an offering ritual. Emery was in no doubt as to what this might mean:

> The juxtaposition of the remains of these two periods was
> indeed significant and at once brought to mind the possibility
> that here, in this place, only about 700 m [2,300 ft] from the
> Step Pyramid enclosure, we might discover the Asklepieion
> and the tomb of Imhotep, the great architect and vizier of King
> Zoser [Djoser] who became in later times the venerated God
> of Medicine. For many years archaeologists have searched, in
> theory and in practice, for the long-lost Asklepieion and the
> tomb of Imhotep at Saqqara. Its location has been suggested
> to lie in various areas of the great burial ground, such as closely
> adjacent to the Step Pyramid, on the edge of the cultivation
> near the pyramid of Teti and south of the Serapeum. But

Reisner, Quibell, and Firth all believed that the tomb, at any rate, would be in the archaic necropolis at the north end of Saqqara...[14]

Mastaba 3508: a first candidate for the tomb

Emery's first act was to begin excavations on the site of the 1956 test pits and he soon uncovered a substantial 3rd Dynasty mastaba, which he numbered 3508. The superstructure was preserved to 3.8 m (12 ft), a far greater height than any other in the area. Pottery and broken offering tables scattered around the bottom of the walls of the mastaba proved to be of 3rd Dynasty date, but frustratingly, as was often the case, no evidence of the name of the tomb owner was found. Fragments of a limestone sarcophagus that had apparently been removed from a second burial shaft were found to have been broken up and thrown to the ground along the western façade of the mastaba, but there was otherwise little trace of the original owner of the tomb. Most interesting, however, was the evidence of much later activity. The surface of the mastaba had been cut into, to a depth of 1.3 m (4 ft), at some point in the Ptolemaic or Roman Period, and a series of sacrificial bulls lain here, in the area of the northern and southern chapels cut into the eastern face of the mastabas –

The superstructure of mastaba 3508 at North Saqqara, taken during the EES excavations.

the ritual spaces where offerings to the deceased would once have been placed. Turning his attention to the burial shaft at the southern end of the mastaba, Emery and his team discovered the burial of another bull on a bed of clean sand and then, underneath that, the first hint of the true nature of the activity that would characterize this part of the site from the Late Period onwards. Up to a depth of 6 m (20 ft) beneath the bull, the burial shaft was filled with clean sand, but beneath that they came across hundreds of ibis mummies, many decorated with embroidered and appliqué designs (see p. i), contained within lidded pots – over five hundred in all. The nature of the designs was intriguing, not only including figures of sacred baboons and ibises – manifestations of Thoth, the god of wisdom and learning with whom Imhotep had by then become associated – but also Imhotep himself. Furthermore, grooves had been cut into the surface of the mastaba's walls, echoing a phenomenon one frequently sees on Egypt's temple walls. These grooves are the result of thousands of devotees scraping away some of the fabric of sacred buildings, believing it to impart magical properties. Clearly, the tomb had taken on a renewed religious significance centuries after the death of its owner – perhaps because of the deification of the individual.

With hundreds more ibis mummies still remaining in the burial shaft, Emery turned his attention to another tomb, this one built of stone and given the number 3509. It was finely decorated with painted reliefs that identified the owner as a man named Hetepka, who lived during the 5th Dynasty. From here, Emery discovered a small street of tombs and another large 3rd Dynasty mastaba.[15] By this point, it had become clear that the much later frenzy of ritual activity extended beyond just tomb 3508. The mastabas of this area had all been deliberately levelled to a height of around 4.5 m (15 ft) above the original ground surface, and the spaces in between the tombs – the 'streets' – had been filled with rubble, creating a single giant platform running across several of the ancient monuments. While this later activity meant removing parts of the original structures, it also ensured they would be preserved to a greater extent than would otherwise have been the case, other mastabas of the period being plundered for their mudbrick or simply eroding into nothingness beneath the force of the winds.

An underground labyrinth is revealed

This platform proved to contain masses of further ritual deposits, including ibis mummies, incense burners, torch-holders, faience amulets and wooden figures of gods including Osiris, Isis and Hathor. The next step was to excavate the burial shaft of tomb 3510, and here Emery made a sensational discovery: the shaft broke into a vast labyrinth of rock-cut passageways. Despite the restrained tone of Emery's end-of-season report, it leaves no doubt that this was a discovery that was simply too complex for him to deal with immediately:

> The extent of this labyrinth is still unknown and we are as yet ignorant of the beginning and end of this great underground structure, although we have explored, with some difficulty, hundreds of yards of its passages. Parts of it are completely clear of debris, but others are filled with sand and rubble to such an extent that we could only crawl just below its ceilings.[16]

> Many of the galleries, which stand 4 m [13 ft] high and 2.5 m [8 ft] wide, are packed with mummies of ibis still undisturbed in their pottery jars. There are literally thousands and thousands of these strange deposits of the bird, which at Memphis in Ptolemaic times was sacred to Imhotep.[17]

This was real Indiana Jones stuff. The galleries ran underneath dozens of tombs of the Archaic and Old Kingdom Periods, and exploration of the passageways was made hazardous by the fragility of the rock, especially in places where the tunnels had broken through into the much earlier burial shafts and features. Emery had gained access to the catacombs via one such accidental collision of older and later building projects, and had yet to locate the original entrance. The passageways provided evidence that pushed the later activity back to the 26th Dynasty, but the Ptolemaic builders had apparently encountered, and deliberately preserved, very ancient features in the course of their construction: one of the galleries was in fact of Old Kingdom date, and contained a frieze of rock-cut statues. The catacombs had, it seems, been known to some of the great 19th-century explorers, including those of the Napoleonic expedition and the Prussian, Karl Richard Lepsius. It was obvious to Emery, however, both that he had seen things they had not, and vice versa. His work was only at its beginning.

Emery's report at the end of this first season of renewed excavations concludes with an extraordinary assertion, which to 21st-century eyes seems quite out of place in an archaeological report, and indeed alongside his earlier, sober account of the season:

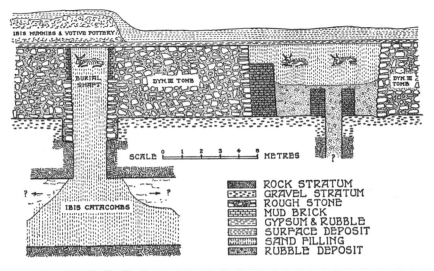

Section drawing showing the stratigraphy in and around the 3rd Dynasty mastabas, including 3508, with the intrusive bull burials and the ibis catacombs running underneath.

Although our excavations are as yet only in their early stages and it is therefore not possible to be dogmatic, I think that in all probability we have located part of the long-lost Asklepieion and that, connected with it, we shall find the tomb of Imhotep.[18]

Emery gave several reasons for this belief. First, it was likely that Imhotep would have had been buried in a large mastaba similar to Hesyra's, at North Saqqara. Secondly, the builders of the ibis catacombs must have believed this was a sacred location, as the presence of so many pre-existing burial shafts made this an extremely inconvenient spot at which to try to build a network of tunnels. Thirdly, a description in the *Hermetica,* a series of Egyptian–Greek wisdom texts of the 2nd century AD, suggests that a temple of Imhotep was situated in the Libyan mountains and close to the 'shore of crocodiles'; the hills to the west are indeed near to North Saqqara, and the 'shore' may refer to the Lake of Abusir, also close by. Fourthly, Imhotep was closely associated with the ibis and baboon, both of which were prevalent in the iconography of the ritual activity uncovered at the site.

Emery believed he was now very close.

The second season of excavations in 1966–67 led to further discoveries. Without the equipment and resources required to investigate the ibis catacombs, which were structurally unstable, Emery transferred his activities to an area to the north where considerable quantities of Saite–Ptolemaic pottery were evident, a large rectangular enclosure was visible in aerial photographs, and to which one of the longest – but not entirely explored – ibis galleries seemed to lead. In search of a safe area to dump the spoil from the excavations, Emery discovered a further large 3rd Dynasty mastaba in an area that must have been prone to flooding, suggesting that all the safer areas for construction had been taken and so demonstrating just how congested this area had become by this time. The excavations revealed a temple enclosure and platform, which had been built on top of further archaic mastabas but dismantled at a certain point. A mass of treasures of various kinds was recovered during the few weeks of excavation in this area, including statues and temple furniture, and numerous papyri and stone flakes (ostraca) providing a wealth of textual material: letters, administrative documents, accounts, lists, jar labels, dedications to gods, and dream texts, in several languages and scripts including Demotic, Hieratic, Greek and Aramaic. To the south of this temple enclosure. Emery uncovered a large courtyard, behind which he discovered a second enclosure that he believed would once have housed a large building, since destroyed, marking the entranceway to a subterranean structure of some kind – more catacombs? Emery had also discovered during the season large quantities of cattle bones and numerous inscriptions mentioning Isis, Mother of Apis.

The cult of the Apis bull, a living manifestation of the patron deity of Memphis, Ptah, had been one of the most important in the Memphite region since the New Kingdom. The Serapeum was a series of catacombs housing the majestic burials of these bulls, a labyrinthine network of tunnels – not unlike the ibis catacombs Emery had found – discovered by Auguste Mariette, founder of the Egyptian Department of Antiquities, in the middle of the 19th century. As with the ibis catacombs, the tunnels of the Serapeum were unstable and unsafe to investigate; today, after years of extensive consolidation, a small number of them are open to the public, but sections remain off-limits and unexplored, and the full extent of the network remains unknown.

Emery was aware that the mother of the Apis bull had also been worshipped, and he now expected that catacombs devoted to the burial of these sacred cows would also be found. He further suggested, in the last line of the report on this second season of renewed excavations, that the cult of the Apis bull was closely connected with that of Imhotep, for when the bull died its successor was taken to the temple of Imhotep so that it might be touched by the god and thus consecrated.[19] Further clues, but still no clinching evidence.

A third season began on 3 February 1968, and excavations resumed in the area of the ritual enclosures. Emery was hoping to uncover the entranceway to the ibis catacombs, but again failed, uncovering instead yet another 3rd Dynasty mastaba and further deposits of ritual objects, deliberately set aside after they had fallen out of use with the care required for such sacred objects, considered too powerful or important to be simply thrown away.

Tellingly, perhaps, although the remains of a very substantial sequence of monuments representing centuries worth of cultic and other activity continued to appear, no mention is made in the report on the 1968 season of either Imhotep or the Asklepieion. Emery, it seems, was losing faith in his earlier convictions.

During the following season a series of small shrines was found in Sector 3, and beneath the pavement of one of these, Shrine D, a fabulous cache of votive objects was discovered. These included a wooden statue of Osiris, bronze statuettes and three wooden shrines containing more bronzes, some of which were wrapped in linen, preserving them in 'mint condition'.[20] Further statues were recovered from other deposits around the shrines, including, tantalizingly, a statuette of Imhotep. Similarly intriguing was the discovery of a stone-built doorway leading to yet another series of galleries with niches containing the mummified remains of yellow baboons.[21]

Even more intriguingly, a series of plaster casts of various parts of the human anatomy were recovered from the debris in what is known as the Upper Baboon Gallery. Emery believed them to be comparable to the *donaria* (votive objects) left at the temple of Asklepius in Rome, as offerings in thanks for, or perhaps hope or expectation of, the healing of a particular ailment relating to the body parts represented.

More sacred animals and a second candidate tomb

The presence of ibises, baboons, healing and Asklepius, all associated with Imhotep, must have tortured Emery, overwhelmed with hints of the man but not the clinching evidence that would certainly identify him – his name. And then, the baboon galleries were found to break through into another monumental mastaba of the 3rd Dynasty – Imhotep's time. Emery decided to return to the surface to try to locate the entrance to the burial shaft, as further investigation from the subterranean galleries would have been too dangerous. The entrance was located by 5 February, and proved to belong to a 'twin' mastaba, designated 3518, of a most unusual design and enormous size – at 52 x 19 m (170 x 63 ft), one of the largest in the necropolis. In a storage magazine next to the southern offering chapel, a clay sealing bearing the name of Netjerikhet Djoser, Imhotep's pharaoh, was discovered; a much later deposit including several more body-part *donaria* was found in front of the main entrance; and, perhaps most intriguingly of all, the mastaba was found to have exactly the same orientation as the Step Pyramid.

Of the *donaria*, Emery noted that 'their position outside the entrance to this large Third-dynasty mastaba is, to say the least, significant'.[22] He did not say it, but he must have been thinking this tomb was a candidate for possible identification as that of Imhotep.

Could it have been? The north shaft and burial chamber, which were not connected with the baboon galleries beneath, had been plundered, although considerable quantities of broken stone vessels were found within them, along with the ceramics from the magazines within the superstructure. Emery perhaps realized that the tomb was not going to yield the name of the owner; it could not be proven to be that of Imhotep, but it's nonetheless interesting that by this point he did not even wish to speculate on it.

The following season in 1969–70 began with the continuation of the work on this mastaba. Perhaps Emery still had some hope at this point. The south burial chamber, which had been cut through by the Baboon Gallery, produced further stone vessels, but 'no evidence of ownership was found'[23] – no doubt to Emery's frustration, who commented, 'It remains a mystery why the builders of the Late Period should select an

The remains of Emery's mastaba number 3518, emerging from the
sand at North Saqqara.

area which they knew was riddled with the burial shafts of the Archaic
Period when fallow sites were available in the vicinity.'[24]

Returning to Sector 3, a select group of Emery's men began investigating the breakthroughs in the south wall of the Lower Baboon Gallery and
in the process discovered yet another sequence of galleries, this time for
the burial of sacred falcons. Within the galleries, a small, round-topped
stela bearing an inscription in black ink was found. It read:

> May Imhotep the great, son of Ptah, the great god, and the
> gods who rest here give life to Petenefertem, son of Djeho,
> together with Paptah, son of Djeho, whom Tamneve bore. May
> their house and their children be established for ever.

Such texts, in which the dedicant invites the blessings of the gods, were
not uncommon. This particular stela, which was dedicated in 'Year 26
which is Year 29' of a pharaoh who is unnamed but who can only be
Ptolemy x in *c.* 89 BC,[25] was significant for Emery because it provided

the first evidence of this kind explicitly associating the ibises and falcons with the worship of Imhotep. Further, opposite this niche was a stone-built gate on which Emery found an inked drawing of the baboon forms of Thoth and Imhotep.

Very substantial caches of statues and other ritual objects were discovered during the season. Emery's original intention had been to leave the many thousands of mummified falcons in place. However, some had to be removed so that the architecture of the galleries could be accurately recorded, and it was in the process of clearing one of the side niches that this latest hoard was found. Excavations in the North East corner of Sector 3 finally revealed the burial place of the Mother of Apis – yet another set of catacombs – the existence of which various finds in previous years had suggested.

At every turn, it seems, Emery made a spectacular discovery. Each new haul of material would give groups of specialists years more work of recording, conserving, studying and publishing, and some of it remains

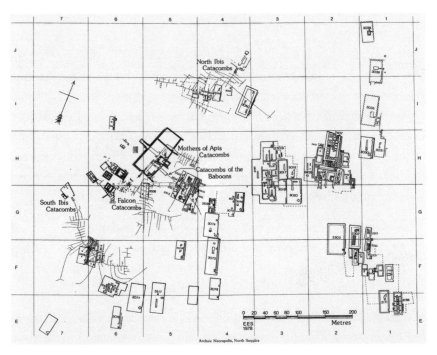

Map of North Saqqara from the EES archives showing the Archaic and Old Kingdom mastaba tombs and main structures of the Sacred Animal Necropolis.

unstudied to this day. And yet mysteries still remained – not least the location of the tomb of Imhotep. One wonders if Emery had become concerned by this point that he had become a victim of his own success; his discoveries, while surely remarkable and exciting, demanded an enormous commitment from him in their research and publication, leaving him little time to dedicate to his original goal.

Sadly, this was the last campaign Emery would complete. Reading his preliminary reports one is entirely unaware that from the middle of the 1960s onwards he had suffered from chronic ill-health. He had undergone a serious operation in 1967, but returned to Saqqara to supervise within weeks. In the following seasons he was in constant pain, but soldiered on in silence. Indeed, by the summer of 1970 it seemed he had recovered. However, the long expeditions in the heat were taking their toll, and on 7 March 1971 he was found collapsed outside his office at the dig-house. He had had a stroke. A second followed two days later when he was apparently making good progress in the Anglo-American hospital in Cairo, and on 11 March he died peacefully.[26]

Whatever Emery's personal strategy and ambitions, his final years had left his successors with decades of work to do, and the research careers of several of today's most senior Egyptologists have been built at least in part on the study and publication of the mass of material that Emery discovered. So much of that material can be connected in some way to Imhotep, but the quest to discover the whereabouts of his tomb died with Emery.

Recent excavations, further possibilities

Of the 3rd Dynasty mastabas Emery uncovered, most were found to have been extensively plundered in ancient times, and therefore yielded no evidence bearing the name of the owner. It is very possible that Imhotep's tomb may be among them. But could the evidence required to identify any of these tombs conclusively as that of Imhotep have been lost even before the site was venerated in the 26th Dynasty? In other words, could the Egyptians of the Late Period who left behind so much material relating to Imhotep, presumably because they believed the area to have been the site of Imhotep's tomb, have got it wrong? There are areas of North

Saqqara never investigated by Emery that may yet conceal the tomb of Djoser's great wise man. Three separate 21st-century expeditions working at Saqqara, close to the area that Emery had focused on in his final years, have uncovered further evidence of monumental construction in the 3rd Dynasty that might be associated with Imhotep.

In 2002, a team of archaeologists from Waseda University's Institute of Egyptology, led by Professors Sakuji Yoshimura and Nozomu Kawai, was excavating a monument of Khaemwaset, son of Ramesses II, when they discovered a massive stone structure built into a wadi (dried water-course) running in a southeasterly direction away from the Khaemwaset monument. The site of their investigation lay approximately 1 mile (1.5 km) to the west of the Sacred Animal Necropolis, in an unexplored area of the desert. The façade of the newly discovered monument measured 34.3 m (112 ft) in length, and the fifteen stepped courses of preserved stone reached a height of 4.1 m (13 ft). These walls were found to slope inwards, strongly recalling the design of the Step Pyramid and other 3rd Dynasty structures. Behind the stepped structure, two chambers were found to have been cut directly into the slope, inside which a variety of votive offerings of the Early Dynastic Period, early Old Kingdom and Middle Kingdom were found. The excavators believed that they had uncovered some kind of cult centre, which had been in use since the time of Imhotep and revived in the Middle Kingdom.[27]

Then, in 2005, the Polish–Egyptian Archaeological Mission directed by Dr Karol Myśliwiec came across yet another substantial monument of the approximate time of Imhotep's life and death. With the permission of the Egyptian authorities, the team had decided to remove part of a large mudbrick platform extending westwards from Djoser's Step Pyramid enclosure wall in order to investigate a series of Old Kingdom structures believed to lie underneath it. The oldest of these layers revealed a rock-cut structure that the excavators believed to date either to the late 2nd Dynasty or the very beginning of the 3rd, due to its longitudinal shape, size and north–south orientation, reminiscent of the 2nd Dynasty royal tombs just south of the Step Pyramid and early 3rd Dynasty private tombs found on the Saqqara plateau.[28] The monument had been partially destroyed by later, Old Kingdom shafts, but a steeply sloping, rock-cut passageway descending southwards was preserved. This led to a subterranean chamber containing pottery used for ritual purposes, suggesting it had been used as a cult place but was probably not a tomb in itself. Though the excavator expected that a tomb of the Early Dynastic or early 3rd Dynasty would be found in the vicinity, possibly to the south,[29] subsequent excavations were dominated by the discovery of later burials, ranging in date from the Old Kingdom to the Ptolemaic Period.

Perhaps most intriguingly of all, at almost exactly the same time another expedition, working across a vast area of the Saqqara necropolis, turned up evidence of two of the largest tomb structures anywhere at the site, which appeared to be of 3rd Dynasty design.

In 1991, a charismatic Scottish surveyor named Ian Mathieson had begun an unusual long-term project to create a topographical and subsurface map of a very large part of the Saqqara necropolis, providing a basis to unify all the archaeological information gathered by various missions over the years, and to identify new features without the need for excavation. Between 2000 and 2007, Mathieson and his colleagues investigated a massive area, from the Step Pyramid enclosure in the south to the village of Abusir to the north, and from the edge of the escarpment in the east to the area around the Serapeum to the west.[30] Mathieson's intention was as much to demonstrate the potential of geophysical and other non-invasive techniques as to discover anything new, but his project was an unmitigated success on both fronts – in showing what could be achieved without digging, it was groundbreaking in pioneering the use of new equipment and expanded our knowledge of the site considerably.

Mathieson's 2007 report in the *Journal of Egyptian Archaeology* includes a wealth of information on 'new' structures revealed by his work, most of which remained as yet unexcavated. Among the numerous mastabas, temple platforms and other monuments that his pioneering techniques revealed scattered across the vast site, two in particular may be relevant to our search. To the north of the Serapeum Way – the route leading from the eastern extent of the site, westwards across the desert towards the burial place of the sacred Apis bulls – and approximately 400 m (1,300 ft) to the west of the house occupied by Emery himself during his campaigns, Mathieson revealed two of the biggest mastabas so far discovered at the site.

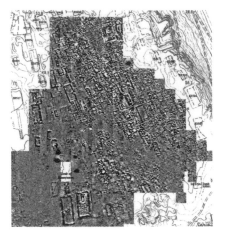

A magnetic map produced by Ian Mathieson showing two very large rectangular shapes – mastabas – one of which Mathieson believed might be the tomb of Imhotep.

By this point, there could be no doubt that Mathieson had succeeded in his aim to demonstrate the effectiveness of his methods and the potential of the Saqqara necropolis to yield further spectacular discoveries. The conclusion to his report is short and to-the-point, but no one reading it could be in any doubt about the significance of what he had achieved: 'it is obvious that we have now been able to provide a fairly complete record of the structures existing in the areas of the north Saqqara necropolis that can be located by magnetic gradiometer methods....

It also means that, without excavation, the SCA [Supreme Council of Antiquities] now has a Geographical Information System plan of the structures that are hidden beneath the sand.'[31]

But what were those structures? Mathieson was not an Egyptologist by background, and for the most part was happy to leave the finer details of excavation and interpretation to others. In one short article published in 2006, however, he allowed himself to speculate a little, and showed that he too had given some thought to the possibility that had once driven Bryan Emery. The article was entitled 'On the search for Imhotep'.[32] In it, Mathieson, as Emery had before him, explained that Imhotep would have wished to be buried near to his king, and that the ritual activity of the Sacred Animal Necropolis had probably sprung up in that area due to its association with Imhotep. He speculated that Imhotep would have built for himself a large tomb within sight of the Step Pyramid, and with at least some of the same features, including an entrance in the southeastern corner. The largest of the two mastabas he had discovered in 2005 and 2006 measured 90 x 40 m (295 x 130 ft) with walls 5 m (16 ft) thick, and had an entrance in the southeastern corner of the east wall, a feature strongly reminiscent of the Step Pyramid. Although there was a little evidence that some attempts may have been made to investigate it in later times, it appeared to be essentially untouched. The second structure lay a mere 20 m (65 ft) further east, and was 70 x 50 m (230 x 165 ft) in size, with thick walls and a complete inner structure suggestive of a temple or house with multiple rooms.

Mathieson concluded his article by saying that it was time to investigate these structures further. Whether he intended to do so himself is unclear. Ian Mathieson died in July 2010 aged 83. His Saqqara Geophysical Survey Project has been continued in recent years by colleagues, but the two huge structures that had caught Mathieson's attention have yet to be investigated further.

Conclusions

And so we are left with several tantalizing possibilities in our search for the tomb of Imhotep. The anonymous mastaba numbered 3508, which led Emery into the animal catacombs for the first time, remains a reasonably convincing candidate for the tomb of Imhotep. Its bull burials, vast quantities of votive offerings connected to Thoth and Imhotep, and the curious scraping of its mudbrick walls by visitors wishing to take away something of its magical properties are clear indications of some perceived special status. Emery himself, however, evidently did not believe that this was the tomb he was looking for, directing his search elsewhere in his later seasons, and it is entirely possible that in the millennia between Imhotep's life and this tomb's apparent veneration by Ptolemaic visitors, the true location of his burial was forgotten. Of the other tombs Emery discovered, perhaps 3518, the massive mastaba precisely aligned with the Step Pyramid and yielding a seal naming Djoser himself, is the strongest contender. The structures discovered by the Japanese and Polish expeditions do not present such good cases. They are significant, however, for revealing new evidence of construction activity on a massive scale connected with subsequent ritual activity – exactly what attracted Emery to his patch of North Saqqara in the 1960s and 1970s. One wonders how the discovery of these monuments might have influenced Emery's investigation, and how they might yet shape the direction of future research at the site. Perhaps the most compelling case of all is made by the massive structures discovered most recently by Ian Mathieson. It is clear that there is a great deal still to be investigated at North Saqqara, and the tomb of Imhotep may yet be lying quietly beneath the sands, a sensational discovery awaiting the next generation of archaeologists.

CHAPTER 2

VISIBLE TO INVISIBLE

Amenhotep I and the

Valley of the Kings

During the New Kingdom, the conspicuous funerary monuments of the previous pharaohs, marked by temples and, of course, pyramids, were abandoned. For virtually the whole of this period, the royals instead favoured hidden, subterranean tombs, secreted away in the desert cemetery we now know as the Valley of the Kings.

Today, the Valley is one of the most famous archaeological sites anywhere in the world, but it was not intended to be so, representing an important step in the evolution of Egyptian royal burial practices – away from ostentatious display and towards secrecy. Although earlier pharaohs' tombs were generally built in the desert, a distance away from the inhabited land of the Nile Valley, they would have been very visible, a constant, enduring monument to the might of the pharaoh. The tombs in the Valley of the Kings, conversely, were built in an even more remote location, a network of high desert wadis, entirely concealed from view in a place that would have been at least an hour or two's arduous walk or donkey ride into the mountains from the nearest villages. They were deliberately hidden from the gaze of unscrupulous would-be plunderers, their location unknown to anyone other than those most closely involved with the tombs' construction and the rituals of royal burial.

The Valley would remain in use as Egypt's royal cemetery for over four hundred years (with the exception of a brief hiatus during the Amarna Period, to which we will return in the next chapter). Although no two tombs in the Valley are exactly alike, it is possible to trace an evolution from one to the next in terms of placement, architecture and decoration, and in their most fundamental features there is a remarkable degree of consistency throughout the cemetery.

A feature of the earliest royal tombs that was incompatible with the new order was the inclusion within the tomb architecture of a place where the cult of the deceased king could be attended to – where offerings could be placed and rituals performed by an attached retinue of priests. As the new tombs were meant to be entirely inaccessible, an alternative solution for the maintenance of the cult would have to be found. The cult place was therefore separated from the tomb; each pharaoh would now build a mortuary temple for themselves much closer to the inhabited lands at the desert edge, alongside the main part of the Theban necropolis. Over time, temples like this came to be built in a line running from north to south. Some, such as those of Amenhotep III, Ramesses II (known today as 'the Ramesseum') and Ramesses III, were among the largest temples ever constructed in a single building phase. These were intended to be accessible to the priests and townspeople who would be employed in the service of the temple and the maintenance of the cult of the deceased king, and visible to all for miles around.

But when exactly did this rift in royal burial tradition occur, and under whose initiative? The individual whose tomb we seek in this chapter seems a likely candidate, and should his tomb ever be found, it would shed light on this compelling question. Djeserkare Amenhotep I, the son of Ahmose I and his Great Royal Wife, Ahmose-Nefertari, was the second king of the 18th Dynasty, the first line of New Kingdom pharaohs. According to Manetho he ruled for twenty years, and though his reign is not very well documented, he seems to have been highly successful in establishing his line within Egypt and beyond. A text in the tomb of the official Ahmose, son of Ebana at el-Kab, provides detail of a campaign into Nubia during Amenhotep's reign, and a building erected in his name on the island of Sai between the Second and Third Cataracts suggests he was successful in ensuring Egypt's domination of the territory to the south. Several cult buildings were erected in Upper Egypt, at Elephantine, Kom Ombo, Abydos and Karnak, but his reign is perhaps most significant as part of the change to the new means of burying the royal dead.

The location of his tomb remains unknown, and scholars disagree as to whether any one of a series of funerary monuments whose owners cannot be identified with certainty might represent all that is left of the monument in question, or if in fact it still awaits discovery. In any case, Amenhotep's reign seems to have fallen at a time of transition. While his predecessors seem to have been buried in the Dra Abu el-Naga precinct at the northern end of the Theban necropolis, Amenhotep's successors came to be buried in the newly established Valley of the Kings, which came into use perhaps in the time of his successor, Tuthmosis I, but certainly no later than the reign of Hatshepsut. Some argue that his tomb should be found among those of the earlier kings, others that it lay in the famous Valley.

Amenhotep, along with his mother Ahmose-Nefertari, became the patron deity of the village of Deir el-Medina, home to the workmen who cut the tombs in the Valley of the Kings, suggesting that he may have been responsible for founding the town. As such his cult came to be celebrated, at least among this community, more than that of any other pharaoh of the New Kingdom, an extraordinary achievement given the competition. To these workmen, who would have known the royal tombs better than anyone else, he was as important as any other pharaoh of the time.

The presence at Deir el-Bahri, the site of royal funerary monuments since Mentuhotep II of the 11th Dynasty built his temple and tomb there, of a sandstone statue of Amenhotep showing the king in the guise of Osiris, suggests that his funerary cult may have been celebrated some distance away from the tomb itself. This separation of burial and cult place was one of the crucial features of the royal funerary practice in the New Kingdom. Could Amenhotep have inaugurated this defining feature of the New Kingdom? The location of the tomb may provide the answer.

The evolution of burial practices to this point, and particularly the transition from the practice of burying the pharaoh within the most visible monuments in the land, to one in which his final resting place was deliberately made as inaccessible, *invisible*, as possible, has been as elusive and difficult to understand as the events. However, in recent years unexpected and spectacular discoveries of previously unsuspected tombs have dramatically improved our knowledge of the situation, and will force the history books to be rewritten.

The evolution of the Egyptian pyramid

Imhotep's achievement in creating the Step Pyramid was considerable, but it was only the first step in Egyptian pyramid design. Inspired by Djoser's great monument, successive pharaohs sought to improve on the original in various ways. With one or two exceptions, the pyramid would remain the standard form for the tomb of the king down to the end of the Old Kingdom almost five centuries later.

Djoser's pyramid itself exhibits signs of continuous experimentation as its architect sought to create the perfect monument. It had originally been conceived as a square-based platform, resembling a mastaba (although these were generally rectangular in plan) but built of horizontal layers, and of stone blocks rather than mud-bricks. This single platform was expanded into a four-layered structure, and then enlarged once more to become a six-stepped structure. For this final leap, the original square base was extended to the north and west, creating a rectangular plan. The six layers of diminishing size created the pyramid shape. The stone blocks used to construct each level were set down in 'accretion layers', in which the blocks sloped inwards, slanted towards a central rubble core.

Pyramids and the buildings associated with them performed several functions: they were intended to house the burial of the king, of course, and to provide for the elaborate rituals performed in connection with the monarch's death and journey to the afterlife. They were also intended as a statement of the power and might both of the individual pharaoh and the institution of kingship. The evolution of pyramid design, particularly in the 3rd Dynasty, seems to have been driven by the Egyptians' desire to mark the burial place of the pharaoh in the grandest way possible.

In this regard, the beginning of the 4th Dynasty seems to have marked an important turning point. The first king of that Dynasty, Sneferu, although not the builder of the greatest pyramid – that honour belongs to his immediate successor, Khufu – was arguably the greatest pyramid builder. At least three pyramids can be attributed to him, one at Meidum and two at Dahshur, both sites part of the sprawling cemetery at Memphis. A further seven smaller pyramids of stepped design attributed to Sneferu are scattered along the Nile Valley as far south as Elephantine, and may have been built to commemorate some kind of royal tour, glorifying the living pharaoh.[1] The main three, however, were probably all designed for the specific purpose of housing the burial of the king. Sneferu's architects built on an unprecedented scale: all three pyramids are approximately 100 m (330 ft) in height, far larger than Djoser's Step Pyramid, which stands just over 60 m (200 ft). The pyramid at Meidum seems to have been the earliest. For the first time, the internal compartments were partly built within the body of the monument itself. Its design was altered not once, but twice during construction: it was originally conceived as a seven-stepped monument but was then enlarged, becoming an eight-stepped monument; finally, and most significantly, it was enlarged again to become a 'true' or straight-sided pyramid, the first of its kind. Sneferu's second monument, this time at Dahshur, was conceived as a true pyramid from the outset, but the builders seem to have encountered problems with the substructure due to the weight of the upper parts of the building. The weight was relieved via a reduction in the angle of incline of the sides towards the top, resulting in the strange form that gave rise to its modern name, the Bent Pyramid. Despite this hitch in the construction, the main

Sneferu's Bent Pyramid at Dahshur. Structural instability forced the builders to adopt a shallower angle of incline for the upper half of the monument.

body of the monument was finished and cased in Tura limestone, the finest and whitest in all Egypt, much of which survives – more than on any other pyramid. Sneferu, however, was clearly not satisfied with the effect either of the Tura limestone or the pyramid overall, and a third monument was attempted to the north of the Bent Pyramid. This time the architects succeeded in creating the first true-sided pyramid, known as the Red Pyramid because the white Tura casing is now missing, leaving the core of reddish limestone blocks exposed.

In attempting to construct chambers within the core of the pyramid, the architects ran the risk of them collapsing immediately under the weight of the stone above and around them. This problem seems to have been solved by the ingenious use of corbelling: each horizontal course of stone was arranged so as to jut a little further into the chamber than the course beneath, creating a vaulted ceiling that distributed the weight of the overlying stone around the sides of the interior voids. This technique was used successfully in all three of Sneferu's pyramids and by his successor, Khufu.

Khufu's place in world history is assured thanks to his construction of the Great Pyramid of Giza, the last surviving ancient wonder of the world. At 146 m (480 ft), this was the tallest man-made structure in the world at the time of its completion in approximately 2540 BC and retained that position for almost four millennia until the construction of the central spire of Lincoln Cathedral, which reached a height of 160 m (525 ft) in AD 1311. (The spire, however, collapsed mere centuries later, in 1549, so the Egyptian architects have the edge in terms of longevity.) The Great Pyramid is one of the greatest feats of engineering and architecture in human history, not only for its size and resistance to ruin, but also for the logistical achievement of maneuvering such a massive number of huge stone blocks into place with astounding precision. The chambers within are equally impressive, the 8-m (26-ft) high corbelled Grand Gallery ascending 46 m (15 ft) to the burial chamber.

No pyramid in the pharaonic age was ever constructed on the same scale; none is so spectacular internally, and none has proven so impervious to the ravages of time. The only one that comes close is that of Khufu's son, Khafra, the second of the three main pyramids at Giza. Khafra's monument is smaller (though not by very much), but seems to take centre stage, being the middle of the three and appearing the tallest from some viewing angles due to its having been constructed on slightly higher ground. Its internal compartments, on the other hand, are distinctly less impressive than those of the Great Pyramid, and the pyramids of the 5th Dynasty were even smaller and less complicated internally. Focus seems to have been placed instead on the surrounding cult buildings, in particular the mortuary temple that lay to the east of the pyramid and would have been regularly attended by priests to maintain the rituals that sustained the king in the afterlife. A further significant change occurred with the construction of the pyramid of Unas, last king of the 5th Dynasty: his burial chamber, its antechamber and part of the entrance corridor were decorated with a series of hieroglyphic texts concerned with the protection of the king's body at death and his journey to the afterlife. We now know this compilation of writings as the Pyramid Texts, and their appearance on the internal walls of the pharaoh's tomb would become standard in the 6th Dynasty, though was not revived in the Middle Kingdom.

The tomb of Pepy II, the last king of the Old Kingdom, was the last substantial pyramid to be built for two centuries. A handful of such monuments found in the Memphite region can be attributed to pharaohs of the 7th to 10th Dynasties – the First Intermediate Period, during which rule of the country was divided between rival lines. When centralized control returned, it was established by a group originating from Thebes that we now recognize as the 11th Dynasty. The kings of this line were buried in their native Thebes, not in pyramids but in rock-cut tombs in the foothills on the western side of the Nile.

The rise of the 12th Dynasty, a new line of pharaohs begun by Amenemhat I, signalled a new era, which involved the founding of a new capital city, Itj-tawy, in the region of the Faiyum Oasis, and an attendant shift of the royal burial ground. Amenemhat also revived the practice of pyramid-building. He and his successor, Senusret I, both built their pyramids at the site of Lisht to designs broadly following those of the Old Kingdom type. The monument of the third king of their line, Amenemhat II, seems, however, to have initiated a new process of innovation relating in particular to the arrangement of the internal compartments, this time driven not by the challenges of erecting a huge monument and preventing it from collapsing in on itself, but by the urgent need to find a means of protecting the king's burial from the threat of robbery.

Amenemhat II's monument is known as the White Pyramid after the scatter of limestone chippings that are all that remains to be seen of the ruin. While the core of the pyramid was constructed using the same technique as his predecessor's, the internal compartments exhibit striking new features that point to an increased concern for security. The king's sarcophagus was made of a series of quartzite slabs and concealed beneath the floor of the burial chamber under a layer of paving slabs and rubble. Furthermore, a niche to hold a canopic chest containing the mummified internal organs lay at the end of a short passageway underneath the main entranceway to the burial chamber, to the north of the sarcophagus, rather than to the south or southeast as had been traditional. This seems to have been an attempt to throw hopeful robbers off the scent.[2]

Amenemhat II's successor, Senusret II, continued to innovate in this vein. His pyramid at Lahun was the first to be built with an inner core of mud-brick, although it was still cased in stone and outwardly would have appeared no different to earlier monuments. Again, the interiors exhibit new features that seem to have been intended to protect the burial. This pyramid was entered not from the north, as had been a constant feature of pyramid design since Djoser's monument, but from the south, and not via a descending passageway but a shaft followed by a deep 'well'. The subterranean elements were tunnelled into the bedrock, rather than being cut at ground level then covered with masonry, and included a corridor that ran around three sides of the burial chamber – a move towards a more labyrinthine design that would become the norm.[3]

Senusret III built a pyramid at Dahshur and again relocated the point of entry, but intriguingly he would also build a second tomb, at Abydos, this time of a completely new, rock-cut type more in keeping with the later, New Kingdom tombs of the Valley of the Kings. Despite this apparent break with tradition, Senusret's successor, Amenemhat III, would build two pyramids. The first, at Dahshur, is now known as the Black Pyramid (in contrast to the Red and White pyramids at the same site) owing to the dark colour of the mud-brick core that is all that remains of the monument. The subterranean elements again increase in complexity, incorporating the burials of two queens. Amenemhat's second pyramid, at Hawara, exhibits the clearest signs yet that a labyrinthine subterranean plan was a deliberate ploy to foil would-be robbers: it was entered via a descending passage on the south side, a little west of centre, which was blocked after a short distance by a portcullis. Beyond, a dummy corridor leading nowhere in particular was filled with blocking stones, a deliberate red herring. Access to the burial chamber was instead via a turning to the right, down a corridor which turned left, and then left again, with a portcullis at every turn. The burial chamber itself was perhaps the most innovative feature of this pyramid: it was constructed of a single block of quartzite sunk into a trench in front of the antechamber, which was covered and sealed by several large blocks of quartzite.

Such colossal blocks of heavy stone were near-impossible to move, and much harder than limestone, making them very difficult to cut into – perfect for keeping robbers out (or so the ancient architects must have hoped). The last of these blocks was lowered into place using a system known as 'sand hydraulics' or 'sandraulics'. In this ingenious arrangement, the last of the series of massive stones sealing the burial chamber was temporarily suspended above the burial chamber, standing on wooden props – like a table top standing on its legs – which themselves stood upon vertical cavities ('chimneys') cut into the walls of the chamber below and filled with sand. The sand was kept in place by removable plugs at the bottom of these cavities. While in this position, the burial equipment could be placed in the chamber, and then, when the moment came to seal it, the plugs would be removed. The wooden props would descend into the cavities as the sand flowed into two trenches either side of the burial chamber, lowering the previously suspended stone block neatly into place. As no ropes or handles needed to be run around the block using this method, there were no gaps that would-be robbers could exploit, making it very difficult for them to reverse the process. Despite this elaborate system to foil the looters, Amenemhat's burial chamber was nonetheless robbed, and his body burned.

Such innovation continued beyond Amenemhat III's reign into the Second Intermediate Period, a period represented by five of Manetho's dynasties and involving nearly one hundred kings. By the end of the Second Intermediate Period, we know that the 17th Dynasty Theban rulers were buried in the Theban hills, in the low desert beneath the high plateau that would become the Valley of the Kings. What happened in between continues to prove difficult for historians and archaeologists to reconstruct. The vast majority of these kings were buried in circumstances that remain obscure to us, but those burials that are known consistently exhibit the familar features that betray a concern with violation of the tomb: winding corridors taking multiple turns, portcullis blockings and burial chambers constructed of a single piece of hard stone, combining the features of both the sarcophagus and emplacement for canopic equipment. And yet, in all cases, the pyramids of this era were robbed successfully. Despite the designers pioneering some of the finest engineering and most innovative security measures yet invented and using the toughest stones they could quarry, the robbers' tenacity always trumped the architects' efforts.

It is difficult not to admire the designers of these royal tombs for their apparently endless inventiveness, and also to feel sorry for them that the robbers – with admirable creativity and perseverance of their own! – continued to foil their plans at every turn. One finds oneself rooting for the architects, and hoping that they might one day succeed, and yet we know that in the end the decision was taken to abandon entirely the idea of burying the king in a monument that was at once grand enough to make a statement about his power, while also remaining secure enough to protect his body, in favour of the hidden tombs of the Valley of the Kings. Might Amenhotep I have been the one to take this decision?

Senebkay and the previously unknown Abydos Dynasty

In 2014, a sensational discovery was made at Abydos, the site of the very first royal tombs and the focus of decades of research and excavation, which showed that the Egyptian sands are still capable of yielding surprises. Dr Josef Wegner of the University of Pennsylvania and Penn Museum of Archaeology and Anthropology has for many years been working on the monuments of the 12th Dynasty pharaoh Senusret III in this area: the temple dedicated to the cult of the king's memory, the town that grew up around it, known as Wah-Sut, and the tomb itself, cut into the cliffs of the so-called 'Anubis mountain' at the western extent of the site.

As Senusret also built a pyramid at Dahshur, it is unclear whether this tomb was used for his burial. Strikingly, Senusret's Abydos tomb breaks with the prior traditions of pyramid-building, and is much closer in many ways to the practices that would characterize the royal burials of the New Kingdom. The tomb is cut directly into the hillside and descends deep into the mountain, in the manner of the later tombs of the 18th, 19th and 20th Dynasty pharaohs in the Valley of the Kings. Perhaps equally interesting, however, is the scatter of smaller tombs built on the slopes just in front of Senusret's, an area that was excavated by the English Egyptologist Arthur Weigall on behalf of the Egypt Exploration Fund at the very beginning of the 20th century. Weigall uncovered two tombs, which he called S9 and S10 respectively, both of which exhibited the same complex internal design as the 12th and 13th Dynasties' royal monuments found further north, including the pyramids of Dahshur. Moreover, the main part of the burial chamber in S9 was made from a single, massive block of stone, in keeping with those same monuments to the north. Weigall could not, however, locate the burial chamber in S10.

In 2013, Josef Wegner's team discovered why. Wegner had already proposed that S9 and S10 were the final resting places of two of the numerous 13th Dynasty rulers whose tombs were yet to be identified. His team had begun re-excavating the area of Weigall's investigations, knowing, following a magnetometer survey carried out in 2002, that there were more tombs present than Weigall had uncovered. Several examples of a type consisting of a sequence of vaulted brick chambers arranged along a single axis and leading to a stone-lined burial chamber were investigated, but all were found to have been robbed, with very little material that might shed light on their date or the identity of their owners remaining. But then the team made a striking discovery: one of the tombs contained another of these massive, single-block burial chambers, but in this case it seemed not to be in its original position. This was the burial chamber that Weigall had been looking for in S10, which, despite its massive size, had been moved by the builders of this, evidently later, tomb, some 75 m (250 ft) away.

Wegner's team now had good evidence for two things. First, that both S9 and S10, on the grounds of their design, may have been tombs of kings of the 13th Dynasty, and perhaps from early in the period given

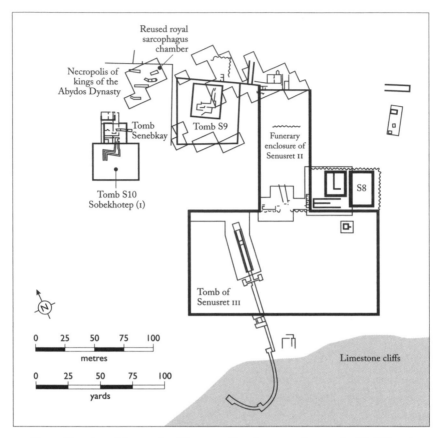

Above: The site of the tomb of Senusret III and surrounding tombs: S9, S10, and that of Senebkay.

Right: Tomb S9 at South Abydos as revealed by the excavations of Josef Wegner. Note the massive quartzite blocks used to seal the combined sarcophagus and burial chamber underneath, a characteristic feature of royal burials of this period.

the similarity with the pyramid of Ameny Qemau at Dahshur. Secondly, at least one of the tombs had been plundered of a part of its structure for use in the construction of a later monument.

They subsequently turned their attention back to S10 in the hope of finding more evidence to identify the owners of these tombs. In the ruins of a chapel connected to the tomb, they found numerous fragments of a stela mentioning the name of a king Sobekhotep, as well as something even more significant: lying so deep beneath the mounds of debris that

The exterior of the tomb of Senebkay at South Abydos as revealed by Wegner's excavations.

it had not been picked up by the magnetometer survey, another tomb built of a sequence of vaulted brick chambers. In this, it resembled the others they had investigated, but it was to vary significantly from the rest. Measuring 16 m (52 ft) in length – not particularly large – the tomb was found to consist of three chambers: the first roofed with wooden beams; the second covered with a brick vault; and the third lined with limestone blocks. Although the roof of the third chamber was now missing, the walls had remained intact, and crucially they were found to be decorated.

In among the images of goddesses and winged sun discs, the team found the simple hieroglyphic inscription they were searching for, furnishing them with the name of the owner: 'the Lord of the Two Lands, King of Upper and Lower Egypt, Useribra, the son of Ra, Senebkay'.[4] Wegner could be in no doubt now that he had found the tomb of a pharaoh, and that the anonymous tombs of the same type nearby probably belonged to further kings. The trouble was that there was almost no record of there having been any such king with this name. Rather than helping to fill in some of the gaps in our knowledge of the Middle Kingdom and Second Intermediate Period by ticking off one of the names of the

Decoration inside the tomb of Senebkay.

many kings whose tombs were unknown, Wegner's discovery added a new name to that list.

The key may lie not in the king's birth name (nomen), Senebkay, but in his throne name (prenomen), Useribra. One of the most intriguing

The epithet 'son of Ra' at top left followed by the name of Senebkay enclosed within a cartouche, inside the tomb of the king.

sections of the Turin Canon, though badly fragmented, contains a list of the names of sixteen pharaohs of uncertain identity, which follows the names of the 16th Dynasty kings. The identity of this group, which apparently does not belong to the 17th Dynasty, is unclear. Previously it had been proposed that it represented a line of kings that ruled at approximately the same time as the 16th Dynasty, whose power was confined to the region of Abydos. The prenomina of the first two kings in this list both begin with 'User-', and end in '-ra' – exactly as with

Useribra Senebkay. The discovery of this king's tomb, and of others perhaps built for his predecessors and/or successors, would seem to support this theory, and Wegner's excavations would lead to further evidence lending weight to this hypothesis.

Inside the tomb, the excavators began to expose the remains of the burial equipment, including the disarticulated body of the king himself, traces of a mummy mask, and a reasonably well-preserved canopic box. It seemed that the box had at one time been gilded but the gold foil had been stripped away, revealing that the wood used to build it had originally been used for something else: the presence of the name 'Sobekhotep' and the nature of the inscriptions made it clear that they had originally been a part of that king's wooden coffin. This strengthened the idea that the builders of this group of tombs had plundered the earlier tomb, S10, to build their own, and therefore that the group including Senebkay's tomb must have belonged to later kings.

The similarities between S9 and S10 and the internal structure of the pyramid of Ameny Qemau suggested a similar date, early in the 13th Dynasty, and their close proximity to one another suggested the individuals buried in these two tombs might have been closely related. Wegner and his team had originally suggested that they may have belonged to the brothers Sobekhotep I and Senbef, the first two kings of the line.[5] However, closer inspection of the wood plundered by Senebkay from Sobekhotep's coffin revealed that it had been decorated with hymns belonging to the corpus of Coffin Texts,[6] a group of spells typically found on burial equipment – and usually coffins, hence the name – of Middle Kingdom date. These inscriptions are a defining feature of the funerary culture of the period, though some appeared as early as the First Intermediate Period, while others are not attested until much later. Because those on the fragments plundered by Senebkay were not, to our knowledge, composed until some time after the beginning of the 13th Dynasty, Wegner and his team revised their conclusion, suggesting instead that the Sobekhotep in question was not the first, but the fourth king of this name.[7] Sobekhotep IV of the 13th Dynasty succeeded his brother, Neferhotep I, as pharaoh, and both were active at Abydos. This conclusion, of course, also pushes back the date of the reign of Senebkay, and the proposed Abydos Dynasty grouped around S9 and S10, into the later Second Intermediate Period.

An ancient inspection of some royal tombs at Thebes

We do not know what ultimately happened to this line of Abydos kings, but their independence had presumably been lost by the time of the great conflict between the Hyksos and Theban rulers.

We know of the whereabouts of the tombs of almost none of the kings of the Hyksos line or the 17th Dynasty. That some of them, at least, were buried at Thebes is clear, thanks to the survival of one of those documents that is so rich in information that reading its texts is like opening a window onto the past. The document in question is a papyrus of the 20th Dynasty, specifically Year 16 of the reign of Ramesses IX, which was bought by the British Museum, where it is kept to this day, in 1857. The seller was one Dr Henry William Charles Abbott, an English doctor who amassed a vast collection of Egyptian antiquities, and it is therefore known as the Abbott Papyrus.[8] The 2-m (6-ft) long scroll consists of seven pages of text on the recto (front), and two lists on the verso (back). It records the inspection of a series of tombs of 'royal ancestors', the discovery that some had been violated, and the judicial dispute between two rival factions as to who was responsible. Aside from the intrigues around the crimes and who had committed them, the papyrus is fascinating as a record of the tombs that were known to the investigating commission at the time, detailing both their location and condition.

In all, nine royal tombs are described,[9] of Amenhotep I, Inyotef II, Intef VI, Intef V, Sobekemsaf I, Seqenenre Tao, Kamose, Ahmose Sapair and Mentuhotep II, apparently listed in the order of their inspection. Of these individuals, the second, Inyotef II, and the last, Mentuhotep II, were kings of the 11th Dynasty. The remainder were all kings of the 17th Dynasty, with the exception of Amenhotep I, second ruler of the 18th Dynasty.

Of the tombs, two have been located by archaeologists. That of Inyotef II is known as the Saff el-Kisasiya (*saff* being an Arabic word meaning 'row' – a reference to the row of rock-cut square-based pillars at the entrance to the subterranean elements to the tombs of this period), which was excavated in the el-Tarif area of the Theban necropolis in the

The Abbott Papyrus.

second half of the 19th century. The Abbott Papyrus mentions that a stela was placed in front of the tomb, on which the king was depicted with his pet dog, Behkay, between his feet. Remarkably, fragments of this very stela were uncovered during the excavation of the tomb.[10] Mentuhotep II, it seems, was buried at the end of a passageway descending deep into the rock behind his great temple at Deir el-Bahri (see pp. ii–iii).

The identification of the two kings named Intef in the papyrus is disputed[11] but they seem to have been two of three individuals named Intef whose coffins are known: Sekhemre-Wepmaat Intef,[12] Sekhemre-Heruhirmaat Intef[13] and Nubkheperre Intef.[14] The tomb of the latter was discovered at Dra Abu el-Naga by Dr Daniel Polz of the German Archaeological Institute in 2001. This area in the Theban cemetery seems to have been dedicated to the 17th Dynasty rulers. A number of items from the funerary equipment of these kings, some of which surely must have come from some of the tombs mentioned in the Abbott Papyrus, was discovered in the 19th century and eventually made its way into some of the greatest museum collections.

In the course of the ancient inspections, only one of the tombs, that of Sobekemsaf I, was found to have been plundered; the others were apparently still intact at this time, and the recovery of coffins and other burial equipment belonging to Intef V, Intef VI and Kamose by archaeologists in the 19th century suggests their tombs were indeed left at least partially unviolated. The bodies of Amenhotep I and Seqenenre

Tao could not have remained in their tombs later than the 21st Dynasty, however: both were discovered in 1881 in the 'royal cache' tomb, TT 320 (see pp. 143–47). The tomb inspection described in the Abbott Papyrus was part of an effort to ensure that the royal tombs remained unviolated in the face of the threat posed by robbers. When TT 320 was found to contain over forty mummies of high-status individuals, including those of ten pharaohs of the 17th to 20th Dynasties, it became clear that ultimately the authorities had felt the only way to guarantee the security of the bodies of the royal dead would be to rebury them in a secret cache. Most had originally been buried in tombs in the Valley of the Kings whose locations are well known to us now, but in a few cases, including those of Seqenenre Tao and Amenhotep, they had been removed from tombs that are now lost.

Amenhotep I in the Abbott Papyrus

In the late 19th and early 20th centuries, excavation of the tombs of the New Kingdom pharaohs – precisely those that the priesthood had been unable to keep secure – in the Valley of the Kings had reached something of a zenith. Excavators such as the Frenchman Victor Loret and the American Theodore Davis, ably assisted by his excavators, including the Englishmen Edward Ayrton, Howard Carter and James Quibell, made a string of discoveries, rapidly ticking the names of pharaohs of the 18th, 19th and 20th Dynasties off the list as they went. By 1900, only a handful of the pharaonic tombs of the period remained to be discovered, and the pace of discovery up to that point must have given them every hope that it would only be a matter of time before there were none left to find.

By the time of the discovery of the royal cache in TT 320, many of the tombs of the pharaohs whose bodies were found there had already been identified in the Valley. Amenhotep I's was not among them, but over the next three decades, while the matter would not be settled beyond doubt, two candidate tombs were discovered, leading various scholars to lay claims in each case. In more recent years, attempts have been made to verify these claims, while a third candidate tomb has been revealed. And now, most recently, a new project is attempting to search for the tomb in an entirely different location.

In the absence of conclusive archaeological evidence, the temptation to use testimony in the Abbott Papyrus to identify various tombs in the area as that of Amenhotep I has proven overwhelming. Amenhotep I's tomb was the latest in the sequence described by the ancient account, the others all belonging to 17th Dynasty or earlier pharaohs. The inspection declared the tomb to be intact – 'examined on this day, it was found in good state by the masons'.[15] The papyrus might even provide some clue as to the location of the tomb, which is described as:

> The eternal horizon of king Djeserkare, Son of Ra, Amenhotep, which measures 120 cubits in depth from its stela[?] called Pa'aka, north of the house of Amenhotep of the Garden.

At first glance this might seem very helpful, not least as the measurement '120 cubits' would suggest, if correct, the possibility that the tomb could be located with precision – we know that one Egyptian cubit is equivalent to approximately 52 cm (20 in.), placing the tomb some 63 m (207 ft) from the given landmarks. The problem, however, is that we cannot be sure exactly what is meant by 'the stela', and although the 'house of Amenhotep' is very likely to have been a temple or other cult building, there are several candidates in the area that we know of, to say nothing of those that may since have been lost.

Arthur Weigall and KV 39

The first of the three most likely candidates for the tomb of Amenhotep I is KV 39. This tomb is in fact located some distance away from the main part of the Valley, to the south, close to the cluster of workmen's huts sometimes known as the 'way station' or 'village de repos', which those who have walked across the cliffs behind the temple of Deir el-Bahri and into the Valley of the Kings will know (although sadly at the time of writing this route is off-limits for security reasons). It was discovered in the late 19th century by two locals, Macarious and Andraos, who had learned of the location of the tomb and were granted permission to excavate it by the Antiquities Service. They were clearly more interested, however, in finding saleable objects (they failed) than making any contribution to the scientific recording of an ancient monument, and left much material relating to several 18th Dynasty burials behind. The tomb was subsequently entered by Arthur Weigall in 1908, when he was the Antiquities Service's Chief Inspector for Upper Egypt, and in an article published in 1911, Weigall announced his belief that KV 39 was the tomb of Amenhotep I.[16] Weigall was a serious archaeologist, and had worked alongside Flinders Petrie, so-called 'Father of Archaeology', at Abydos, but even though he observed that Macarious and Andraos had hardly been thorough in their work he attempted no further clearance himself. In fact, no such work was undertaken until the retired British engineer turned Egyptologist Dr John Rose applied for permission to revisit the tomb over seventy years later to see if the matter of its owner's identity could be settled once and for all. Rose and his team cleared the tomb over the course of five seasons between 1989 and 1994, showing the previous plans of the tomb to have been flawed and discovering considerable quantities of new material, the first recovered from the tomb under scientific conditions.

The tomb is entered via a short descending staircase heading towards the west and leading to a simple L-shaped Entrance Chamber. This provides access to a rectangular vestibule, dubbed the Upper Chamber

The entrance to KV 39.

directly ahead and opening out to the right. Into the floor of this room are the beginnings of a descending staircase continuing further westwards into the bedrock. However, this has been blocked and damaged by debris brought into the tomb by floodwaters, and it has so far proven impossible to establish whether or not it continues any further or is simply unfinished.[17] The Upper Chamber also provides access to two further descending corridors, their entrances to the left of that to the Upper Chamber, both of which lead the visitor much further down into the rock.

The first corridor proceeds in a southerly direction, at right angles to the vestibule, and is entered via a staircase cut into the floor. At the bottom of the staircase, the passage continues to slope downwards, dropping a further three times by single steps, before a second staircase is reached, at the end of which lies a rectangular chamber. The second, longer passageway begins with a gently downwards-sloping corridor leading in an easterly direction to a series of staircases, doorways and passageways, eventually concluding, after a total distance of almost 40 m (130 ft), in the burial chamber.

Certain features of the architecture and masonry techniques evident in the entrance, east passage and burial chamber suggest that the tomb dates to the early 18th Dynasty.[18] It has no protective 'well' – a sudden and deep, but brief, drop in the floor level of the corridor designed to prevent robbers from proceeding further along the corridor and to capture any debris that might enter the tomb as a result of flash flooding. These became a regular feature of royal tombs from the reign of Tuthmosis III, the fifth king of the 18th Dynasty, onwards.[19] Furthermore, a recess cut into the floor of the chamber at the end of the south passage may have been an emplacement for a coffin, a feature common to pre-New Kingdom tombs.[20]

Rose and Buckley also argue that the tomb lies at the 'head' of the Valley, precisely where you might expect construction of the cemetery to have begun. KV 39 does lie at the base of the Meretseger mountain, the natural pyramid-like peak overlooking the Valley, which would seem to make for an ideal spot to inaugurate a new cemetery. It certainly is in an unusually prominent, or at least high, place, and perhaps anticipates the move towards the Valley of the Kings, even if it sits slightly aside from the tombs in the main part of the Valley. It is perhaps curious that it should have been assigned a 'KV' number, which in itself lends something of a bias among academics, perhaps – a tomb with a 'KV' designation is perhaps simply more likely to be interpreted as a royal tomb than one without.

The material discovered within the tomb demonstrated beyond doubt a connection to several pharaohs of the early part of the 18th Dynasty, although not as early as the reign of Amenhotep I, including a series of dockets naming Tuthmosis I, Tuthmosis II and Amenhotep II, and a gold signet ring bearing the cartouche of Tuthmosis III. The excavator suggests

The mountain of Meretseger overlooking the Valley of the Kings, taken from the main entrance to the Valley by Francis Frith, c. 1857.

that the presence of multiple, later royal names might be explained by the mummies of these pharaohs having lain in the tomb temporarily during the period of their rewrapping by the priests of the 21st Dynasty while they were preparing to move them to the royal cache, a theory supported by additional evidence of mummification having been carried out in the tomb. Of these four pharaohs, Amenhotep II was returned to his original tomb, while the others were reburied in TT 320, which lies only a short distance away.

Weigall's hypothesis seems to have been based mainly on his having drawn a connection between KV 39 and the resting place of Amenhotep I as described in the Abbott Papyrus. His belief was that the 'stela' mentioned in the text is a reference to the 'way station', which does indeed lie approximately 120 cubits above the entrance to KV 39.[21] He interpreted the 'house of Amenhotep of the Garden' as a now lost monument of Amenhotep I's at Medinet Habu, which was the administrative base for those who carried out the inspection of the tombs. This suggestion has proven impossible to verify of course, and ultimately, although the more recent investigations have undoubtedly brought much interesting material to light, they have not significantly strengthened the case for arguing that KV 39 was the tomb of Amenhotep I.

Howard Carter's rebuttal: Tomb AN-B

Weigall's conclusion had barely been published before it was called into question. His fellow Englishman, Howard Carter, was not convinced, and within a couple of years had formulated a theory of his own. Carter had in fact been interested in locating the tomb of Amenhotep I for several years before Weigall made his assertion, writing to Lady Amherst, an excavator herself and daughter of one of the foremost private collectors of Egyptian antiquities of the day, in 1903, 'I wonder if Lord Amherst would like me to look for the tomb of Amenhotep I.'[22] Nothing came of this, however, until 1912, when Carter was visited by a local antiquities dealer, Gad Hassan. Hassan showed Carter some fragmentary alabaster vessels, some bearing the names of Amenhotep I and his mother, Ahmose-Nefertari. Of course, these captured Carter's attention, and he persuaded Hassan to show him where the fragments were found. Hassan led Carter to a high point in the Dra Abu el-Naga cemetery. Here Carter came upon a tomb consisting of an entrance shaft, a corridor from which two side chambers could be entered, a protective well, then a second corridor leading to a burial chamber with two pillars. These features convinced Carter it was a tomb of the 18th Dynasty, and the location was also known as the burial place of the kings of the 17th Dynasty, so it was entirely possible that it continued in use for royal burials beyond the transition to the 18th. The tomb, which he designated AN-B, was in a very ruinous state and no doubt had been since antiquity, but Carter would have known that the mummies of both Amenhotep I and his mother had been found in TT 320, the 'royal cache' tomb, presumably following – or in anticipation of – the violation of their original resting place, and so would not have been expecting to find the king's tomb undisturbed. He decided it was worth investigating further, and in the spring of 1914, he took his chance. Although these excavations yielded only a few fragments of burial equipment pointing to the (re-)use of the tomb at a later date, in the Third Intermediate Period, Carter and Lord Carnarvon, by that time his patron, were both convinced. Little, if any, further evidence came to light to change the picture over the following seventy years.

A third candidate

In 1991, a new archaeological mission under the auspices of the German Archaeological Institute in Cairo (DAIK) and led by Dr Daniel Polz began exploring Dra Abu el-Naga with the explicit aim of identifying tombs of the 17th and 18th Dynasties, including those of the pharaohs of the period.

An enormous concession of 160,000 m² (1,700,000 ft²) was granted by the Egyptian authorities in order to allow the DAIK to tackle thoroughly the question of the location of these missing tombs.[23] Two and a half decades later, the project has revealed a massive quantity of material of those periods and succeeded in identifying certain tombs, including, most spectacularly, the pyramid tomb of the 17th Dynasty king Nubkheperre Intef (see p. 74), and fragments of a probable second such monument built for Nubkheperre's predecessor, Sekhemre Wepmaat Intef. But it is another part of the site, with a complicated later history, that is of particular interest to us here.

Polz had uncovered a structure referred to in the *Topographical Bibliography of Ancient Egyptian Hieroglyphic Texts, Reliefs and Paintings* (first published in 1927 and considered the 'Bible' of Egyptian archaeology) as 'Theban Tomb (TT) 293'. The very brief entry describes it as being the tomb of the Chief Priest of Amun, Ramessesnakht, of the time of the 20th Dynasty pharaoh, Ramesses IV. All fairly straightforward and unremarkable, but from the outset of their investigations, Polz and his team were convinced that this simply could not have been the tomb of a non-royal individual; both its scale and location were more suggestive of a royal burial. Over the course of three seasons between 1993 and 1995 the area was cleared and the outline of the tombs planned, revealing it to be a far more complicated monument than previously thought. It is, in fact, a double tomb, and has been given the new designation K93.11/12.

The entrances to the two tombs are cut side by side into the hillside, fronted by a grand double forecourt, built on a levelled plateau

View across the site of K93.11/12 on the low hills of Dra Abu el-Naga, looking south, with the Nile Valley and cultivation to the left in the distance.

and delimited by a very substantial dry-stone wall. This wall was made from limestone blocks and chippings cut from the bedrock during the construction of the tombs, and seems to have been constructed in a single phase, demonstrating that the tombs were built simultaneously, and thus the monument as a whole was always intended to be a double burial. The forecourt at the front of each tomb entrance is divided into inner and outer areas by a pylon, in front of each of which the remains of a colonnaded portico were recovered. Located as they were high on the Dra Abu el-Naga hillside, these pylons would have created a very striking impression. Clearly this was not a monument that was intended to be kept secret, and indeed Polz and his team have also found evidence of shrines that he believes were placed here in later times in veneration of the original tomb owners. Imposing superstructures and provision for cult offerings and ritual activities were also found in association with the nearby 17th Dynasty tombs of Nubkheperre Intef and Sekhemra Wepmaat Intef, but analysis of the ceramics discovered at the complex shows it to have been in use from the early 18th Dynasty onwards.

Polz and his team had undoubtedly unearthed something intriguing: a substantial, probably royal, tomb of the late 17th or early 18th Dynasty, designed for a pair of individuals. We know of very few such pairs whose equality of status would have warranted the construction of such a double-tomb. Ahmose I, founder of the 18th Dynasty, and his wife Ahmose-Nefertari are one; the only other of this period is their son, Amenhotep I, and his mother. Of these two pairs, it is the latter couple that was most celebrated after their deaths.

Perhaps most striking of all is the connection between the tomb complex and the nearby 'Meniset', a temple dedicated to the divine form of Amenhotep I and his mother. This curious temple was discovered in the 1890s by Wilhelm Spiegelberg, but was not thoroughly documented until Howard Carter investigated the site in 1916. The temple once lay at the edge of the cultivation, where the fertile strip of land nourished by the Nile flood meets the desert, but is now surrounded by the modern village of Gurna and has all but vanished beneath the silt. Its association with Amenhotep I and Ahmose-Nefertari is, however, clear from the objects recovered during the excavations.[24] Most significantly perhaps, its builders did not follow the later practice of aligning the temple at right angles to the river; rather, it was quite precisely aligned on a north–south axis, and if this axis is projected in a northerly direction, it coincides exactly with K93.11/12. This could be coincidence, but it is difficult not to see a connection, especially given what we know of the Egyptians' preoccupation with the symbolism of, and skill for, geometry in their architecture.

This view is perhaps strengthened by the presence, revealed by the German excavations, of a pylon running along the southern side of the forecourt of K93.12, and a causeway extending from it. The causeway is lined on both sides by a wall of limestone boulders and runs for 60 m (200 ft) in a southerly direction, until it meets a small wadi known as the Shig el-Ateyat. This wadi runs in an easterly direction down the hillside, and eventually meets the temple of Meniset.

K93.11 seems to have modified for reuse as a tomb-temple by Ramessesnakht, the Chief Priest of Amun during the reigns of Ramesses IV to Ramesses IX in Karnak. Ramessesnakht is believed to have died as early as Year 2 of Ramesses IX, some years before the Papyrus Abbott inspection in the same king's Year 16, at which time the tomb of Amenhotep I was thought still to be intact. Assuming the date of the inspection, and the tomb's unviolated state at that time, are not in doubt, then if K93.11/12 was the tomb of Amenhotep I, then we must revise our dates for Ramessesnakht. His son and successor as Chief Priest, Amenhotep, adapted K93.12 for the same purpose, and seems to have been responsible for the construction of the causeway leading to the Meniset. The German excavators argue that the Chief Priest Amenhotep's causeway simply developed a pre-existing pathway between the Meniset and the tomb complex, implying that the two had been connected all along.[25]

Further strengthening the case for the identification of the tomb as that of Amenhotep I and his mother is a fragment of relief decoration from the time of the Chief Priest Amenhotep, which shows an image of a pharaoh, perhaps Amenhotep I himself, alongside a short hieratic (the handwritten form of hieroglyphics) graffito that includes the word *mahat*, meaning 'tomb'.

Finally, although Polz himself has rejected the use of the Abbott Papyrus as a source of information in locating the tomb of Amenhotep I – 'there seems to be only one way to step on methodologically solid ground: we simply have to disregard pAbbott as a source for any attempt to locate the royal tombs of the late 17th and early 18th Dynasties'[26] – it is difficult not to recall the text's 'high place...north of the house of Amenhotep of the Garden...'.

Polz sensibly rejects the Abbott Papyrus in favour of a more purely archaeological approach, on the grounds that the text can be interpreted to fit any number of archaeological sites in the area. This has not deterred all of his colleagues however, and one final candidate site for the tomb, which is very definitely in a high place, is the subject of perhaps one of the most improbable, incredible but ultimately fascinating excavation projects currently under way anywhere in Egypt.

The Polish–Egyptian Clifftop Mission to Deir el-Bahri

This project began its extraordinary work in 1999. Led by Professor Andrzej Niwinski of Warsaw University, it traverses a vertiginous landscape of ledges, slopes and pathways, some covered in very loose

The cliffs at Deir el-Bahri. The chutes employed by the Polish–Egyptian Clifftop
Mission to remove debris away from its excavations to safety below are
visible to the left of the temple of Hatshepsut.

scree, directly above the temples of Mentuhotep II, Hatshepsut and
Tuthmosis III at Deir el-Bahri. From the ground the project appears
completely impossible: these famous cliffs, which form such a spectacular backdrop to the temples, seem completely vertical, like an arcing
set of cinema curtains, and yet they are not. Professor Niwinski, surely
as spry and energetic as even the most youthful of his workmen, has
been working here for almost two decades now, demonstrating his
own head for heights and agility, but also those of the ancients, traces
of whose activities he has been uncovering all across the cliff's face
(see pp. ii–iii).

Contrary to what one might expect, given the site's precarious position,
Niwinski has uncovered a considerable amount of evidence of human
activity. Given the difficulty even of getting to the site, let alone making
use of it, Niwinski believes the ancients must have had a very special reason
to have been there. Indeed, he believes this spot was chosen precisely for
its remoteness, as the perfect place to conceal an important tomb.

What has he found? Approximately 60 m (200 ft) below the top of the cliffs lies an enormous boulder, the area around which seems to have been covered with an artificial cement composed of limestone powder and chippings, flint and Esna shale slate bonded together with water. Once dried, this composition would have looked very much like the surrounding limestone,[27] and appears to have been used to create a level platform on top of an area of cliffside sloping naturally in places at an incline of as much as 45 degrees. Niwinski proposes that this platform served several purposes: it was used to seal and conceal a tomb lying beneath it; it created a ledge upon which the ancient craftsmen could work, presumably carrying out the final stages of the concealment; and finally it played a vital part in what, if Niwinski's interpretations are correct, was an unparalleled and audacious final means of preventing access to the tomb. A second huge boulder, of an estimated 60 tonnes, is also present in the same area. Niwinski hypothesizes that this second stone was deliberately dropped from the top of the cliffs onto the ledge below with such precision that it nudged the pre-existing boulder from its earlier position, the two finally coming to rest directly above the tomb entrance, forming an impenetrable barrier to the chambers concealed within.[28]

Six tectonic fissures have been discovered in the area by the team, two of which were found to have been deliberately filled in with the same orange-coloured sand that is present in the cement mixture, perhaps protecting something underneath from the ingress of floodwaters.[29] Ten man-made drains may have served a similar function.[30] Most intriguingly of all, ten robbers' tunnels – according to Niwinski's interpretation – were also found in the area,[31] suggesting to the archaeologist that he was not the first to think there was something to find.

A further clue is provided by seven graffiti in hieratic around the site. Five of them mention the name of a 20th Dynasty official named Butehamun, who is well known from a corpus of documents known as the Late Ramesside Letters.

Butehamun seems to have played a more prominent role in the inspection and reburials of the royals than any of his contemporaries. His name occurs frequently in tomb-inspection graffiti around the Valley of the Kings, and he is also mentioned in dockets attached to mummies as having been responsible for various acts of restoration, including the

'Osirification' (rewrapping) of the mummy of Ramesses III. He clearly had a high position in the royal court, holding the title of 'Scribe of the Necropolis', as did his father Djehutymes, and also those of 'Opener of the Gates of the Necropolis' and 'Overseer of Works in the House of Eternity' (meaning the tomb, or sometimes the burial chamber). Furthermore, the lid of his own outer coffin, now in the Museo Egizio in Turin, is painted with the images of several named members of New Kingdom royal families, confirming a very close and privileged connection between the scribe and the royal dead.

Niwinski had originally argued that the graffiti naming Butehamun in the Deir el-Bahri cliffs must have been written immediately after the sealing of a tomb, and that the tomb can thus only have belonged to one of the two royal individuals of that period whose tombs have so far not been identified: Herihor (see Chapter Four) and his son, Neferheres.[32] But further discoveries have led Niwinski to revise this conclusion, and instead suggest that the tomb had in fact been adapted for one of these individuals, having originally been cut for someone else: Amenhotep I.

In the year 2000, the team discovered the central part of an unusual dagger made from bronze, the closest known parallel to which is a dagger made of gold and silver, discovered buried alongside the mummy of the 17th Dynasty pharaoh Kamose, a predecessor – and uncle – of Amenhotep I.[33]

Could Deir el-Bahri have been the setting for the elusive tomb of Ahmose's son and successor? It is noteworthy that, according to the Tempest Stela, it was during Ahmose's reign that a great storm befell Egypt, damaging numerous monuments including the royal necropolis: 'It was then that His Majesty was informed that the funerary conces-sions had been invaded [by the water], that the sepulchral chambers had been damaged, that the structures of funerary enclosures had been undermined, that the pyramids had collapsed[?]'[34] Might this have prompted the authorities to search for a new, less vulnerable site for the place for the burial of pharaoh, and might the drainage system dis-covered by Niwinski have been part of the response to this apocalyptic event?

It is also well established that Amenhotep I was active and venerated in this area. He built a small mudbrick chapel on the site later occupied by the temple of Hatshepsut. This may have been where, originally, a very striking sandstone statue of the king now in the British Museum was erected; it was discovered during the Egypt Exploration Fund's excavations led by Edouard Naville at the nearby temple of Mentuhotep II, and was perhaps moved to that site when construction of Hatshepsut's monument was begun. Amenhotep's temple was perhaps not a mortuary temple,[35] but the statue depicts the king in the Osirid pose, associating him with the great god of the afterlife, and the temple of Mentuhotep II certainly was a funerary monument, marking as it did the burial place of that king. A stela also discovered by Naville at the temple of Mentuhotep II and now in the British Museum shows a series of four Osirid statues of Mentuhotep II and Amenhotep I,[36] indicating that the temple was associated with both kings equally at some point. Futher, the courtyard of the temple is known to have incorporated a substantial garden, in which the evidence of fifty-five sycamore trees and eight tamarisk has been found.[37]

Could this have been the 'house of Amenhotep of the Garden' mentioned in Papyrus Abbott? The text tells us that the 'eternal horizon of… Amenhotep [I]' lies directly to the north of this temple, and Professor Niwinski's site lies directly to the north of the temple of Mentuhotep…[38] Furthermore, the bedrock in the area of the cement platform discovered by Professor Niwinski and his team lies, he claims, 63 m (207 ft) – that is, 120 cubits – below the top of the cliffs, which he argues represents the 'high place' referred to in the Abbott Papyrus.[39] Finally, we know that Amenhotep's wife Meritamun and son Amenemhat were both buried at Deir el-Bahri, in tombs discovered by Herbert Winlock.[40]

Could Niwinski be right? The suggestion that the tomb could be at Deir el-Bahri somewhere seems sound, given Amenhotep's relationship with the temples there. However, despite Niwinski's optimism and enthusiasm for committing to it in print – 'numerous archaeological premises make me believe that exactly here the mouth of the tomb shaft can be expected'[41] – no tomb has been found, and indeed the evidence remains circumstantial.

Conclusions

When the various hypotheses are compared against one another, Niwinski's case seems to be the weakest, purely on the grounds that in all other cases a tomb has certainly been found. Tombs AN-B, KV 39 or K93.11/12 are all undeniably tombs, and can all be associated with Amenhotep I on various grounds. Conversely, Niwinski's argument is essentially that the Deir el-Bahri cliffs present evidence for the concealment of *something*, that that something is probably a tomb, and that it could be expected to be that of Amenhotep I. It's there somewhere, Niwinski hopes, but he has been unable to locate it so far. Understandably, most archaeologists and Egyptologists are sceptical about his claims. Nonetheless, his arguments are not inherently flawed, and his project is one of the most extraordinary in the history of Egyptology if only because, to the casual observer with their feet firmly on the ground looking up at that most dramatic backdrop, it seems impossible to believe there could really be an archaeological excavation in progress halfway up the cliffs. There is something quintessentially Egyptological about the improbability of the project, and about Niwinski's undimmed determination and enthusiasm.

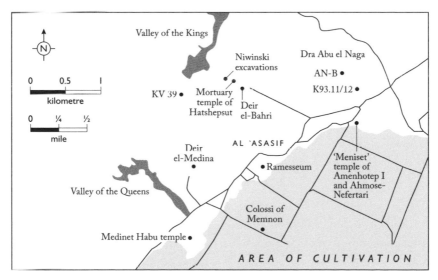

Map of the cemetery of Thebes, at the edge of the cultivation on the West Bank opposite Luxor.

The use of the Valley of the Kings as the royal necropolis is one of the most distinctive characteristics of the New Kingdom. The deliberate concealment of the tombs constructed there is the Valley's defining feature, and contrasts sharply with previous practices, particularly those of the Middle Kingdom, when pyramid-building was still de rigueur. So in a sense, the search for Amenhotep I's tomb is about determining his place in the changing traditions of royal burial practice. If it turns out that his tomb was at Dra Abu el-Naga, as were those of the 17th Dynasty kings before him, then he was perhaps a follower of tradition, with the relocation to the Valley of the Kings occurring after his reign. Professor Niwinski argues for a change of location to a deliberately inaccessible spot, but that we should expect the tomb of Amenhotep I to have been very visible, as were those of earlier kings. In his eyes, the Deir el-Bahri cliffs would have provided Amenhotep with the ideal location. If this is the case, and the tomb was not at Dra Abu el-Naga, it would represent a break with tradition. But if Weigall's suspicions were right all along, and Amenhotep was buried in KV 39, we should know him as the founder of one of the most celebrated burial grounds in history.

CHAPTER 3

THE MISSING
AMARNA ROYALS

The enduring mystery

In the popular imagination and on the screen, the archetypal archaeo-logical discovery involves a professorial type entering a previously sealed chamber with lamp held aloft, its flickering light gently illuminating a hoard of treasures. It never really happens like that – except in Howard Carter's case, it actually did.

What Carter had found in 1922 was the intact tomb of a then little-known pharaoh, Tutankhamun of the 18th Dynasty. His discovery caused a sensation internationally and a wave of 'Egyptomania' rolled across the globe. Egyptian motifs began to appear in art, clothing, jewelry and even hairstyles; novels, films and songs inspired by the discovery were written; and Tutankhamun became a household name, used to advertise all manner of products, from lemons to cigarettes. Carter's job was to manage the documentation of the objects and their safe removal to the Egyptian Museum in Cairo, all the while battling against the public and media interest, and the squabbling among those who wanted to control and take ownership of the discovery. This was a massive task, which, given the circumstances, Carter accomplished admirably. However, the comprehensive, scientific study of this vast haul of material was more than he could manage, and great enough, even, that the collective efforts of dozens of Egyptologists working ever since have been insufficient to give the material the thorough study it deserves.

It just so happens that Tutankhamun – whose mummified body, covered except for his head and feet, can now be viewed in the antechamber of the tomb – lived and died at the end of one of the most compelling and scrutinized periods of Egyptian history. He reigned shortly after the time of the Amarna 'heresy'. His predecessor, the pharaoh Akhenaten, in a reign lasting less than two decades, had brought about a revolution in Egypt's religion, art and politics. He proscribed the worship of the traditional gods in favour of just one, the sun disc called the Aten, completely transformed the way that he as pharaoh, along with the royal family, was portrayed in art, and built an entirely new capital city, to which thousands of courtiers and others were moved over the course of just a few years. The discovery of his tomb, though the sensation of the initial discovery has died away, is the starting point for a debate that concerns just a few individuals, and events that unfolded over just a few years – out of all the millennia of ancient Egypt history – but nonetheless continue to capture the public imagination. The focus on the surviving evidence of this period is so intense that any new material has the potential to transform our knowledge, and inevitably there is therefore a great hunger for more. The precedent set by the superabundance of such material discovered in the tomb of Tutankhamun raises expectations still higher. Could there be another tomb belonging to a member, or members, of the royal Amarna family waiting to be unearthed? If so, where is it? And to whom might it belong?

In this case, we are not necessarily talking about a single tomb, or a single individual. Debate rages as to how many individuals in the Amarna royal house might have received a royal burial, what their names were and even what gender they might have been. As we will see, our evidence suggests that some of these individuals may have been buried more than once, disinterred and reburied somewhere else, or their burial equipment deliberately damaged or destroyed as attitudes towards their memory changed – and thus put almost, but not quite, out of the reach of archaeologists, tantalizing us with just enough information to set imaginations racing, but insufficient evidence for firm conclusions to be drawn. It's the perfect setting for an archaeological tale. The one thing we can be certain about is that Tutankhamun, whose death represents the end of this fascinating era, was buried in the tomb we now know as

KV 62, the 62nd to be discovered in the Valley of the Kings. Could the tombs of the other leading royals of the period – Akhenaten, Nefertiti, Smenkhkare, Ankhesenamun and possibly others – still await discovery?

Akhenaten and the Amarna 'heresy'

Akhenaten was the son of Nebmaatre Amenhotep III, and was crowned pharaoh of Egypt as Neferkheperure Waenre Amenhotep IV in approximately 1353 BC. In the early years of his reign, he departed from the rigid conventions of the Egyptian artistic canon, having himself depicted with highly exaggerated – even grotesque – features in a series of extraordinary colossal statues erected in and around buildings he constructed at the margins of the great temple complex of Karnak (see p. vi). Karnak, established as one of the great religious centres in the Middle Kingdom, was the cult centre of the god Amun. By the 18th Dynasty, Amun had become the pre-eminent deity in Egypt, particularly when combined with the sun god as Amun-Ra. As such, Karnak became the most important cult centre in the country and the focus of massive construction projects, as each successive pharaoh sought to demonstrate their devotion to the god by building on a grander scale than anything that had come before. It was therefore entirely conventional for Akhenaten to follow his predecessors in pursuing a programme of building at Karnak, but he did so in an unconventional – even heretical – manner. The buildings differed from earlier constructions in their location at the eastern extent of the Amun enclosure, and in that they featured the king, but also his wife, playing an extremely prominent role alongside one god only: the Aten, a very particular manifestation of the sun god represented in the art of the era as the many-armed sun disc. The buildings' form, iconography and focus on divine actors other than Amun must have seemed treasonous to the temple authorities.

In Year 4 or 5 of his reign, Amenhotep IV ('Amun is Satisfied') changed his name to Akhenaten ('Effective for the Aten'), and founded an entirely new capital city on virgin territory in Middle Egypt. This was a phenomenal achievement: within a few years approximately 30,000 people inhabited this new city, which he named Akhetaten, the 'Horizon of the Aten'. Its remains can be found at the site of Tell el-Amarna, or simply

Amarna, which gives its name to the period and the culture associated with it. This radical cultural upheaval was not to last, however; around twelve years after establishing his new order, Akhenaten died, and his great project began to come apart. Within a few years of his death, the conventional religion had been restored, Akhetaten was abandoned in favour of a return to the old capitals of Memphis in the north and Thebes in the south, and draughtsmen, craftsmen and builders resumed their work in the traditional artistic style. Akhenaten's reign came to be seen as a heresy. The old gods and their cults were restored, and his successors set about erasing all trace of the heretic pharaoh and his revolution from the monumental and historical records.

Akhenaten's Great Royal Wife, Nefertiti, has come to be recognized as one of the great icons of ancient Egypt. She is perhaps best known for the famous bust discovered at Amarna in 1912 by a German archaeological expedition, now kept in the Ägyptisches Museum in Berlin (see p. 25). This remarkably well-preserved bust, made of stuccoed limestone, depicts the queen wearing the distinctive, flat-topped headdress that is unique to her, gazing confidently forward, relaxed but assured, strong and invulnerable. She is beautiful in a strikingly modern way, with high cheekbones, a shapely nose and strong chin, and though one of the inlaid eyes is missing, the other is enough to convey a sense of someone very alive. The moulding around the edges of the mouth and beneath the eyes suggest someone perhaps not in the very prime of youth but stronger and wiser for it. She looks hauntingly real, and a good fit with modern ideas of beauty.

Limestone trial piece on which an artist has practised sculpting the head and shoulders of Nefertiti in profile. Discovered by the Egypt Exploration Society at Amarna in 1932 and now in the Egyptian Museum, Cairo.

An unfinished head of Nefertiti discovered by the Egypt Exploration Society in 1933 and now in the Egyptian Museum, Cairo.

There is no doubt that the survival of this extraordinary object, which is now one of the most recognizable images from the ancient world, has contributed to an elevation of Nefertiti's status in the popular imagination but she clearly did enjoy a status in her own lifetime that was at least equal to, if not higher than, any king's Great Royal Wife before or since.

Nefertiti features prominently in the decoration of the structures that Akhenaten built early in his reign at Karnak, and in one of the temples she even appears more frequently than her husband. She was also prominently depicted in the boundary stelae that Akhenaten had set up to mark out the limits of his new city. She would continue to feature in scenes decorating the palaces, houses and non-royal tombs at Amarna, especially in the new scenes of the royal family that are a defining feature of the art of the period.

These scenes, in which Akhenaten and Nefertiti were shown with their daughters, serve to emphasize the close relations between the royal family and the one god, the Aten, where previously such close correspondence with the gods had been the exclusive preserve of the king. Furthermore, a relief found at Hermopolis, but originally from Amarna and now in Boston's Museum of Fine Arts, depicts Nefertiti on a royal barge receiving the benevolent rays of the Aten and smiting a foreign enemy, standing in a typically Egyptian pose – but one usually reserved for pharaoh.

Besides Nefertiti, reconstructing the house of the Amarna Period royals continues to provoke discussion and disagreement among scholars. The existence of a pharaoh named Smenkhkare who reigned during the Amarna Period has been known since the mid-19th century, when the decoration on the walls of the tomb of Meryre ii were recorded. Here, Ankhkheperure Smenkhkare-djeserkheperu is shown rewarding the tomb owner with tribute, alongside Meritaten. The latter, Akhenaten's eldest daughter, is here given the epithet 'Great Royal Wife', confirming she was wife to this pharaoh. The scene appears on a wall adjacent to a scene of foreign tribute that dates to Year 12 or 13 of Akhenaten's reign. As Akhenaten is known to have reigned for several years beyond this, it seems that Smenkhkare must have been a co-regent of his, and this would seem to be confirmed by a vase discovered in the tomb of Tutankhamun that features the names of the two kings side by side. But our understanding of the period of transition between Akhenaten's death and the revival of the old ways is fraught with uncertainty. The key questions are: Who ruled Egypt after Akhenaten? How many members of the royal family (or the noble ranks around them) took the throne, either independently or jointly with others? Where were these individuals buried? And can the remains of those burials be identified among the vast jumble of material already found in various funerary contexts, or are they yet to be discovered? Is it possible that we already have the remains of all the tombs, mummies and burial equipment, or are pieces of the puzzle still missing?

Right An elaborately wrapped animal mummy, the bandages decorated with an appliqué image of a seated Thoth with the head of an ibis and wearing the Atef crown.

Right Professor Andrzej Niwinski exploring the clifftop site of his excavations.

Below View looking west down onto the temple of Mentuhotep II Nebhepetre at Deir el-Bahri from the site of Professor Andrzej Niwinski's excavations. In later times the temple may have been the 'house of Amenhotep of the Garden' mentioned in the Abbott Papyrus.

Above Chute used by Professor Niwinski and his team to convey the debris from the clifftop excavations to ground level.

Below Deir el-Bahri from the air. The temples of Hatshepsut (extensively restored, to the right) and Mentuhotep II Nebhepetre (to the left) are clearly visible. KV 39 lies just beyond the ridge of the cliffs.

Above The head of a statue of Amenhotep I in the Luxor Museum.

Opposite The coffin of Amenhotep I, discovered as part of the royal cache in TT 320 and now in the Egyptian Museum, Cairo.

Left The main descending passageway in the royal tomb at Amarna.

Left The main burial chamber in the royal tomb at Amarna.

Below The scene of the royal family mourning the death of Meketaten, in Room gamma within the royal tomb at Amarna.

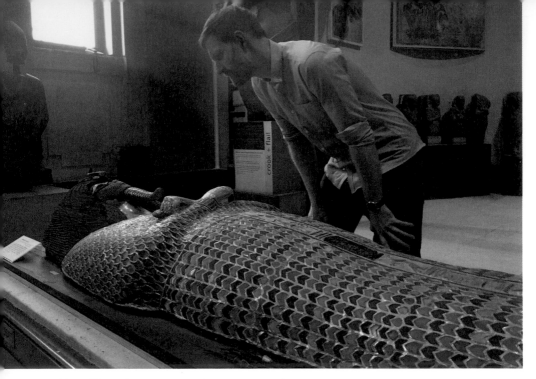

Above The author examining the reconstructed coffin from KV 55 in the Egyptian Museum, Cairo.

Below Canopic jars found in KV 55; the heads are thought to exhibit the features of Kiya, Akhenaten's secondary wife.

The royal tomb at Amarna

At the beginning of Akhenaten's reign, while he was still known as Amenhotep IV and prior to the establishment of Akhetaten as the new capital, construction would presumably have begun on his tomb – in the Valley of the Kings. Where exactly this may have been, or whether it might even eventually have come to be used for the burial of one of his successors or for another purpose, we may never know.[1] What is certain is that whatever plans were made, they were changed as part of the relocation of the royal house. Akhenaten could not have been more explicit about his intention to be buried at Amarna itself, and he provides what might, had history played out differently, have been some helpful clues as to the location of the burial of some of the other characters of this period:

> There shall be made for me a tomb in the eastern mountain of Akhetaten...and the burial of the Great Royal Wife Nefertiti shall be made therein...and the burial of the King's Daughter Meritaten shall be made therein.[2]

Notably, only one tomb is mentioned here, implying that Akhenaten's intention was that he, Nefertiti and Meritaten would all be buried in the same tomb, although there is some ambiguity as Akhenaten later speaks of a 'cemetery' (semet) of 'tomb chapels' (ahaut) to be built for various officials, all of whom will be buried in 'it'.

It was not until long after Western scholars had become aware of Akhenaten's city that the tomb seemed finally to have been found. One might expect this to have been one of the great, iconic moments in Egyptology, and yet the discovery remained unknown for several years – it seems the royal tomb at Amarna was found by locals before any archaeologists could get to it. Petrie, writing in 1892, believed that the tomb had been discovered 'four or five years ago' by locals, who kept it a secret while removing any and all items they thought could be sold on.[3] It was presumably only once this process had been completed that the secret was allowed out, which then prompted several senior members of the Antiquities Service staff each to lodge their own claim to have made the discovery, when none had done any such thing. There was, by this point, no sensational discovery to be made, and as a result the tomb did not receive the attention it should

The royal wadi at Amarna.

have had for many years after its official clearance by Italian archaeologist Alessandro Barsanti in 1891. English Egyptologist Geoffrey Martin of the University of Cambridge set out to rectify the situation in the 1960s, and we now rely on the two volumes arising from his comprehensive study of the tomb and the objects that he found left in it for our knowledge of what was intended to be Akhenaten's final resting place.[4]

The tomb was given the designation TA 26 by Norman de Garis Davies, who documented the tomb in the early 20th century, some sixty years before Professor Martin investigated it more systematically. Its architecture broadly follows the pattern established for earlier 18th Dynasty royal tombs in the Valley of the Kings. It lies some distance from the Nile Valley in a wadi running through the high desert. Its entrance is cut into the bedrock of one of the sloping sides of the wadi, and from here is formed of a long, descending passageway, with staircases cut on either side. This central ramp was left smooth so that the sarcophagus – made of finer stone, granite, brought from elsewhere – could be lowered down into the burial chamber (E), which lies at its end, just beyond a deep shaft or well (D), a typical feature of tombs of this period designed to thwart would-be robbers and to capture any incoming floodwaters that might threaten the burial chamber. Before reaching the well, the visitor encounters two subsidiary sections. First, a series of chambers arranged along a curving corridor leads off to the right of the descending passageway, and terminates in an unfinished chamber. Secondly, also to the right of the descending corridor, is a suite of three rooms named alpha, beta and gamma (see p. vii).

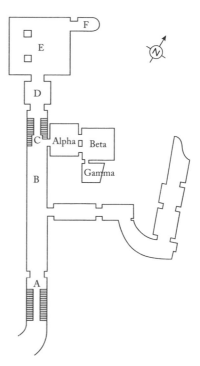

Plan of the royal tomb at Amarna.

That the tomb belonged to Akhenaten seems to have been assumed from the outset. Its location and its shape and size, strongly reminiscent of the royal tombs in the Valley of the Kings, distinguish it from the non-royal tombs at Amarna, which were already known to have been cut into the cliffs at the edge of the desert plain on which Akhetaten was built, clustered in two groups, one to the north of the city, the other to the south. Moreover, although very badly damaged, the decoration remaining in the tomb was clearly of the Amarna style, with the distinctive linear rays emanating from the sun disc and elongated cartouches very much in evidence, and showed enough of Akhenaten himself to suggest that indeed this was his tomb. Recalling that Akhenaten himself announced that he would build a tomb for himself and that Nefertiti and Meritaten would be buried in it, it would seem straightforward enough to surmise that Akhenaten himself was to be buried in the main burial chamber, and the other two sections of the tomb would receive the burials of his Great Royal Wife, Nefertiti (perhaps the first, larger but unfinished, suite of rooms), and their eldest daughter, Meritaten (the second, smaller set of three rooms).

Indeed, there are good reasons for us to conclude that Akhenaten was buried in the tomb as intended, but there are also reasons to believe that his body did not stay there very long. Furthermore, while it seems likely that other members of the royal family were buried alongside him, these were probably not in fact the two most important women in his life mentioned on the boundary stela inscription – neither Nefertiti or Meritaten were ever buried there at all. To understand the situation better, we must take a closer look at the two main kinds of evidence: the decoration on the walls, and the objects recovered.

Fragments tell an unexpected story

The tomb had already suffered very badly by the time archaeologists became aware of it, both from the depredations of flash-flood damage and at the hands of men. There may have been many dozens of episodes of the latter, but we might hypothesize that two were of particular interest and importance in helping us to reconstruct the history of the tomb: the first shortly after Akhenaten's death, when the turbulent years of the 'heresy' he had brought about came to an end; and the second in the short period of a few years prior to the official discovery of the tomb, when its existence was known to the locals and many objects were removed from the tomb for sale on the antiquities market. Some of these artefacts have since come to light and provide conclusive evidence of this illicit activity. But there are also rumours that far more than we currently know about was removed from the tomb at the time and may yet lie unidentified in museum or private collections.

The quality of the stone into which the tomb was cut has a bearing on this. Had it been of very fine quality it is conceivable that the scenes and inscriptions might have been cut directly into the rock surface. However, such fine work requires a particular kind of stone, of a consistency soft enough to permit for the most delicate carving, but stable enough not to crumble or crack under the impact of the chisel. That quality can vary quite dramatically across relatively small spaces, so that the ancient craftsmen could never have known exactly what they were going to be working with until the quarrying had finished and the finer work of dressing and sculpting the stone could begin. Where the stone itself does not offer the right consistency, a layer of fine plaster is used to cover the surfaces, providing the 'canvas' onto which the craftsmen can add their decoration. This is less ideal than using the finest-quality rock, but a good pragmatic alternative, and has the added advantage of taking some of the pressure off the draughtsmen tasked with the decoration: when you are working directly on the rock you have only one chance – make a mistake and an unsightly repair will be required. A plaster surface, on the other hand, can simply be reverted to its previous condition by the addition of a new layer of plaster should any mistakes need correcting. But the great disadvantage of plaster in the long term is that it has a tendency to move, especially upon drying out completely, and then to separate from the wall behind it, at which point the decoration is lost.

The decoration of Akhenaten's Amarna tomb was mostly carved directly onto such a layer of gypsum plaster, and much has been lost. Nevertheless, what remains tells us a great deal. The tomb is decorated in the area above a well shaft, in the main burial chamber and in the second suite of three rooms, named alpha, beta and gamma.

The side walls above the well shaft preserve traces of a scene of Akhenaten and Nefertiti offering to the Aten, and the end walls those of one or more princesses.[5] On entry into the main burial chamber, it is very difficult to make out much more than the typical images of the Aten, with its rays extending downwards, and the remains of cartouches of the Aten or Akhenaten. These and other fragmentary inscriptions provide the name and titles of the Aten, Akhenaten and Nefertiti. One scene, which is now almost invisible to the naked eye, was reconstructed by Professor Martin[6] and provides something of a surprise. The scene shows Akhenaten, Nefertiti and one or more of their daughters standing before a figure standing in a kiosk. The top half of this figure is almost completely missing now, but crucial details remain. In front of the individual's legs a sash is present, identifying her as a queen. As Nefertiti, identified by the tiny trace of the top of her distinctive, flat-topped crown is present elsewhere in the same scene, it cannot be her. The only other candidate would seem to be Akhenaten's mother, Tiye, Great Royal Wife of Amenhotep III.[7]

Amenhotep III was responsible for some of the most striking monuments to have survived from ancient Egypt, including the so-called 'Colossi of Memnon' that stood in front of his mortuary temple in the Theban necropolis, a unique open court at the temple of Luxor, and a colossal statue now in the central part of the Egyptian Museum in which Amenhotep and Tiye are shown seated together. Tiye is mentioned frequently in the diplomatic correspondence of the age, and seems to have played an unusually active role in Egypt's foreign policy alongside her husband. She is more visible in the iconography of the period alongside her husband than previous queens had been, even being shown as a sphinx, a form previously reserved for the pharaoh, and also on occasion with aspects of the iconography of the goddess Hathor, such as cow horns and a sun disc. Amenhotep built a temple dedicated to her worship at Sedeinga in Sudan, to accompany his own, built some 10 miles (15 km) away at Soleb, at which his divine form was worshipped alongside Amun-Ra. The elevated status of this royal couple perhaps in part provided the basis for Akhenaten's new religion, in which he and his wife, Nefertiti, were the principal actors along with the Aten.

We know that Tiye survived her husband and made the journey to her son's new capital city to live alongside him, and it seems likely that she would have continued to have an influence over his activities.

The decoration in rooms alpha and gamma is generally much better preserved (room beta was not decorated). One particularly legible scene, found on a wall facing the door through which the visitor enters room gamma, is one of the most touching to be seen anywhere in ancient Egyptian art. At left, a princess is shown standing in a kiosk. In front of her, Akhenaten, Nefertiti and their daughters Meritaten, Ankhsenpaaten (who would later change her name to Ankhsenamun) and Neferneferuaten-Tasherit – all identified by the labels above their heads – are shown raising their right hands to their faces in a gesture of mourning. The princess in the kiosk is the second daughter of the family, Meketaten, who, clearly, has died. It seems beyond doubt that she, at least, was buried in this suite of rooms.

The scene is reminiscent of that including the female figure in a kiosk in the main burial chamber, as far as its fragments can be pieced together. It seems likely, therefore, that that individual, probably Queen Tiye, was buried in the main chamber.

The evidence leaves plenty of room for speculation in the finer details, but the big picture seems clear enough. The main burial chamber was prepared for the burials of Akhenaten and Tiye. Room gamma appears to have been given over for the burial of Meketaten.[8] Room alpha, within the same suite of rooms, may also have been at least prepared as a burial chamber, to receive the bodies of one or perhaps two individuals.

Bearing in mind, however, that we have good reason to believe that some of the individuals with whom we are concerned in this chapter may ultimately not have been buried in the places originally intended for them, we might next ask whether Akhenaten, Tiye and Meketaten were ever really buried in the tomb. It is safe to assume that the preparation of Akhenaten's tomb would have begun very shortly after the decision to move to Amarna was taken. The decoration would have been one of the final stages in the preparation of the tomb itself, but there is no reason to think that this would not have been under way, and could even have been completed, long before the king's death. Therefore, the presence of scenes connected with his death does not necessarily tell us whether or not his body was ever interred there. In the case of Tiye and Meketaten the situation is perhaps different. Strikingly, neither are the women Akhenaten explicitly stated would be buried with him, and yet the decoration clearly demonstrates an intention to bury both within the tomb. This deviation from his original plan seems most likely to have been brought about by the death of each individual, which in both cases may have meant something unexpected – if not the death of Tiye, who had presumably reached a good age by this point, then her presence at Amarna and the necessity of burying her in the new city, but probably a sudden death in the young Meketaten's case.

In addition to the decoration on the walls, a few hundred broken bits and pieces of burial equipment offer further insight into the intended and eventual functions of the tomb. These have found their way into scholarship in various ways. Some were recovered by Barsanti's team during the first official clearance following the discovery of the tomb, but many had by this time already come onto the market and begun to make their way into the major museum collections. These, we assume, must have come from the royal tomb at a time before archaeologists knew of its location. We cannot know precisely where they were found, however, and such information might potentially transform our interpretation of the necropolis. Were we to discover, for example, that they were not found in TA 26 but in another of the tombs in the royal wadi area, we might draw different conclusions about the final or intended resting place of the individuals for whom the burial equipment was prepared. Sadly, a very significant proportion of the material evidence for ancient Egypt was removed from its archaeological context, depriving us of valuable information. Fortunately, a number of further fragments of evidence were recovered and thoroughly documented by the Egypt Exploration Society team led by John Pendlebury during its work in the early 1930s, and further re-clearances in the 1980s[9] and 2000s[10] added still more.

The objects can be divided into several groups, each represented by numerous fragments. Two, or perhaps three, sarcophagi seem to have been present, and belonged apparently to Akhenaten, Tiye and, possibly, Meketaten. The first of these has been reconstructed and is now on display in the gardens of the Egyptian Museum in Cairo. It is reasonable to assume that large, heavy items, such as the sarcophagus and perhaps the more elaborate canopic chests, would have been put in place prior to the burial itself, while any smaller, more portable items would have been brought into the tomb along with the body as part of the funerary procession. As with the decoration on the walls, therefore, the presence of the sarcophagi should not be taken as conclusive evidence of burial. The same goes for a fragmentary canopic chest found to belong to Akhenaten.

Other items recovered from the tomb do, however, suggest that these individuals were buried there. First, numerous *shabtis* – figurines representing servants intended to carry out necessary manual tasks on behalf of the deceased in the afterlife (see pp. 12–13) – belonging to Akhenaten have come to light, some through the market at a time consistent with

The reconstructed sarcophagus of Akhenaten in the garden area outside the Egyptian Museum, Cairo.

the looting of the tomb by the locals in the period immediately before the official discovery, others during controlled excavations. One of these shabti figures, confusing the picture somewhat, bears the inscription: 'the Great Royal Wife, Neferneferuaten Nefertiti, living forever'. Evidently, this figure did not belong to Akhenaten, but his royal consort, Queen Nefertiti. But this is the only evidence to suggest that she was buried here and certainly not enough to argue convincingly that this was the case.

Finally, it is alleged that a mummy was observed close to the tomb entrance by French Egyptologist Georges Daressy at the time of its official opening.[11] Its reported location and general condition were consistent with it having been dismembered by robbers searching the wrappings for saleable items such as jewelry and amulets. Agonizingly, it has since been lost. Of course, the mummy may have been nothing to do with the original owners of the tomb – tombs were often reused, over and over again, for centuries, so the discovery of human remains unrelated to the original burial in and around them is not uncommon. But what if these were the remains of a member of the Amarna royal family, which had survived in the tomb for over three thousand years until a matter perhaps of no more than a few months before the archaeologists' arrival? A rumour that a group of locals had been seen carrying a golden coffin down from the high desert not long before the official opening of the tomb adds another tantalizing, if unlikely, footnote to the story.[12]

Further tombs in the royal wadi

TA 26 was not the only tomb in the royal necropolis at Amarna: three further tombs, numbered 27, 28 and 29 are present, while another structure – TA 30 – appears to have been an embalmers' cache. All are in the vicinity of Akhenaten's Amarna tomb, and were originally cleared by Barsanti as part of the operation in the early 1890s when the necropolis was first identified. All were subsequently re-excavated in the 1970s and 1980s by Geoffrey Martin and Aly el-Khouli, and then again in the 2000s by Marc Gabolde and Amanda Dunsmore. At first glance they do not amount to very much: none of them is decorated, and only a small number of fragmentary objects has been found in or around them, but such is the degree of scrutiny to which we must subject anything associated with the royal burials of this period that it is nonetheless worth reviewing what little information they do provide.

Tomb 27 was found on the south side of the main wadi, not far from the side wadi in which TA 26 can be found. It is unfinished and consists only of a single corridor. Access from the surface is via a staircase with a central ramp, as in TA 26, and its dimensions are the same as those of Akhenaten's tomb, implying an owner of the highest status.

Proceeding eastwards along the main wadi, a branch extends off to the south, a little way along which tombs 28 and 29 can be found, immediately adjacent to one another. Tomb 28 is smaller than the other two but, uniquely, seems to have been finished. It consists of an entrance corridor and three chambers, all of which are similar in size to rooms alpha, beta and gamma in TA 26, suggesting that the tomb may have been intended for the burial of one or more of the royal princesses. The excavators have also suggested that its proximity to the much larger TA 29 may signify that the latter was intended for a relative (perhaps a parent?) of those princesses.[13]

Tomb 29 is the most substantial of the group. Four corridors were cut and plastered but no other, larger chambers are present, and it was therefore clearly never finished, architecturally at least. Its dimensions are similar to those of the unfinished suite of rooms in TA 26, which as we have seen may have been intended for Nefertiti. The excavators believe its location suggests that it may have been cut for a (lesser) royal wife of Akhenaten, but there is nothing to suggest that it was ever used to receive a burial, and indeed in its unfinished state it could not ever have been used as such.

The excavators nonetheless remained convinced that a burial was made in this side wadi, on the basis of the discovery of a number of blue-green faience plaques in the area, which must have come from a luxurious item of funerary furniture. However, knowing the extent to which the royal funerary material of this period was disturbed – as evidenced by the destruction of the large stone items from TA 26, and the probability that some, at least, of the material discovered in KV 55 (see below) came from the royal necropolis at Amarna – it is entirely conceivable that these plaques may have come from items originally placed in TA 26. There is nothing more to suggest that any of these tombs was ever used for burial, let alone of *whom*.

The discovery of KV 55: more questions than answers

Up until 6 January 1907, Egyptologists might have thought the question of the final resting place of the Amarna rulers easily answered. Akhenaten's tomb had been found – admittedly without much evidence of his actual burial, but this was not uncommon. At this time, a number of New Kingdom pharaohs' tombs were yet to be discovered, but the expectation was probably that, as had been the case for a few decades, the missing ones would be unearthed as excavations proceeded in the Valley of the Kings. Some may have thought the burial of Nefertiti might yet turn up elsewhere at Amarna, it now having been shown that this site possessed a royal necropolis; equally, her name might simply have been added to the much longer list of queens whose burial places remained unknown. The significance that we now attach to her – as probable pharaoh in her own right – was not recognized until much later.

The discovery shortly after the beginning of 1907 of a tomb in the Valley of the Kings that would be given the number 55 made things far more complicated than anyone would previously have imagined. Theodor Davis, a wealthy American lawyer turned Kings' Valley treasure hunter, set the scene:

> With a large gang of men, we commenced clearing on the apex
> of the hill, within a few feet of the tomb of Ramesses IX. In
> the course of a few days we reached the level of the door of
> his tomb, finding nothing but the chippings of the surround-
> ing tombs. But down we went some thirty feet [9 m], when we
> found stone steps evidently leading to a tomb.[14]

The western face to the south of the mound into which Ramesses IX excavated his tomb was found to have been covered with a massive heap of limestone chips from the excavation of the tomb of Ramesses VI, across the other side of the modern pathway that leads visitors up through the Valley. Davis's colleague, the English archaeologist Edward Ayrton, described the next steps:

> …we made a thorough clearance down to the entrance of the
> tomb which had evidently been begun on a smaller scale and

then enlarged. We found the doorway closed by a loosely-built wall of limestone fragments resting not on the rock beneath but on the loose rubbish which had filled the stairway. This we removed and found behind it the remains of the original sealing of the door. This was composed of rough blocks of limestone cemented together and coated on the outside by cement of so hard a quality that a knife could scarcely scratch it; on this we found the impressions of the oval seal of the priestly college of Amun-Ra at Thebes – a jackal crouching over nine captives. This wall we also removed and began the clearance of the corridor, which we also found filled with rubbish to within three feet [1 m] of the ceiling, near the first doorway, and sloping towards the other end until the space from the ceiling was almost six feet [2 m].[15]

This was an intriguing situation, to say the least. It seemed that what Ayrton had first encountered was the final sealing of the tomb, which was relatively intact and yet clearly imperfect, as if undertaken in somewhat strained circumstances. The presence of an earlier, more carefully executed sealing showed that the tomb had been officially closed once, before being opened and then closed again. Hearts must have been racing at the prospect that this new tomb in the Valley might be at least partially undisturbed. What Ayrton found next must have heightened the sense of excitement, but only confused the picture further. On top of the debris a few metres beyond the entrance lay:

a large wooden object resembling a broad sled in shape. It was covered with gold leaf with a line of inscriptions running down each side. On it lay a wooden door with copper pivots still in place; this also was covered with gold leaf and ornamented with a scene in low relief of a queen worshipping the Sun-disk. On both objects lay fragments of limestone which had injured the gold. When we examined the gold we found the cartouche of the famous Queen Tiyi.[16]

From here Ayrton and his colleagues continued into a 'large oblong room' that seemed to be 'in a state of complete confusion'. They were able to see further sections of the same gilded, wooden structure, other small boxes, four canopic jars in a niche in the right-hand wall and, most significantly, a wooden coffin covered in gold leaf and inlaid with carnelian and glass (see p. viii), which had been partially broken so as to expose the head of a mummy within, wearing a crown of gold. Agonizingly, a cartouche in the centre of the inscription of the coffin lid that would have contained the name of the deceased had been carefully and completely removed. The face of the individual had evidently been recreated in gold, but this had also been almost completely removed – only a small part of the brow and the right eye remained – exposing the anonymous wooden surface underneath. Whose face was this?

According to Ayrton's description, work was then suspended so that the situation and the objects could be photographed without any further attempts to move anything.[17]

KV 55: the coffin as found by Ayrton.

....presently we cleared the mummy from the coffin and found that smallish person, with a delicate head and hands....I gently touched one of the front teeth (3,000 years old) and alas! it fell into dust, thereby showing that the mummy could not be preserved....We then took off the gold crown, and attempted to remove the mummy-cloth in which the body was wrapped, but the moment I attempted to lift a bit of the wrapping it came off in a black mass, exposing the ribs. We then found a beautiful necklace....Subsequently the wrappings of the mummy were entirely removed, exposing the bones. Thereupon, I concluded to have them examined and reported upon by two surgeons who happened to be in the Valley of the Kings. They kindly made the examination and reported that the pelvis was evidently that of a woman.[18]

At that point, the situation seemed straightforward. This was the body of Tiye, whose name had been observed immediately. However, as Davis himself records in the same paragraph, 'the bones' (to which the mummy had been reduced) were sent for a more detailed examination by the renowned anatomist Grafton Elliot Smith, Professor of Anatomy in the School of Medicine at the University of Cairo, who pronounced them to be of a male individual, and not, therefore, Queen Tiye.

Inscriptions bearing the names of Akhenaten and Tutankhamun were also present. In the case of the latter, these were confined to fragmentary clay seals, which were not part of the burial equipment as such but rather were connected with the activities surrounding the deposition of the equipment. Akhenaten's name was found on items of funerary equipment, however. Indeed, the coffin itself, from which the cartouche and face had been removed, bore the titles of Akhenaten, if not his name.

This discovery has proven to be one of the most enduringly fascinating for Egyptologists. Davis's volume, which included brief descriptions of events both by himself and Ayrton, was provocatively entitled *The Tomb of Queen Tïyi*, but even Davis was prepared to admit on the pages of his own report that the body found inside the chamber was not that of the famous queen. What he and Ayrton had found was clearly in a very confused and fragile state that would have tested the skills of any

One of the gilded wooden panels from the shrine in KV 55, depicting Queen
Tiye receiving the beneficent rays of the Aten.

excavator. With hindsight, it would have been best if it could have been
afforded the same kind of treatment as modern forensic investigators give
the scene of a murder, with nothing moved, or even touched, until every
aspect of the situation could be recorded. There is no way that Ayrton,
Davis and their team could have avoided disturbing the situation in the
tomb, staggering, as they were, around an unfamiliar space cluttered with

debris of all kinds and lit only by lamplight. All 'invasive' archaeological work, whether excavation or 'clearance', is inherently destructive to a degree; at best it separates the material the archaeologist is trying to recover from its context, and at worst that material might be so fragile that any attempt to move it results in its complete destruction, as Davis found in his encounter with one of the mummy's teeth. Yet one cannot help but wonder what more we might have been able to learn, had the excavators shown a little more care and patience. Still, the deficiencies in the execution of the clearance, the recording process and subsequent reporting have provided fertile ground for Egyptologists; their intention has been to reconstruct the situation as found in the tomb in greater detail than the original excavators provided, and, in turn, to try to reconstruct the sequence of events that took place there in ancient times.

It seems the tomb was sealed, reopened, then sealed again. The shrine of Queen Tiye was discovered dismantled and lying in several sections, scattered throughout the tomb. Some parts remained in the main chamber, but others were found in the descending entrance passageway, just inside the point at which it was sealed. The suggestion is that when the tomb was reopened an attempt was made to remove it, but then aborted when it became clear that the shrine could not be brought through the opening, which was narrower than when the tomb was first sealed because of the remains of the original blocking and an accumulation of debris. Otherwise, many of the objects recovered showed no sign of disturbance, and seemed to be more or less in place where they had been left quite deliberately at the time of the original burial. If this is correct, the shrine would originally have been placed in the centre of the room and the coffin over to one side (where it was found).[19] It has been argued that the presence of the shrine suggests the body of Tiye would originally have been inside the tomb as well.[20]

The original owner of the set of canopic jars, with beautiful stoppers carved into the shape of human heads wearing elaborate wigs (see p. viii), seems to have been Kiya, a secondary wife of Akhenaten, and it has been argued that the coffin was originally prepared for her as well. They seem to have been reworked for a king, however, and it has been argued that the king in question was Akhenaten;[21]

although the inscriptions on the coffin, defaced as they are, do not mention his name, they include his epithets. Furthermore, the 'Osiris Neferkheperure' referred to on at least two of the magical bricks must be Akhenaten, as he was the only king to have borne this name (his prenomen).[22]

On the basis of the iconography in the tomb it seems most likely that the mummy of a male individual found in the coffin was that of Akhenaten, and that the heretic was lain to the rest in this tomb on the orders of Tutankhamun; seals bearing the name of Tutankhamun were discovered in the tomb, suggesting that he was responsible for the deposit. This would seem to make sense, particularly if Tutankhamun was Akhenaten's son (see p. 128). The problem with this interpretation is that most anatomists who have examined the remains of the KV 55 mummy have concluded that he was an individual in his twenties, and Akhenaten, who ruled for approximately seventeen years and displayed a burst of creative activity from the earliest years of his reign, and so was surely not an infant when he came to the throne, must have reached a greater age than that by the time of his death. The only other royal male individual who we might expect to have received similar treatment is Smenkhkare, Akhenaten's apparent co-regent, but there is almost nothing to connect the material in the tomb with that king.

One intriguing note to this concerns the more recent history of some of the material discovered in the tomb. The coffin found in KV 55 was lined with several sheets of gold foil, which had become detached from the badly decayed wooden case, and were subsequently kept in storage separately in Cairo's Egyptian Museum. These subsequently disappeared, but resurfaced on the art market in the 1980s, and were then purchased by two German museums. Those sheets that were part of the original coffin basin – by now perished – were restored to a plexiglass substitute, which was repatriated to Egypt in 2001, along with the fragments that had once been attached to the lid. It has long been rumoured that one of the sheets preserves the remains of a cartouche of Smenkhkare, although this has never been verified. In 2016, it was reported that a project was under way to study the fragments from the lid, leading to speculation that the rumours might be proven one way or another, once and for all,[23] but at the time of writing, no verdict has been given.

Reused material in the tomb of Tutankhamun

At the start of this chapter we said that the one thing that we know with certainty of the Amarna royalty is that Tutankhamun was buried in KV 62. While this is true, even here the situation may not be quite as straightforward as it might seem at first glance. Certain other royal names crop up in the inscriptions on the items found in the tomb. It is not that unusual for objects bearing the name of one king to appear among the burial equipment of another, but here things are a little different.

This part of the story starts with a box discovered by Howard Carter in KV 62. The box is inscribed with three royal names: Akhenaten, Ankhkheperure-mery-Neferkheperure Neferneferuaten-mery-Waenre, and Meritaten. The first and last of these names were familiar to Egyptologists, but who was this other person, who was 'beloved' ('*mery*') of Neferkheperure and Waenre (Akhenaten)?[24] The conclusion drawn in 1928 by Percy Newberry, which would hold for many years, was this Ankhkheperure was one and the same as the Ankhkheperure Smenkhkare-djeserkheperu depicted in the tomb of Meryre ii, next to Meritaten, his Great Royal Wife (see p. 96). The prenomen Ankhkheperure matched, and the name was obviously followed on the box by Meritaten as this was his wife.[25]

All seemed simple enough. But during the 1970s, the British Egyptologist John Harris noted that the longer version of the Ankhkheperure part of the name often included the hieroglyphic 't' sign, which is used to feminize names, and suggested that this was therefore the name of a woman. So was Smenkhkare a woman? Harris suggested that yes, *she* was a woman, and that it was none other than Nefertiti, who, it was known, had also used the name Neferneferuaten – as on the box found by Carter – alongside her much more famous name.

Finally, however, James P. Allen argued in a paper published in 1988 that Smenkhkare and Neferneferuaten were not one and the same after all.[26] The former was male – solving the problem of his having been shown as male and with a Great Royal Wife in the tomb of Meryre ii – and the latter definitely female. The idea of Neferneferuaten's femininity was further strengthened in 1998 with the publication of Marc Gabolde's observation that her name was often followed by the epithet 'effective for her husband'. The debate as to which royal woman of this period Neferneferuaten really was continues, but a consensus seems to be building around the idea that she was Nefertiti. It is not impossible that this individual is not known to us by any other name, and should not be identified with any of the other prominent royal women of the time, but while we cannot rule this out as a possibility there is no good reason to pursue the argument. Of those we know, we should probably look to the most prominent – Nefertiti and the royal daughters. Of the latter, Meritaten can be ruled out on the grounds that her name also appears on the box discovered by Carter, showing that she was a different individual. Akhenaten's second daughter, Meketaten, died at Amarna, apparently young, and was buried with that name and certainly not, it seems, having assumed the trappings of kingship as Neferneferuaten did. Ankhesenamun appears prominently later in the story as the Great Royal Wife of Tutankhamun, and we have no reason to think that she assumed another guise at any point. The remaining daughters are less well known, and presumably younger. One, Neferneferuaten-Tasherit, was given a name that fits, and Allen has argued that she may have become Pharaoh Neferneferuaten. However, neither Neferneferuaten-Tasherit or any of the other daughters appear to have held anything like the same prominence as Neferneferuaten Nefertiti.

For many years it seemed there was no evidence of Nefertiti from after the time of Meketaten's death, as depicted in the royal tomb at Amarna. This is generally thought to have taken place around Akhenaten's Year 14, a few years before the king himself died, in the seventeenth year of his reign.[27] Had she fallen from grace, or died? If so, this would seem to mitigate against her having reigned as Ankhkheperure Neferneferuaten after her husband's death. Recently, however, an inscription has been discovered in a quarry near to Amarna, at a site called Dayr Abu Hinnis. This includes a date in Akhenaten's Year 16, and mentions the 'Great King's Wife, his beloved, mistress of the two lands, Neferneferuaten Nefertiti'. She was still alive almost at the very end of the reign therefore, and still apparently the principal female actor in Akhenaten's world – there is no mention of Smenkhkare, Meritaten or anyone else.[28] Nefertiti – named 'Neferneferuaten Nefertiti' here, note – therefore seems as strong a candidate as any to be identified with Ankhkheperure Neferneferuaten.

The surface of a wooden box discovered by Howard Carter in KV 62 and inscribed with three royal names: Akhenaten, Ankhkheperure-mery-Neferkheperure Neferneferuaten-mery-Waenre, and Meritaten.

The presence of other royal names among the material from the tomb of Tutankhamun is well documented, and the notion that some of the material found in the tomb had originally been intended for one or more other royal individuals accepted for some time. However, in recent years, the evidence for much of the equipment having belonged to Neferneferuaten in particular has been building, and Egyptologist Nicholas Reeves has now taken this idea a step further, with the revelatory theory that Tutankhamun's death mask, perhaps the most iconic ancient Egypt object in existence, was itself also made for this same individual (see p. xiii). Reeves has been building the case for this suggestion for years, on the basis of several different types of evidence: the face seems to have been modelled separately from the rest of the mask, and the ears exhibit evidence that they were originally intended to receive earrings, and were therefore those of a woman.[29] Furthermore, the mummy trappings (including a scarab and ornamental side straps) belonged to Ankhkheperure Neferneferuaten, as did the coffinettes.[30] Finally, in 2015, close inspection of the inscriptions chased into the gold of the mask showed that the cartouche of Tutankhamun was added over the top of an earlier name. The traces are barely visible, but have been reconstructed as 'Ankhkheperure-mery-Neferkheperure', the prenomen of Pharaoh Neferneferuaten.[31] Reeves now believes that not only was *some* of the equipment in KV 62 originally made for Ankhkheperure Neferneferuaten, but *most* of it was.

Hidden chambers in KV 62

In many ways, these details and new conclusions simply provide the backdrop to an even more sensational story that gripped the public imagination in summer 2015. Dr Reeves published a paper online in which he articulated a theory that there may yet be hidden chambers

The underside of one of the inlaid bands placed on Tutankhamun's mummy inscribed with the cartouche of Ankhkheperure-mery-Neferkheperure (at left).

in the tomb of Tutankhamun, lying behind what up to then had been considered to be walls of solid bedrock, and that these chambers had been deliberately concealed by the ancient Egyptians, to prevent anyone from gaining access to what lay beyond.

This fascinating idea began to develop when Reeves examined a series of high-resolution photographs taken by the conservation team Factum Arte during the construction of an exact replica of the tomb. These photographs digitally removed the painted decoration from the walls of the tomb, allowing the physical surface beneath to be examined. Superficially, the surfaces are entirely flat, but the photographs reveal a more complicated situation, the walls being dotted with uneven areas, blemishes and other anomalies. Even then, however, to the untrained eye there might have appeared to have been little of interest. However, Dr Reeves noticed that certain of the marks seemed to define linear features, in particular parts of two of the walls of the burial chamber: one in the bottom right-hand corner of the west wall, and a second a little way to the right and at the bottom of the north wall. Reeves suggested these were the outlines of concealed doorways.

Reeves's scholarly paper was made freely accessible online. In it he built the case to explain the presence and concealment of the doorways. That in the west wall lay more or less directly opposite the entranceway to the small room leading off the burial chamber, which was discovered by Howard Carter, who labelled it 'the Treasury'. Many of the finest objects were found in this storage room, including the jackal shrine and canopic chest. Reeves's suggestion was that the supposed concealed doorway in the west wall would lead to a similar storage chamber, presumably containing even more 'wonderful things'.[32]

Far more compelling, however, was the question of what might lie beyond the north wall. When looking at the face of this feature in its

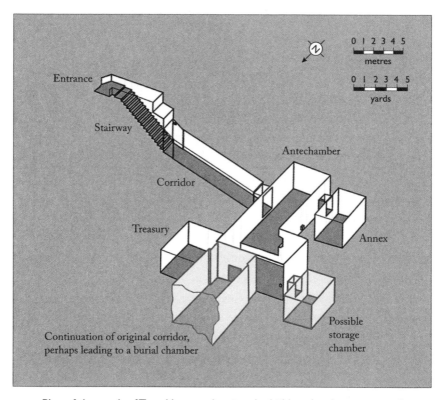

Plan of the tomb of Tutankhamun showing the hidden chambers proposed by Nicholas Reeves.

The tomb of Tutankhamun. Taken from the antechamber towards the north wall of the burial wall, behind which Nicholas Reeves has suggested may lie a concealed corridor and further chambers.

entirety, the supposed doorway seems to be 'off-centre', appearing towards the right, which perhaps sits uncomfortably with the Egyptians' taste for symmetry. However, when viewed from the antechamber, which leads to the burial chamber, things are a little different. There is no doorway as such between the antechamber and burial chamber;[33] the burial chamber opens out in a leftward direction, but to the right the (east) wall simply continues uninterrupted. If one ignores the leftward extension that defines the burial chamber as a distinct space, and imagines both the left (west) and right (east) walls continuing uninterrupted towards the north wall, the supposed doorway appears to have been placed right in the centre of that axis.

Reeves's suggestion was that the antechamber, which we now think of as the first chamber in KV 62, may originally have been no more than a corridor, and what became Tutankhamun's burial chamber, no more than a well shaft, beyond which the corridor continues, albeit concealed by the north wall, which is no more than a screen designed to conceal what lies beyond. He suggests that KV 62 is therefore a larger monument than we realize at present and predates the burial of Tutankhamun.

At the time of the boy-king's death, the burial chamber was reworked in order to receive Tutankhamun's burial.

Reeves's suggestion caused a sensation, not merely on the basis that there was *something* more to be found, but because he went further, by suggesting exactly what he thought it would be. Provocatively, the paper in which his theory was carefully articulated was entitled 'The Burial of Nefertiti?'.[34] There are Egyptologists who consider such sensationalism to be unworthy of serious scholarship. But we must remember that one of the main reasons that Egyptology has flourished as an academic discipline is that it has captured the imagination of the public, who are eager to read books, watch documentaries and visit exhibitions, or even Egypt itself, and who are often hooked in because of stories like this – the possibility of some fantastic treasure being revealed or a mystery being solved. I admire Reeves for embracing the sensational element of his research despite knowing, as he must have done, that some of his colleagues would not accept it, while also allowing the world to make their own minds up about his theory by presenting his arguments in full in a freely accessible scholarly paper.

Is there anything there? At the time of writing we do not know. The doorway in the west wall can be more or less disregarded. Reeves himself argues that this would be nothing more than a storage chamber to mirror that leading off the eastern wall (the Treasury), perhaps also completing a quadruplet of rooms at the four corners of the monument, along with the so-called 'annex' at the southern end of the west wall of the antechamber, and the entrance passageway at the south end of the east wall. While another room stuffed full of the kind of material Carter found would be a sensation in itself, it might only provide more of the same.

The supposed doorway in the north wall is a different matter. Concealing an entranceway leading to further rooms cut deeper into the bedrock is something we know the Egyptians did. The tomb of Horemheb, a military general turned pharaoh who reigned not long after Tutankhamun, exhibits clear evidence that the builders of the tomb attempted to conceal the innermost chambers of the tomb using just such a device. In that case, access to the tomb was provided by a descending passageway incorporating a staircase, then a ramp, a second staircase and second ramp, which leads to a well shaft decorated with scenes of the king and various deities.

The remains of a false wall in the tomb of Horemheb.

On completion this would have appeared to be the end of the monument, the rear wall seeming solid, with the painted decoration covering
its surfaces. However, this was in fact a false wall, concealing a pillared
hall, a continuation of the descending passageway, and finally the burial
compartments.[35]

The marks Dr Reeves observed on the high-resolution photographs
may be nothing more than blemishes resulting from the imperfect
preparation of the surfaces prior to painting. Even if he is correct, and
they amount to anything at all, it is possible that they may relate to
chambers that were started but never finished when time ran out before
Tutankhamun's burial, due his untimely death. But if they conceal something more, then it seems highly unlikely that much effort would have
been expended on concealing further storage rooms leading off the
north wall; if anything was being concealed, it would have to have been
something special. Reeves suggests that, if we should now think of the
antechamber of KV 62 as being a corridor, it must be one belonging to
the tomb of a queen, for two reasons. First, on reaching the end of the
entrance passageway the tomb takes a turn to the right, a feature generally observed in the tombs of royal women, but not of royal men, which
generally turn to the left. Secondly, the decoration in the burial chamber

seems to have been reworked – Reeves suggests it had originally been decorated for Nefertiti, the images of a deceased king now labelled as Tutankhamun exhibiting in fact the features of Nefertiti, and those now labelled as Tutankhamun's successor, Ay, depicted with features that closely resemble those of Tutankhamun.[36] Reeves argues that these figures were simply relabelled when the chamber was adapted for Tutankhamun's burial.

Furthermore, Reeves argues that this must have been the tomb of a queen who became a king: if the antechamber should be regarded as a corridor, it would have been a large one, and was made that way in order to permit the ingress of the large wooden panels of a shrine, of exactly the kind that Carter discovered surrounding the sarcophagus of Tutankhamun. There is one obvious candidate queen who became king in the late 18th Dynasty: Ankhkheperure Neferneferuaten, or Nefertiti as she was known earlier in her life.

Reeves argues that Nefertiti became co-regent with Akhenaten late in the king's reign under the name Ankhkheperure Neferneferuaten, and that a substantial quantity of funerary equipment was created for her in this name.[37] When, after Akhenaten's death, the co-regent Neferneferuaten became sole ruler under the name Ankhkheperure Smenkhkare-djeserkheperu, this equipment was cast aside as being inappropriate for a full pharaoh. The cast-off equipment was subsequently repurposed for Tutankhamun, when his early death necessitated the very swift assembly of the necessary items for a royal burial. That no burial equipment belonging to Ankhkheperure Smenkhkare-djeserkheperu has been found is due to the tomb remaining undiscovered and intact up to now.

Reeves's theory has been criticized on a number of grounds. First, there are those who simply cannot see in the Factum Arte photographs any evidence for the doorways Reeves believes to be there. Further, some have taken issue with various aspects of the argument thereafter. Reeves's proposal that what became the burial chamber of Tutankhamun was originally the well shaft of an earlier tomb seems unlikely: the 'well' in this case would be approximately 1 m (3 ft) deep, far shallower than one would expect.[38] Reeves argues that the figures now labelled as Tutankhamun and his successor, Ay, on the north wall, are stylistically closer to known images of Nefertiti and Tutankhamun respectively. However, it has also been argued in response that the figure that is supposed to be King Tutankhamun does in fact look like other known representations of King Tutankhamun, and the figures of Ay look like known representations of Ay.[39]

Lastly, of course, there is the argument about the burial equipment. If Nefertiti/Ankhkheperure Neferneferuaten is to be identified with Ankhkheperure Smenkhkare-djeserkheperu and died as full pharaoh under the last of these names, then it makes sense that she would have been buried at Thebes,[40] providing support for the theory that her tomb is intact and has yet to be discovered.

However, it seems more likely that Nefertiti was not one and the same individual as Smenkhkare. Despite Reeves's arguments to the contrary,[41] the image of Smenkhkare in the tomb of Meryre ii seems clearly to represent a male, and the fact that the majority of the evidence of the reign of this individual has only been found at Amarna[42] is consistent with the idea that he was active there only, while Akhenaten's Amarna revolution remained in full swing. The Meryre scene was carved sometime around Akhenaten's Year 12, suggesting this was the point at which Smenkhkare came to the throne as Akhenaten's co-regent, and the meagre evidence for his reign suggests that he did not live long. The theory that Nefertiti's status was elevated only after this,[43] and perhaps as a direct result of the death of Smenkhkare – who presumably had been made co-regent as part of a succession plan of Akhenaten's – is preferred here.

In this scenario, Nefertiti would have died as Ankhkheperure Neferneferuaten; an assemblage of burial equipment was prepared in her name, but subsequently reworked for Tutankhamun for reasons we cannot yet explain with certainty. Tutankhamun's early and unexpected death – prior to his own assemblage having been prepared – presumably made it necessary for pre-existing equipment to be requisitioned, and as Neferneferuaten's standing was in decline by this point, the appropriation of her assemblage for this purpose seems plausible.

In this case, we must assume that her burial was disturbed. Some equipment, and a separate tomb – along with her mummy – may have been left, and therefore may yet be discovered. There are those who believe her body at least has already been found, however, many years ago, prior to the discovery of the royal tomb at Amarna, of KV 55 and of the tomb of Tutankhamun.

KV 35: a cache of royal mummies

On 8 March 1898, an excavation in the Valley of the Kings directed by Victor Loret came upon a man-made opening in the cliffs between KV 12 and 13. By the evening of the following day, Loret was able to enter the tomb with his foreman. A descending passageway with a staircase halfway along led to a well shaft. Beyond, Loret could see that the tomb continued further into the rock, leading to a two-pillared hall with a further staircase in the corner. Curiously, the most striking feature of this room was the presence of four model wooden boats (barques), on top of one of which lay the 'frightful spectacle' of an unwrapped mummy. This proved to be one of the original inhabitants of the tomb, whose body had been ravaged and cast aside by robbers looking for jewels within the wrappings. It formed something of a prelude to what for scholars would become the most important aspect of the discovery. Descending the staircase Loret entered the next room, a grander hall of two rows of three square pillars, lavishly decorated with scenes from the Book of Amduat – a set of scenes and texts reserved for the burials of pharaohs, describing what is to be found in the afterlife – and the same simple stick-figures familiar from the decoration in the 18th Dynasty tomb of Tuthmosis III, which Loret himself had found the previous month. Here, the Frenchman was able to read the name of the king for whom this tomb was built: Amenhotep II, son and successor of Tuthmosis III. At the end of the pillared hall a sunken crypt contained the king's quartzite sarcophagus. All around, the floor was littered with broken funerary equipment, and inside the sarcophagus lay a coffin with garlands of flowers still in place at the head and feet. Loret knew that Amenhotep II's mummy was not among those discovered in the famous 'royal cache' (see pp. 143–47) that had been discovered and partially looted by the Abd er-Rassoul brothers some two decades earlier. This was the first mummy of a pharaoh to be found in place in the tomb designed for it (although it would later become clear that it had been disturbed in antiquity and replaced in a new coffin – see Chapter 4). It was a momentous discovery, but there was more to come, for this was more than just the tomb of one of Egypt's great 18th Dynasty pharaohs.

Four side chambers led off the six-pillared hall, two on each side. Loret explored each in turn. In the first, leading off the sunken crypt to the left of the sarcophagus, he came across a group of thirty large jars; in the second, to the left as the visitor enters the pillared hall, he found that the floor had been cleared on the left-hand side of the room, while a clutter of broken funerary material had been left on the right. In the fourth Loret would find further mummies. This was another sensational discovery, that of a second cache of New Kingdom royal mummies, including the bodies of Tuthmosis IV, Amenhotep III, Merenptah, Sety II, Siptah, Sethnakht and Ramesses IV, V and VI.

But before that, in the first chamber to the right when one enters the pillared hall, he came upon the extraordinary sight of three unwrapped mummies lying side by side. In the centre was a young male, identified as such by the 'sidelock of youth', well known from Egyptian iconography as a means of signifying childhood. To the right, a shaven-headed adult was mistaken by Loret for a young man – it was in fact a young woman, now known as the 'Younger Lady' – and to the left, Loret was

The group of mummies discovered by Loret in KV 35; the 'Elder Lady' is on the left, and the 'Younger Lady' on the right.

The remarkably well-preserved face of the 'Elder Lady' discovered in KV 35.

confronted by perhaps one of the most haunting images ancient Egypt has provided. The mummy of an older woman lay beneath a pile of rags, partially covering her otherwise unwrapped body. The right hand had been wrenched off, leaving just the left lying across her chest, with the hand at the top just beneath her throat, fingers closed, thumb exposed, almost as if she were clutching something tightly towards her for protection. Her face was extraordinarily well preserved. She had 'brown, wavy, lustrous hair'[44] and a piece of cloth covered the top of her head and most of the left side of her face, amplifying the sense that she was sheltering from something. The overall effect, to judge from the photographs, is quite moving; the pose, and the way the linen was casually draped over the body, serve almost to animate it, and that face must have seemed so alive to Loret in the lamplight.

As if meeting someone from the ancient past like this was not enough, the question of who these two women might be has been the subject of speculation ever since, and as an important consideration in our hunt for tombs. In 1978, the mummy of the 'Elder Lady' (as she has come to be known) was 'examined from the viewpoint of Egyptology, x-ray cephalometry, biostatistics, and biochemistry'.[45] The chemical composition of her hair was also found to be of the same composition as several locks found inside a nest of miniature coffins found in the tomb of Tutankhamun. These were inscribed for Queen Tiye, and thus it was proposed that the 'Elder Lady' was the queen herself, wife of Amenhotep III and mother of Akhenaten. More recently, the mummy has been shown on the basis of DNA analysis to have been the daughter of the non-royal individuals Yuya and Thuya, whose mummies were discovered intact in their Valley of the Kings tomb by Theodore Davis and James Quibell in 1905.[46] They had long been known from inscriptional evidence to have been the parents of Queen Tiye. Combined, this evidence puts the identification of the 'Elder Lady' with Queen Tiye almost beyond doubt.

Between 2007 and 2009 a team led by Dr Zahi Hawass undertook a project to extract and analyse DNA from a total of sixteen royal mummies, including eleven suspected of being related to Tutankhamun, in an attempt to confirm or clarify the precise nature of the relationships between each.[47]

The mummy that, according to the ancient label placed on it by the priests responsible for the royal caches, is Amenhotep III, was identified as the father of the individual whose remains were found in KV 55.[48] Furthermore, the combination of the DNA of the mummy labelled Amenhotep III and that of the 'Elder Lady' matches the KV 55 mummy perfectly; they are very likely therefore to have been the parents of the individual in KV 55.[49] As we have seen, there are only really two males with whom this mummy might be identified: Akhenaten – who we know was the son of Amenhotep III and Tiye – and Smenkhkare. Akhenaten has been ruled out by many on the grounds that anatomists have suggested that the remains are those of a male who died in his twenties,[50] and given that Akhenaten reigned for sixteen or seventeen years, and began his programme of reforms from the beginning of his reign onwards, it seems he must at least have reached his thirties by the time of his death. However, doubts have been expressed about the reliability of the anatomists' conclusions.[51] Furthermore, the evidence provided by the funerary items discovered by Ayrton and Davis in association with the mummy, weigh strongly in favour of the identification of the body as being that of Akhenaten: the canopic jars and coffin seem to have been inscribed for Akhenaten, even if they had originally been made for someone else (probably Kiya), and the magical bricks seem to have been made for him.

By contrast there is no epigraphic evidence at all to support the identi-fication of the mummy as that of Smenkhkare.[52] And recent CT-scan investigation of the royal mummies suggests that the KV 55 individual may have been as old as forty, which, if correct, would remove the previ-ous objection that the individual was not old enough at death for it to have been Akhenaten. Whoever it is, the KV 55 individual was also the father of Tutankhamun.[53]

The identity of the 'Younger Lady' remains the subject of much specu-lation. In 2003, it was revealed that Dr Joann Fletcher had identified the mummy as being that of Nefertiti. She was not the first to make this claim, but her hypothesis gained much more attention than similar assertions had previously. Fletcher argued that one of the mummy's arms had been bent in a pose that indicated this was a royal individual; furthermore, damage to the front of the individual's skull was suggested to have been the result of the *damnatio memoriae* inflicted on Nefertiti and others involved in Akhenaten's reforms after they had died, and a wig found in the tomb and piercings to the mummy's ears were suggested to have been in keeping with the iconography of Nefertiti. However, the case was by no means watertight, and the more recent CT-scan investigation has shown that it is more likely both arms were straight, and the damage to the face was inflicted pre-mortem and was probably the cause of death, rather than the posthumous *damnatio memoriae* proposed.[54]

The recent DNA study has contributed much in this regard. It sug-gests that, along with the KV 55 mummy, the 'Younger Lady', too, was a daughter of Amenhotep III and the 'Elder Lady'. She and the KV 55 mummy were therefore full brother and sister, and also the parents of Tutankhamun. The marriage of brothers and sisters within the royal family, a measure designed to ensure the purity of royal line, was not uncommon, and so in this respect the results are not surprising. Neither Nefertiti or Kiya are known to have been a daughter of Amenhotep III and Tiye; neither are categorically ruled out, and some of the foremost scholars on the period continue to believe it is most likely that the Younger Lady is Nefertiti (in which case Joann Fletcher was right all along);[55] however, on the basis of the conclusions outlined above, it is just as possible that Akhenaten fathered Tutankhamun by an as-yet unknown wife.[56]

Reconstructing the end of the Amarna Period

On the basis of all of this evidence, we can broadly reconstruct the history of the death and burial of the principal members of the royal family in the Amarna Period.

Meketaten, a daughter of Akhenaten and Nefertiti, apparently died prematurely and was buried within TA 29, the tomb intended for Akhenaten at Amarna during his reign. Tiye, the mother of Akhenaten, also died some time during Akhenaten's reign, and was almost certainly buried in the same tomb. Akhenaten himself died in his seventeenth regnal year and was also buried as intended in the royal tomb at Amarna. After his death, he was succeeded by his Great Royal Wife, Nefertiti, who reigned as Ankhkheperure Neferneferuaten, and may in fact have been co-regent with Akhenaten, possibly already under this kingly name, some years before her husband's demise. Nefertiti may have reigned either prior to, and/or alongside, Tutankhamun. In any case, Nefertiti died first, and when Tutankhamun himself died he was succeeded by the God's Father – a priestly title – Ay, as the decoration in KV 62 makes clear. Before his untimely demise as a young man, between seventeen and nineteen years of age, Tutankhamun had overseen the removal of the body of his father, Akhenaten, from Amarna to Thebes, where it was reburied in KV 55. Some of the burial of equipment of Akhenaten's mother, and Tutankhamun's grandmother, Tiye, was also taken from Amarna to Thebes; some of the equipment ended up in KV 55, but her body came to be placed, finally, almost completely separated from any of the trappings of the lavish burial she must originally have been given, in a side-room in KV 35. On the death of Tutankhamun, much of the burial equipment that had been prepared for Nefertiti – as Ankhkheperure Neferneferuaten – was recycled for his burial.

Many questions remain. If the above analysis is correct – and many would disagree – we can now account for the bodies of Tiye and Akhenaten, as well as Tutankhamun, and his unidentified mother, the 'Younger Lady'. But even if this is right, and we also assume that some of the royals of the period who were of lesser status, and may have died and been buried in Amarna and never moved to Thebes, will never be found – including Meritaten, Meketaten and even Smenkhkare – what of Nefertiti? It is difficult to avoid wondering whether the puzzle might yet be solved once and for all by the discovery of yet more material. And perhaps even another tomb.

Radar scans in the tomb of Tutankhamun

Nicholas Reeves's theory was greeted with a mixture of scepticism and optimism on the part of the Egyptological community, and by great excitement among the wider public. In the weeks following the initial announcement it seemed the possibility that there were further chambers yet to be discovered in KV 62 was about to be proven. In November 2015, a radar scan of the walls in the tomb was undertaken by Japanese radar specialist Hirokatsu Watanabe. He seemed convinced immediately that the results supported Reeves's theory that there was more than just solid bedrock behind the walls:

> He reached the section of the wall that Reeves had pro-
> posed was a blocked-over partition. 'There is a change from
> here,' Watanabe announced. After he was finished, he studied
> the multicoloured bars that ran across the computer screen.
> 'Obviously it's an entrance to something,' he said through a
> translator. 'It's very obvious that this is something. It's very
> deep.' He scanned the wall again and confirmed the initial
> reading. Reeves asked him if he wanted to do another round.
> 'I don't need to,' Watanabe said. 'It's good data.'[57]....the initial
> analysis of the data was extremely encouraging. It showed at
> least two materials: bedrock and something else. 'The transition
> from solid bedrock to non-solid bedrock, to artificial material,
> it seems, was immediate,' Reeves said, speaking of the north
> wall. 'The transition was not gradual. There was a strict, straight,
> vertical line, which corresponds perfectly with the line in the
> ceiling. It seems to suggest that the antechamber continues
> through the burial chamber as a corridor.' He continued: 'The
> radar people tell me that we can also recognize that behind this
> partition there is a void.'[58]

Watanabe was also reported to have found evidence of the presence of organic and metallic objects behind the walls.[59] However, a few months later, in April 2016, a second series of radar scans was carried out by Eric Berkenpas, an electrical engineer at National Geographic and mechanical engineer Alan Turchik. Their data was sent to a series of specialists in the US and Egypt for independent analysis, and all reached the same conclusion: there was nothing behind the walls. Dean Goodman, one of the specialists involved, reported that:

> If we had a void, we should have a strong reflection....But it just doesn't exist....Radar data can often be subjective....But at this particular site, it's not. It's nice at such an important site to have clear, convincing results.[60]

That this analysis has been supported by a number of experts working independently gives the results of the second round of radar scans a greater degree of validity over the first. Mysteriously, Watanabe has refused to release his data. Nonetheless, at the time of writing, it seems the world is not yet ready to let go of the possibility of further chambers being found in KV 62; a third radar investigation was undertaken by Professor Franco Porcelli of the Polytechnic University of Turin later in 2017, but the results have yet to be announced.

Many Egyptologists were hesitant from the beginning to accept Reeves's theory: if not about the presence of undetected chambers in KV 62, then about what was likely to be found within them. Some believe that Nefertiti never achieved the status required for a burial of the kind Reeves suggests she would have had as Pharaoh Ankhkheperure Neferneferuaten. In any case, it would seem to have been very beneficial for Egyptology and for Egypt: it has got people excited, and even the most sceptical of specialists could not deny that Reeves's scholarly paper is well argued and presented, with copious references to further reading. It has also revived the endlessly fascinating and still-unresolved debate over the death and burial of the Amarna royals, and the distinct possibility that there may yet be more to be found, if not in KV 62, then perhaps elsewhere in the Valley.

Recent and future research in the Valley of the Kings

Howard Carter's remarkable discovery in the Valley of the Kings marked an end of the search for further tombs in the Valley, and little work prospecting previously unexcavated areas was undertaken in the decades that followed. However, further work has been undertaken and in recent years 'new' tombs have been discovered. Tutankhamun's tomb was the sixty-second to be discovered in the Valley, and KVs 63 and 64 have now been added to the list.

In 2006, the Amenmesse Project, a mission of the Supreme Council of Antiquities led by Professor Otto Schaden, uncovered KV 63 (see pp. 30–31). The project's focus was in fact KV 10, the tomb of Amenmesse, the fifth ruler of the 19th Dynasty. Schaden and his team intended to clear it completely in order to clarify its history. The project had already been working on the tomb for many years and had begun clearing the area around the entrance in search of associated funerary deposits when they came across a group of workmen's huts, underneath which was a layer of clean, undisturbed limestone chippings.[61] Underneath this layer the team discovered a shaft 5 m (16 ft) deep leading to a doorway opening onto a simple L-shaped chamber. The tomb contained seven wooden coffins, five piled side by side along the left wall, one at their feet and one placed lengthways across the top of the row of four, at the head end. The tomb walls were undecorated and the coffins did not contain any mummified remains; rather, they and the twenty-eight storage jars that were also present contained various materials connected with the embalming process. The style of the coffins in particular was suggestive of a late 18th Dynasty date, and it now seems most likely that the deposit represents a cache of equipment used in the burial of Tutankhamun.[62]

Given what we already know about the use, reuse, removal and reburial of equipment like this in the Valley of the Kings, one might ask how we know that material that was *made* in the late 18th Dynasty was also deposited at that time. Thanks to some brilliant detective work undertaken in recent years by Stephen Cross, we can now be almost certain that this was the case. Cross knows his Egyptology very well but his formal training is in geology, an expertise that most Egyptologists do not have. Cross carefully reviewed the reports of Ayrton, Davis, Carter and others who carried out their excavations in this area, and embarked on field-walking the Valley itself to build up a picture of the way the Valley evolved in terms of the original natural landscape, and the man-made and natural events that have occurred since it first came into use. He came up with a fascinating hypothesis that has great relevance for the period under study here.[63] KV 55, KV 62 (Tutankhamun's) and KV 63 were all cut into the bedrock floor in the central area of the Valley, and are among the earliest known tombs in that part of the cemetery. They also lie at a point of confluence of several side wadis leading down from the higher ground in the mountains. We have known for a long time that the Valley is, from time to time, hit by devastating flash floods, formed of rainwater that gathers volume and momentum as it starts its journey from the mountains in the west towards the lower ground of the Nile Valley floor. The floodwaters carry with them limestone chippings and other debris. These deposits have occasionally come rushing into the tombs in the Valley of the Kings, wreaking havoc inside. The ancient Egyptians were aware of this and put in place various measures to ensure that the kings' burials could withstand such events. This debris, destructive though it is, can also be useful: when it dries it forms a distinctive archaeological layer in the stratigraphy of the Valley, a tell-tale sign, very obvious to a geologist like Cross, that a flood event happened at a particular point in the sequence of events in the Valley.

It is of course very well known that the tomb of Tutankhamun was discovered undisturbed since antiquity, whereas most of the other tombs in the Valley had been comprehensively robbed, and some of them had even lain open since ancient times, available for anyone venturing into the area to enter them at will. Cross noted that just such a flood event seemed to have taken place after KV 62 had been sealed, but *before* the construction of a series of workmen's huts, built over the top of the flood deposit, a relatively short time later, during the Ramesside Period. Furthermore, the absence of a layer of wind-blown sand deposits, which accumulate very quickly in this part of the world, above the entrance to the tomb but beneath the flood layer suggests that very little time elapsed between the sealing of the tomb and the flood. This event deposited an approximately 1-m (3-ft) depth of alluvium across the central area of the Valley and concealed completely not only KV 62 but also KVs 55 and 63 under a thick and impenetrable layer of what was effectively cement. It would have made it extremely difficult for anyone to find them afterwards, not least enter them. This explains why Tutankhamun's tomb and KV 63 were never plundered; perhaps even more interestingly, it makes it very likely that the disturbances evident in KV 55, which was sealed, then re-entered and sealed again, took place before this flood episode, not long after the death of Tutankhamun. What is most interesting perhaps for our investigation is that this part of the Valley, which we know was used for the construction of tombs at the end of the 18th Dynasty, and we now also know was completely concealed by the flash flood identified by Cross, has never been completely excavated.

Two more excavation projects

Two projects have been active in this area in the recent years, with the explicit aim of uncovering tombs of the Amarna royals. The first, named the Amarna Royal Tombs Project (ARTP), was led by Professor Geoffrey Martin and Dr Nicholas Reeves, and worked in the Valley between 1998 and 2002.[64] They were drawn to excavate the area around a side wadi close to KV 58, a simple tomb consisting of a single, undecorated chamber, in which gold foil bearing the names of Tutankhamun and Ay had been found.[65] Ancient graffiti from the 20th Dynasty that recorded the inspection of tombs had been found in this area, but no tombs had yet been found. The excavations revealed workmen's huts, which had been exposed by Ayrton but not excavated. The ARTP completed the work, shedding important light on the sequence of construction of the huts in the area, under the lowest (i.e. earliest) of which were found 18th Dynasty artefacts. The project also carried out a ground-penetrating radar survey of the Valley and detected an anomaly that was later discovered to be KV 63.

From 2007, a Supreme Council of Antiquities mission led by Dr Zahi Hawass undertook to clear two sections of the Valley down to the bedrock, again in the central area. The first focused on the side wadi leading to KV 8, the tomb of the 19th Dynasty pharaoh Merenptah. Here, some evidence of human activity, including perhaps the commencement of a tomb that was never finished, was discovered but nothing more than that.[66] In the area just in front of the rest house, which anyone who has visited the Valley will know, a second excavation trench was opened. It was known that Ayrton had revealed another group of workmen's huts in this area but it was uncertain whether or not he had excavated them down to the bedrock. However, it became clear during the work that Ayrton had indeed done this and that no tomb would be found.[67] Remote sensing work undertaken at the same time suggested the possibility that a corridor exists beneath the rock in the area directly opposite KV 62;[68] however, apparently attempting to bring the matter to a close for good, the expedition eventually concluded that 'there are no tombs in the area indicated by the radar anomaly identified by N. Reeves and the Amarna Royal Tombs Project, or in those locations cited by L. Pinch-Brock and S. Cross'.[69]

Future discoveries?

Nonetheless, the same expedition had clearly not finished its work. Its most recent report concluded with a list of 'Future goals for the project', which included continuing the excavations to the southwest of KV 55, parallel to the side of the rest house, and starting or continuing investigations in nine other locations in the Valley of the Kings, several of which lie in the central area around the rest house.[70]

A number of scholars of the period remain open to the possibility that there are one or more tombs still to be found. And until the Valley can be fully excavated – the job Howard Carter was in the process of attending to when he was inconvenienced by the discovery of KV 62 – the possibility will continue to capture the imagination. Three areas in the main, eastern branch of the Valley, and one in the Western Valley where the tombs of the pharaohs who ruled immediately before and after the Amarna royals – Amenhotep III and Ay (the depiction of twelve baboons in the latter tomb gives the Western Valley the name it is known by locally – the 'Valley of the Monkeys') – were buried, have yet to be excavated. Until they are, many scholars will remain convinced that the tombs of some of the most famous individuals from the ancient world, including Nefertiti, are yet to be found.

CHAPTER 4

HERIHOR

A tomb to 'make Tutankhamun
look like Woolworths'?

The collapse of the 20th Dynasty, the last of the New Kingdom, brought about one of the most fascinating periods in Egyptian history. As early as the reign of Ramesses II of the 19th Dynasty the Egyptian capital was moved from Memphis to a new city, Pi-Ramesse, in the northeastern Delta. Ramsesses's family came from this region, but more importantly the site lay closer to Egypt's border with its vassal states in the Levant, the territory that its Near Eastern rival, the Hittite Empire, also aspired to control. During the 20th Dynasty, as the influence of the Egyptian royal line began to wane, its control of the southern portion of Egypt began to loosen, allowing for a corresponding rise in the power of the priesthood of the temple of Karnak at Thebes, which was significant not only in religious terms but also economically, given its control of resources – manpower, agricultural lands, materials for building and so on – and therefore politically as well. During the reign of Ramesses IX, towards the end of the 20th Dynasty, the Chief Priest of Amun at the temple of Karnak, Amenhotep, was depicted in a relief in the temple as the same size as the king, indicating an unprecedented equality of status between the two.[1]

In recent years, Thebes had suffered from repeated disturbances brought about by groups of invading Libyans, declining economic conditions and, consequently, a spate of strikes and tomb robberies. After the ten-year reign of Ramesses X, during which time this strife persisted, the situation continued into the reign of Ramesses XI and indeed appears to have worsened. At a certain point no later than his Year 12, Panehsy, the Viceroy of Nubia – a title given to the deputy of the king in the territory to the south of Egypt – arrived in Thebes to restore order, but the economic situation made it difficult for him to feed his troops. He thus claimed the role of Overseer of the Granaries, bringing him into conflict with the Chief Priest, Amenhotep, who otherwise maintained control over the stores. The latter was at one point besieged in the temple complex of Medinet Habu by Panehsy and appealed to the king for help. Panehsy began marching north, ransacking the town of Hardai in Upper Egypt and perhaps even reaching further north, but was eventually pushed back to Nubia by an army of the king, led probably by a general named Payankh.[2] Payankh subsequently took over the titles of Panehsy, including Viceroy of Nubia, and also that of vizier, the highest non-royal position in the country, and became Chief Priest of Amun on the death of Amenhotep.

All of the most important Upper Egyptian titles were thus concentrated in a single individual, and Payankh's 'coup' brought about the beginning of a new era known as *wehem mesut*, meaning 'repeating of births' a formula signifying the beginning of a new era (and sometimes referred to by Egyptologists as the 'renaissance').[3] The period seems to have begun around the nineteenth year of the reign of Ramesses XI, and events in Thebes would now be dated to the new era – 'Year 1 of *wehem mesut*', and so on, independent of the northern pharaoh.

The beginning of the period of *wehem mesut* in the south marked the end of the central authority of the 20th Dynasty pharaohs, whose northern base must have seemed increasingly distant at this time, even though Ramesses XI would continue to reign for another seventeen years or so. During this time, another key figure was to emerge: a Delta official named Smendes who had taken control of the north, and was therefore an equal of Payankh in the south.[4] The line of 20th Dynasty kings came to an end with the death of Ramesses XI in his twenty-ninth regnal year, in approximately 1069 BC, and thus Egypt was now divided between Smendes, pharaoh of the new 21st Dynasty line in the north, and the Chief Priest of Amun, Payankh, in the south.

Herihor and the priests who became 'kings'

The next individual in the sequence of powerful Upper Egyptian rulers based at Thebes took his authority a step further. Herihor came to prominence as a military commander under Ramesses XI, but gradually took on additional titles, in particular those of Chief Priest of Amun and vizier (a title which had historically been held by the principal administrative official in the court of the king, and gave the holder control over the judiciary), which combined gave him, as Payankh before him, control of all the main areas of the administration in Upper Egypt – the armies, the principal temple, the economy and legal affairs. His wife Nodjmet may have been a daughter of Ramesses XI, implying a mutually advantageous relationship between Herihor and the Dynastic line in the north. Most significantly, when Herihor succeeded Payankh,[5] he also broke with convention by adopting some of the trappings of kingship himself although he was not of royal blood, and despite there being a pharaoh in the north. He enclosed his name and the title of Chief Priest inside a cartouche,[6] previously one of the most important and exclusive prerogatives of the pharaoh. The cartouche enclosed the birth and coronation names of the king, and was therefore an indicator of ultimate power and status in Egypt. In adopting the cartouche, Herihor was thus implying that even though he was not king himself – he could not have been while another pharaoh to whose line he was at least at one point allied was still in existence – his role as Chief Priest of Amun gave him the equivalent level of authority. This was a watershed moment in Egyptian history and the precedent set – of individuals other than the established pharaoh declaring themselves to have equivalent authority – would recur from time to time throughout the following period, at least until the 26th Dynasty. Herihor was followed in this by two further chief priests during the period of the 21st Dynasty, Khakheperre Setepenamun Pinudjem I and Menkheperre.[7] This was a profound departure from the conventional world view of the Egyptians, for whom pharaoh alone was at the centre of everything, the sole communicant between men and gods. Herihor demonstrated that even this privileged connection with the divine was now within his reach – he is depicted frequently in the hypostyle hall of the temple of Khonsu at Karnak in direct communion with Amun-Ra. The implications seemed

A relief showing Herihor making offerings to Amun from the first court of the temple of Khonsu at Karnak.

clear: Herihor and his successors as Chief Priest (and also, significantly, of the title of 'Commander of the Armies'[8]) enjoyed the same status as pharaoh. We will see in the next chapter what this power dynamic – the collapse of the country's central authority – meant for the burial of the pharaoh in the period that followed. Here we will examine what happened to the first of them, Herihor, whose burial remains a mystery.

The Valley of the Kings at the end of the New Kingdom

The Valley of the Kings, which as we have seen was perhaps inaugurated by Amenhotep I, was in use as the royal cemetery right up to the end of the New Kingdom – with the exception of the Amarna Period – and the tombs of some of the 20th Dynasty rulers are among the most extensive and lavishly decorated anywhere in the Valley. Towards the end of the Dynasty, however, reigns were becoming shorter, and this is reflected in the quality of the tombs. One particularly elaborate tomb, KV 9, was used for the burial of Ramesses VI despite having been intended for Ramesses V, who reigned for only four years and whose burial has not been found. Ramesses VII similarly reigned for only a short time – seven years – and his tomb is notably smaller than those of his predecessors. No tomb, or even any burial equipment, is known for Ramesses VIII, who reigned for only a very short time; it is not impossible that the tomb still awaits discovery, but it is likely that it would not have been very extensive at the time of his death and would not have left a substantial impression in the Valley, if he was buried there at all. His successors, Ramesses IX, X and XI, maintained the tradition of burials in the Valley, but their tombs (KV 6, KV 18 and KV 4 respectively) were never finished, and only that of Ramesses IX seems to have been used for burial. Of Ramesses X and XI, no trace has been discovered, even in the caches of royal mummies; as with Ramesses VIII, it is therefore unclear whether they were even buried at Thebes.

Overall, the picture is one of a decline in the practice of burying pharaoh in the Valley of the Kings, and this is in keeping with the troubles of the period that affected Thebes and the royal line in particular. Several factors seem to have been at play. The first of these was the persistent threat of foreign invasion. Ramesses III, second pharaoh of the

20th Dynasty, had his mortuary temple at Medinet Habu decorated with extensive scenes recording his victories over a coalition of invaders from the area of modern Libya, including the Libu, Meshwesh and Seped groups in his Years 5 and 11. In his Year 8, he engaged and defeated the 'Sea Peoples' – a coalition of seafaring foreigners, who apparently plagued the coastal settlements of the Mediterranean at this time – in the Delta. These 'victories' failed to put an end to the threat, however, and by the reign of Ramesses v, the workmen of the village of Deir el-Medina, the community of artisans dedicated to the cutting and decoration of the royal tombs of the Valley of the Kings, had to suspend work for 'fear of the enemy',[9] presumed to be further groups of Libyan invaders. And a few decades later, in the reign of Ramesses x, the 'necropolis journal' recording the activity of these workmen suggests they were idle much of the time, due in part to the ongoing threat posed by the Libyans.[10]

A further threat to the dominance of pharaoh was the increasing economic power and influence of the temple of Amun at Karnak. The Wilbour Papyrus, which is now kept in the Brooklyn Museum, New York, is dated to Year 4 of a king whose name is not mentioned but is thought to have been Ramesses v. The information it records is similar to that which might be found in a census, dealing with land ownership, farming and taxes. It shows that by this point most land was owned by the temple of Amun, which by extension therefore had control of a very significant part of the Egyptian economy. It was this trend that must have led to the increasing power of the head of the Amun clergy, the Chief Priest Amenhotep, being depicted as having equal standing to the king at the time of Ramesses ix. This limited the pharaoh's ability to command the best resources in the land, including the skills of its craftsmen and artisans, and in Year 29 of the reign of Ramesses iii, the first recorded strike in history took place: the workmen of Deir el-Medina refused to work and staged 'sit-ins' at the mortuary temples of Tuthmosis iii, Ramesses ii and possibly Sety i in response to their rations not having been provided to them.[11] Further disputes were recorded during the reigns of Ramesses x and xi. The picture overall is one of an increasingly fractious situation, in which the royal house's economic authority became ever more precarious.

One final aspect of this trend, emblematic of the decline of the influence of the pharaoh in general but particularly in Thebes, is the wave of tomb robberies that plagued the reigns of the 20th Dynasty kings. In turn, these contributed to the eventual abandonment of tomb-building in the Valley of the Kings, bringing an end to a tradition that had lasted centuries.

A spate of tomb robberies

No part of the history of the Valley of the Kings is better attested in the evidence than that of its end, as a royal cemetery at least. The story of inspections, robberies, court cases, convictions, punishment and the eventual reburial of all the famous pharaohs of the New Kingdom in two secret caches, can be pieced together thanks to a variety of sources, both textual and archaeological. It is one of the most compelling and detailed chapters in the history of ancient Egypt.

Our information about the robberies comes principally from a series of papyri,[12] mostly comprised of court records detailing thefts, inspections, lists of suspects and so on. The robberies documented by these texts seem largely to have taken place during two phases, under the reigns of Ramesses ix and xi respectively – that is to say, right at the end of the period in which the Valley of the Kings was in use. The robberies targeted not only tombs in the Valley of the Kings but also those of royal family members and high-ranking courtiers elsewhere in the Theban necropolis, and the funerary temples associated with royal burials. In fact, only three of the documents relate directly to thefts in the Valley, specifically to those of the tombs of Sety ii,[13] Ramesses ii[14] and Ramesses vi.[15]

The papyrus records can be supplemented by evidence from the tombs themselves, several of which exhibit evidence of having been entered illicitly in ancient times, and the material within rearranged or repaired and blockings resealed.[16] It seems these were often opportunistic robberies, perhaps carried out by the very people involved in burying the deceased, or on occasions when the construction of a new tomb led inadvertently to entry into another.[17]

Despite the efforts made by the robbers to cover their tracks, it is clear that regular inspections were carried out – that described in the Abbott Papyrus (see pp. 73–76) being one of the best attested – and that robbers were caught, and their crimes taken very seriously, to judge from the punishments meted out to the guilty parties: anyone caught violating a royal tomb was sentenced to impalement. Such legal proceedings were evidently felt insufficient to deter the looters and protect the historic tombs of the Valley, however; in the 19th century, two caches of royal mummies were discovered, demonstrating that ultimately, the authorities felt drastic action was necessary if the bodies of the royal dead were to be protected from desecration. The mummies were removed from their tombs and reburied together in these caches, which presumably were more easily protected than numerous individual tombs. One of these caches, KV 35, the tomb of Amenhotep II, was discussed in Chapter 3; the second, TT 320, was well hidden in the cliffs a little to the south of the temples of Deir el-Bahri.

The circumstances surrounding the discovery of TT 320 remain somewhat obscure to this day. It became known to archaeologists in 1881, but in a curious echo of the circumstances that led to the assembly of the caches in ancient times, it had been entered for the first time perhaps as long as a decade before that,[18] and partially plundered in the years that followed by two men from the local area who have become the archetypal modern-day tomb robbers: the Abd er-Rassoul brothers.

During the 1870s the authorities of the museum in Bulaq – forerunner of the present-day Egyptian Museum in Cairo – had noticed that a number of very fine items relating to the 21st Dynasty Chief Priests of Amun had begun to appear on the antiquities market. Auguste Mariette, then Director of the Egyptian Antiquities Service, had purchased two very fine papyri for the museum, and his successor Gaston Maspero had seen a number of shabtis, further papyri and wooden stelae of similar date in private collections. Maspero suspected that an important tomb had been discovered and that further objects – and vital archaeological information – might still remain to be recovered for the museum. The items had been traced to a consular agent acting for the British, Russian and Belgian governments in Luxor, Mustafa Aga Ayat, and ultimately to the Abd er-Rassoul brothers. In 1881, during his first tour of inspection as Director of the Service, Maspero interviewed one of the brothers, Ahmed, but was unable to extract any information from him. Ayat attempted to provide some level of protection to the brothers, but under pressure from Maspero and the governor of the province of Qena, Daoud Pasha, the secret was given up. A reward of £500 for information was offered, and the eldest Abd er-Rassoul brother, Mohamed, travelled to Qena and secured an amnesty for himself – as well as the reward – by revealing the location of the tomb. He also admitted that he and his brother were well aware of the importance of what they had found: not just two or three mummies, but closer to forty, and most of them in coffins decorated at the brow with '*un petit serpent*' – the *uraeus*-cobra that sits on the brow of pharaoh.[19]

Maspero had by this time departed Egypt for a vacation in France, but clearly the matter could not wait. On 1 July, Maspero's deputy, Emile Brugsch, and the Egyptian Egyptologist Ahmed Kamal departed for Luxor to investigate. On their way they stopped in Qena, where Daoud Pasha informed them that the Abd er-Rassoul house had been searched and was found to contain numerous precious objects from the tomb, probably the last to have been removed by the robbers.[20]

On 6 July, Mohamed led the group to the tomb. Its entrance, a simple shaft, was concealed in one of the rock 'chimneys' that characterize the landscape of the Theban hills, behind a huge boulder. The Abd er-Rassouls had taken care to conceal their secret by partially refilling the shaft, which thus had to be cleared before Brugsch and Kamal could proceed.

The shaft proved to be approximately 14 m (46 ft) deep. From here Brugsch and Kamal encountered a corridor roughly 10 m (33 ft) in length, which then took a turn to the right; a second, roughly cut corridor then lay in front of them, proceeding in a northerly direction for a further 30 m (100 ft). At this point a rough and irregular stairwell took the visitors 5 m (16 ft)

The approach to TT 320.

TT 320: the author at the entrance.

downwards, via a niche to another corridor, which terminated after a further 30 m (100 ft) or so in a burial chamber.[21]

The accounts do not provide as much detail as we might like, and we can only imagine what entering the labyrinthine tomb must have felt like for Brugsch and Kamal. They must have known as soon as they left Cairo that there was a good chance they would find something spectacular, but even they could not have imagined the riches that the tomb contained. It was full to bursting with coffins, the first of which Brugsch and Kamal encountered more or less as soon as they reached the bottom of the shaft, in the first corridor.[22] Brugsch made a preliminary examination of the tomb over the course of two hours. It must have been apparent to him quite quickly that here lay not only the mummies of a group of important 21st Dynasty Chief Priests and their families, but those of a series of New Kingdom pharaohs. The importance of the find and the splendour of the material must have rushed over him like a tsunami, but he had no time to dwell on it.

> I took in the situation quickly, with a gasp, and hurried to the open air lest I should be overcome and the glorious prize still un-revealed be lost to science.[23]

The time taken to clear the shaft and to make the initial inspection seems to have taken them close to the end of the day, and Brugsch must have known that the security of the material would be under threat. He feared for his own safety, too, and even for his life, recording that he was 'armed to the teeth'[24] and that his assistant Ahmed Effendi Kamal was the only person he could trust, as everyone else around him knew that he was about to deprive them of a great source of revenue.

It was clearly vital that the material be removed and sent to Cairo as quickly as possible. Brugsch seems to have worked through the night assembling a workforce to undertake the clearance and removal of the material to a boat belonging to the museum, which was moored on the Nile a few miles away across the desert and cultivation.

Once everything had been removed, Brugsch re-entered the tomb for a final inspection, during which he seems to have made a first sketch of its dimensions. He also discovered a small niche at the bottom of the entrance passage containing the glorious leather funerary canopy of Istemkheb now on display in Cairo's Egyptian Museum.[25]

On 9 July, the objects began their journey down to the Nile. The scene was recreated in the wonderfully atmospheric Egyptian film *Al-Mummia* (1969), directed by Shadi Abdel Salam and known to English-speaking audiences as *The Night of Counting The Years*,[26] shot in and around the hills where TT 320 is located. The burial assemblage is depicted by Abdel Salam being carried across the desert in solemn procession, the locals, dressed in black – as was and still is traditional, and lends the images a distinctly funerary feel – looking on silently, reverently. The sequence also evokes the ceremonial processions that would have brought the mummies and their grave-goods to their tombs in the first place, thousands of years earlier. This was no mere cinematic conceit: the locals really did turn out in numbers as if for a funerary procession, the nature of the ceremony quite in keeping with the objects they watched passing them by, but their attitudes perhaps motivated more by the loss of the treasure that might otherwise have provided the area with lucrative income.

The journey seems to have taken seven or eight hours, and in some cases the coffins required a team of twelve to sixteen men to carry them, and a second team to guard against ambush.[27]

Once everything had safely arrived in Cairo, the immense significance of this discovery could finally be appreciated. What they had found, even now, seems staggering. Forty mummies were present in total, ten of them belonging to pharaohs, from Seqenenre Tao of the 17th Dynasty to Ramesses IX of the 20th. Some of the most famous individuals from the ancient world were among them, including Tuthmosis III, Sety I and Ramesses II (the Great). Three of the 21st Dynasty Chief Priests were also present: Pinudjem I, Masaharta and Pinudjem II. Inscribed items of burial equipment brought the total number of individuals represented in the tomb to forty-five.[28] Maspero quickly realized that the mummies divided into two groups, the first including the 17th Dynasty and New Kingdom individuals contained in coffins of poor condition, and the second including the later individuals, whose mummies were much better equipped.[29] He also noted that several of the mummies were in the wrong coffins; short inscriptions in ink naming individuals were written on coffins and mummy bandages, and in the latter case seem to provide the most reliable means of identifying the bodies.

The implications of the discovery must have been overwhelming to Brugsch and Maspero, and the discovery attracted much publicity. Of all the important aspects of the find, there is one that is perhaps not the most significant historically, but that allows a unique connection with the leading characters from the distant past in Egypt: thanks to the discovery of these mummies, it is possible to look upon the face of a famous pharaoh like Ramesses II himself.

Bodies still missing

Although the number of royal mummies discovered in each of the caches must have seemed overwhelming – one can imagine that, for a moment, Brugsch might have wondered if he had discovered all of the missing New Kingdom pharaohs in one place – it is nonetheless clear that TT 320 and KV 35 do not represent the whole picture.

In fact, the relocation of the mummies to these two caches was the last of a number of measures taken over the course of a century or so in an effort to protect the royal dead. The first steps seem to have been taken in Years 4 to 7 of the *wehem mesut*. At this time, the burials of Sety I and

Ramesses II were restored, and two initial caches were created within KV 14 (the tomb of Siptah and Tausret) and probably KV 57 (belonging to Horemheb).[30] A graffito in the latter, combined with the discovery of the remains of four mummies in the tomb when it was found in 1908, suggest that it was used as a cache, the mummies possibly including those of Horemheb himself, and perhaps his immediate predecessor, Ay, both of whose bodies are otherwise unaccounted for.[31] During the priest-king Pinudjem I's floruit, the mummies that had previously been gathered in KV 14 were transferred to their final resting place, the tomb of Amenhotep II, KV 35 (see pp. 124–28). He also created a cache in KV 17, the mummies of Ramesses I and II being added to that of the tomb owner, Sety I.[32]

The dockets on the mummies in TT 320 suggest that before they came to rest there, they were kept in anoher cache in the tomb of Ahmose-Inhapy, an 18th Dynasty queen, though this tomb has yet to be identified with certainty. In Year 10 of Siamun, the mummies of Ramesses I, Sety I and Ramesses II were added to it, following that of Amenhotep I, which had arrived sometime beforehand.[33]

Perhaps as much as sixty years then elapsed before the first burials, those of the family of Pinudjem II, were introduced into TT 320, beginning in Year 5 of Siamun.[34] The royal mummies, including those that had previously been in the tomb of Ahmose-Inhapy, were introduced sometime after this. The sequence and dates of the removal of the various royal mummies to the Pinudjem tomb are uncertain, and in this we have cause to regret the speed with which TT 320 was cleared, necessary though Brugsch and Kamal may then have felt it. The way in which the coffins were removed from the tomb left a lot to be desired, and much seems to have been lost as a result. The objects were damaged: many years later, in the late 1990s and early 2000s, during a re-clearance of the tomb led by Erhart Graefe, fragments of the coffins were found, suggesting that they were dragged out through the tomb and lifted up and out of the shaft without any protection.[35] But more importantly, no one involved in the original clearance seems to have taken even so much as the briefest of notes. Tragically, if any record was made of the position of the coffins within the tomb, it has not survived. This moment, one of greatest in the history of Egyptology, thus presents something of a paradox: the revelation of the contents of the tomb, even after untold years of secret robbery by the Abd er-Rassoul brothers, provided an unparalleled windfall of material and information, and yet much was also lost, first in the tomb's initial plunder and then in the hasty and almost entirely undocumented removal of the material by the archaeologists.

In any case, the deposition of the royal mummies in TT 320 seems to have been conducted piecemeal over a considerable amount of time. The last documented activity in the tomb dates to Year 11 of Sheshonq I of the 22nd Dynasty, when the mummy of the Fourth Priest of Amun Djedptahiuefankh was brought into the tomb, thirty to forty years after the burial of Pinudjem's family members.[36]

Missing mummies, further caches?

The cached mummies included the bodies not only of pharaohs, but also of queens, royal children and other high-ranking individuals, including the 21st Dynasty Chief Priests of Amun. The evidence from this deposit, poorly documented though the discovery was, combined with the cache in KV 35, allows us to account for the bodies of most of the New Kingdom pharaohs and several of the Chief Priests of the period. But there are noteworthy exceptions. Along with Herihor, a number of the Chief Priests – Menkheperre, Djedkhonsuiuefankh I, Nesubanebdjed (Smendes) II, Pasebkhanu (Psusennes III/IV) – and New Kingdom pharaohs remain unaccounted for, and the absence of these individuals from either of the two surviving caches has led some to conclude that a high-status cemetery of the period remains to be found.

Romer's search for Herihor

We know that Herihor died at a time when burial practices were changing; we also know that he was not a king in the conventional sense, and there should not, therefore, be any expectation of his having had a tomb in the Valley of the Kings. His status was almost equivalent to that of a king, however, so could he perhaps have had a lavish, rock-cut tomb like those of the pharaohs of earlier years?

In 1982, the British Egyptologist John Romer featured in a BBC television series entitled *Romer's Egypt*. Romer subsequently became one of the best-known presenters of history and archaeology programmes, thus making an enormous contribution to bringing Egyptology to the public. This first film is a 'fly-on-the-wall'-style documentary, which begins by setting out Romer's ambition to locate the tomb of Herihor, and follows his attempts to put together an archaeological expedition – acquiring funding, expertise, permits and so on. In the course of his preparations, he struck a deal with New York's Brooklyn Museum, but was consequently diverted away from his desire to investigate the remote areas further into the desert from the Valley of the Kings and onto the first serious exploration of the tomb of Ramesses XI, which, though a worthy project, was not his mission. This led to some frustration and conflict with his colleagues at the Brooklyn Museum – high drama, all of which was captured in the film and secured its popularity, though perhaps not for the reasons that Romer would have hoped.

Romer did not fit the mould of the typical establishment Egyptologist, preferring to operate independently from traditional academic institutions, but had good experience of Egypt and its history and monuments. He had spent several years working for the Luxor-based Epigraphic Survey of the Oriental Institute, University of Chicago, and clearly had a great passion for his subject. He was also clearly very driven by a desire to make his great discovery. The narrator of the film tells us: 'He seeks the tomb of the priest-king Herihor....A tomb that would, in his own words, make Tutankhamun['s tomb] look like Woolworths.'

A lavish tomb, then, but one hidden well away from the main part of the Theban royal necropolis, Romer believed. The narrator tells us: 'From the sad experiences of the preceding decades we can hardly believe that they would have begun new monuments amidst the ruins of the Great Place [the Valley of the Kings]. From their graffiti and other clues in the southern wadis, however, we may assume that the High Priests were buried there, in that most remote section of the Theban mountain, in the valleys holding the ancient cemeteries of queens and princes.'[37]

The 'graffiti and other clues' of which Romer speaks comprise a body of evidence first scientifically documented by Howard Carter during a single season in 1916–17. This expedition, which has come to provide the basis for a considerable amount of further archaeological work and much speculation, was in fact largely unplanned: Carter was on holiday in Luxor when it came to his attention that a discovery had been made in a 'lonely and unfrequented region'.[38] A tomb had been found by a group of local plunderers, who had been driven away by a second group who had got wind of the news. Carter was asked by the notables of the village to intervene to head off any further trouble. Gathering the few workmen who had managed to avoid conscription as part of the war effort, he set off in late afternoon, the majority of the climb up into the mountains taking place by moonlight.

> It was midnight when we arrived on the scene, and the guide pointed out to me the end of a rope, which dangled sheer down the face of a cliff. Listening, we could hear the robbers actually at work, so I first severed their rope, thereby cutting off their means of escape, and then, making secure a good stout rope of my own, I lowered myself down the cliff. Shinning down a rope at midnight, into a nestful of industrious tomb-robbers, is a pastime which at least does not lack excitement.[39]

Carter managed to shoo the robbers away, and stood guard at the site overnight before making a thorough investigation the next day. What he found was of considerable interest, not least as the tomb was in an extraordinary location, cut directly into the vertical wall of a cleft in the rock, some 40 m (130 ft) from the top of the cliff and 70 m (230 ft) from the bottom of the valley below. It would seem to have been the perfect place to conceal and protect a tomb, and it is difficult not to marvel at the robbers for having spotted it, and then managing to get themselves inside. More astounding, however, the ancients managed to place within it a sarcophagus of yellow crystalline sandstone, the inscriptions on which revealed the identity of the owner: the famous Hatshepsut, but at a time before she became pharaoh in her own right, while she was still the consort of Tuthmosis II. The tomb was undecorated and never finished, it seems, the only other objects that Carter found being fragments of two jars of the kind that were used by the ancient workmen.[40]

This was perhaps not quite the sensation that Carter – and presumably the robbers – had hoped for, but there was a wider significance to the find, which Carter recognized immediately: the wadi in which the tomb was located was one of several covering a vast area, remote and distant from the main part of the Theban necropolis. Indeed, the area had not yet attracted archaeological attention, but if, in the early part of the 18th Dynasty, the ancient tomb builders had taken the trouble to locate a royal tomb here, then perhaps it was worth a more thorough investigation.

Once Carter had cleared the tomb, he spent ten days surveying the wadi system,[41] in sequence from the southeast to the northwest, and produced a sketch map including seven areas of interest, which he gave the designations 'A' to 'F'. Carter found numerous tombs concentrated in the least accessible or visible spots, the clefts and crevices of the cliffs. He also found ancient pathways, groups of stone huts, graffiti and some worked material, including heaps of chipped fragments of both the local stone and stone of finer quality, including granite, basalt, crystalline sandstone and alabaster.[42]

The cliff-tomb of Hatshepsut was found in 'Wadi A', the terminus and northern extent of a wadi known locally as Wadi Sikket Taqet Zaid (the 'Valley of the Window of Zaid'),[43] in which Carter found a further three tombs: two simple pits and a corridor-type monument.[44] Several other areas were also found to be of significance. Within a bay at the end and east side of a further wadi, that of the Gabbanat el-Qirud (the 'Valley of the Ape Cemetery'), Carter found several pit-tombs and a cliff-tomb of considerable size. Below the latter, a large fallen block of limestone was inscribed with the name 'Neferure' inside a cartouche.[45] This was the name of a daughter of Hatshepsut, and the tomb was taken by Carter to have been hers, although no further evidence survived to confirm it.

At the head of the same wadi, a tomb cut into a crevice had been discovered by robbers earlier in 1916 before Carter got there. This was in fact the most spectacular find yet made in the area. The tomb belonged to 'the three foreign wives of Tuthmosis III', and has come to be known by that name. The treasure recovered included canopic jars, silver canisters inscribed for Tuthmosis III, goblets of blue glass, alabaster and gold, ointment jars, a silver mirror, and bracelets and headdresses of gold.[46] Most of these items were removed by the modern looters, but have since been tracked down on the antiquities market and are now kept in the Metropolitan Museum of Art, New York.

The westernmost of the wadis surveyed by Carter is known as the Wadi el-Gharby, where he identified three locations of significance, designated 'E', 'F' and 'G'. The main part of this large and impressive valley was described by Romer as 'an isolated, completely silent place, a ruined slab-filled area that holds in it the imminence, the same sense of expectation as an empty theatre, but on a colossal scale'.[47] It runs parallel to the Wadi Gabbanat el-Qirud, and terminates in location 'F', a sharply cut watercourse between high rocks – 'a narrow canyon cut in the lower stratum and ending sharply under a cascade once fed from the upper stratum overhung by the great cliffs'.[48] Here Carter identified traces of significant ancient activity; there were apparently no tombs to be found, but all around there were the tell-tale signs:

> At the beginning of this canyon, among great fallen blocks of limestone, are heaps of *débris*, stone chippings from some ancient excavation. On the right, as you enter, is a small lateral valley containing stone huts of workmen, pottery and various graffiti. Above the cascade are more heaps of ancient origin and upon the larger limestone fragments fallen from the cliffs are numerous hieratic inscriptions such as also occur at the bases of the cliffs themselves.

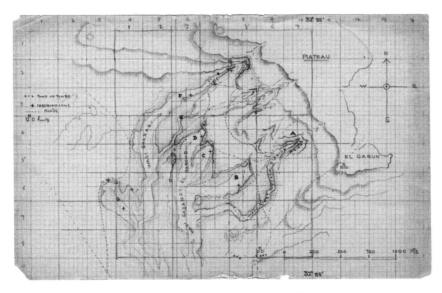

Carter's map of the western wadis.

The graffiti and heaps of rubbish indicate the presence of tombs in the vicinity, as the natives have recognized; but the extensive excavations made by them have apparently been without result.

As the Wadi el-Gharby is far away and difficult to protect against depredations I am making more extensive soundings here in the hope of revealing lost tombs. I have already found a piece of crystalline sandstone from a sarcophagus – the projection for the levers used in transportation.[49]

In other words, although Carter found no tombs in this particular wadi, he suspected he might yet do so, having apparently found all the classic signs of tomb-building activity – workmen's huts, graffiti and a fragment from a sarcophagus – along with numerous tombs in the neighbouring wadis, establishing beyond doubt that this locale was known to the tomb builders of the New Kingdom. Still, Carter's efforts came to naught. He refers to his work as being 'preliminary' in nature, and was convinced that the area was worthy of further investigation, saying especially that the wadi Gabbanat el-Qirud 'may possibly have a tomb secreted in it.... The debris here covering the rock is very deep and may conceal burials.'[50]

He was unable to devote limitless time to the work, however, as he was involved with the war effort for British Intelligence in Cairo. By the time his commitments in this direction allowed him to return to his archaeological work in December 1917, it was to the site that he had really set his heart on, the Valley of the Kings. He would, of course, remain preoccupied with that site, and Tutankhamun in particular, and never returned to the remote wadis.

The evidence for a tomb

Although the tombs of Hatshepsut and (probably) her daughter, Neferure, suggest that the wadis were in use as a burial ground by members of the royal family during the earlier part of the 18th Dynasty, numerous graffiti found in the area relate rather to the late 20th Dynasty. These graffiti suggest that the 18th Dynasty burial ground might still have been in use by the elite at that time; might Herihor have been among them? According to a note at the foot of the first page of Carter's report,

The house of Butehamun at Medinet Habu.

apparently written by the editor, 'the vast majority of them [the graffiti] refer to the well-known "scribe of the necropolis Butehamun" or to persons known to have been connected with him'.[51] Butehamun (see pp. 86–87) was a contemporary of Herihor's, active during the reigns of Ramesses XI and Smendes I, and indeed the name that appears more than any other is that of Herihor, particularly in the Wadi el-Gharby. Some broken water jars found in the area date to the same period.[52]

It was these inscriptions that led John Romer to the site. He supplemented what had been learned from Carter's survey with his own survey work and extensive field-walking undertaken during his years working in Egypt prior to initiating his Theban Royal Tombs Project.

He set down his case in his book, first released in 1984, *Ancient Lives: The Story of the Pharaohs' Tombmakers* and the documentary series that accompanied it, in addition to *Romer's Egypt*. He drew on several types of evidence coming from the western wadis, and specifically the Wadi el-Gharby, noting of the graffiti there that the ancients 'drew the sign signifying "tomb" over and over again, and often they scratched a group of signs that held the same meaning, but expressed the ancient phrase

Graffito of the supposed 'tomb sign' in Wadi 'G'.

"the house of life", a term which was in fashion again in Butehamun's time and signified "royal tomb"'.[53]

These simple signs appear to show a square-shaped enclosure with a central opening along one side. They are not part of the canon of established hieroglyphic symbols, but resemble the much better-known glyphs used to denote structures such as houses or temples. Their meaning is not entirely clear, therefore, but Romer's interpretation that they indicate built structures of some kind, and specifically tombs, seems reasonable, even if some scepticism has been expressed.

Romer also cited the presence of Herihor's name and that of the royal scribe Butehamun,[54] the presence of huts and access routes that might have been used by tomb builders, and the sinks and connecting canals they may have used to collect flash-flood water, as compelling evidence that Herihor's tomb might yet be found at the site.[55] He also mentions the presence of chippings, 'like those from the work in the royal tombs still covering much of the great place' (the Valley of the Kings),[56] and 'the discovery [by Carter] in this same valley of the bosses from a granite sarcophagus'. This last piece of evidence would seem to bring us closer than any of the others to the much sought tomb itself; Carter himself noted only that he had found 'a piece of crystalline sandstone from a sarcophagus'[57] – had Romer found more? It seems he may well have uncovered material not seen by Carter: in *Ancient Lives* he also mentions several offering tables 'inscribed in the characteristic village style' and includes a drawing of the inscribed surface of one of them, based on a photo he had taken, suggesting that he did find and at least photograph more material.[58]

Romer also refers to an 'inspection' of Year 6 of the *wehem mesut* period of 'the tomb of the Great General', recorded in Papyrus Ambras.[59] This document is a record of the assessment of a series of administrative documents, whose contents are described in brief. Several of the papyri inspected were 'records concerning the thieves', and some can even be identified with known tomb-robbery papyri. Papyrus Ambras notes that one of these papyri dealt with 'The examination of the tomb of the Generalissimo which was made [because of?] the coppersmith, Waresi 1.'[60] However, although Papyrus Ambras itself is dated to Year 6 of the *wehem mesut*, it is not clear when the papyri it documents were written – as has been noted elsewhere, most of the texts it mentions were written some time before the *wehem mesut*. Romer himself admits that 'it is not clear whether this was the tomb of Herihor who had died in that year, or of...Piankh', but if the examination took place before the *wehem mesut*, it cannot have been the tomb of either of them. Indeed, it has been argued that the 'generalissimo' in question may be a king, but a much earlier one: Ramesses II.[61]

The New Kingdom Research Foundation Survey

Romer, in spite of his convictions, did not find the tomb of Herihor and after he gave up his hunt, archaeological work in the wadis surveyed by Carter all but ceased. But in 2013, the Egyptian Ministry of Antiquities granted a team led by Professor Geoffrey Martin and Piers Litherland under the auspices of the New Kingdom Research Foundation (NKRF) permission to revisit the site. A comprehensive monograph on the initial stages of the project appeared with admirable speed in 2014. The report is generously illustrated, including a reproduction of Carter's original sketch map, satellite images more accurately showing the terrain and locations of the important sites, and annotated colour photographs of the archaeological features taken from the ground.

In essence, the survey's aim was to revisit the areas investigated by Carter, to confirm – or debunk – his findings, to improve the accuracy of his sketch maps where necessary, and to supplement his findings with any additional observations made or material identified.

Of most relevance to us here of course are the sections dealing with the Wadi el-Gharby and the evidence used by John Romer to build his case. The survey established that this wadi contains by far the most graffiti of the 7, and even discovered a further 39 groups of graffiti, bringing the total to 115.[62]

Having already cast some doubt on Romer's interpretation of some of the graffiti as 'tomb signs',[63] Litherland confirms that the graffiti seem to have been left during two distinct periods, the first in the 18th Dynasty and the second in the late 20th to early 21st, indicating a second phase of activity devoted to the extraction of 18th Dynasty burials hidden here. In other words, Litherland agrees that there are tombs still to be found, but believes they would belong to 18th Dynasty royals.[64]

The NKRF team included geologists, and their observations seem to have done the most to advance the discussion of the possibility that Herihor's tomb might be found in the area. Their assessment suggested that the larger piles of stone chippings that Carter and Romer proposed were man-made were in fact composed of natural debris, washed down the hillside by flooding. Such chippings flake in the same way naturally as when cut from a tomb, and so human activity can only be demonstrated conclusively by the presence of chisel marks, which these flakes did not exhibit. The report is clear that on this basis Carter himself was mistaken in identifying them as chippings from tomb-cutting.[65]

If correct, this is a serious blow to Romer's theory; although the absence of man-made chippings does not mean there aren't any tombs in the wadi, their presence would make the case far more compelling. Furthermore, in Litherland's view, the Wadi el-Gharby is in fact not as fruitful a location as some of its neighbours, in which such natural accumulations were apparently used to gain access to high places and then cut away after the tombs were sealed.[66]

As Litherland notes, the evidence of an as-yet-undiscovered tomb therefore comes down to the workmen's huts and the sarcophagus boss. On the first of these, the NKRF survey casts doubt on Romer's suggestion that the site was well provided with access routes by which water and other necessities could be supplied. They found that the pathways do connect with the high desert road, but not without difficulty, and furthermore what might have appeared to be reservoirs or wells on this high desert plateau proved to be excavations for quartzite or gypsum. Neither the supposed 'settlement' nor the sarcophagus fragment can indisputably be connected to the time of Herihor; both could just as well relate to another period, for example, the 18th Dynasty, when we know tombs were cut in the area.

Further fieldwork has now lent more weight to Litherland's theory. Beyond his wadis A–G, Carter had also examined five 'open pit-tombs' that had been cut into an area of raised ground a few hundred metres out into the plain,[67] where he found a fragment of alabaster from a canopic jar bearing the Egyptian word for 'king'. The NKRF survey relocated these tombs, observing workmen's huts and three blocking stones in the area, and around the tombs themselves, spoil heaps, pottery, fragments and pieces of green stone, perhaps from a stone vessel. The team entered the tombs via a shaft, encountering six rooms and establishing the possibility of a further five.[68]

Since the initial report was published, the mission has focused on the re-clearing of four shaft tombs at a site at the mouth of the Wadi Bariya, identified as the family burials of two wives and a son of Amenhotep III (father of Akhenaten), his sister Ti'aa and at least thirteen court women. This exciting news, announced in 2015, would seem to confirm the view that further 18th Dynasty tombs were more likely to be found than that of Herihor. Full publication of the results is eagerly awaited.

A hoard of gold and treasure?

Romer seems convinced – or at least wants *us* to be convinced – that not only is there a tomb waiting to be found, it's going to be full of treasure. In his view, 'Herihor is most likely to be buried in a coffin of gold, like Tutankhamun [250 years before]. There are likely to be canopic chests, objects of alabaster, gold-plated statues, and thrones, though possibly not chariots.' It is true that, to some extent, Egyptology thrives on – is even dependent on – such possibilities.

But we should remind ourselves of a problem presented by the vastly rich hoard of treasures discovered in Tutankhamun's tomb. It is the only royal tomb of the period to have been discovered intact (after an ancient robbery). We cannot say therefore to what extent it was *typical* of the burial of New Kingdom pharaohs in the quality and quantity of the grave-goods. Should we assume that all pharaohs would have been buried with such treasures? Or was there something unusual about the circumstances surrounding Tutankhamun's death that meant he was laid to rest with an abnormally rich stash? The material from other royal burials demonstrates that the quality of the artefacts found in Tutankhamun's tomb was by no means unique – but the quantity? It's impossible to say. We must also ask ourselves whether or not we would expect Herihor in particular, or any other pharaoh or Chief Priest of his era, to be buried in similar fashion to Tutankhamun. The answer on this specific point would seem to me to be 'no'.

Herihor was in power at a time when reburials and the creation of caches was undertaken in part as a response to the persistent threat of robberies, but this process also involved the reappropriation of some of the more precious materials with which the deceased had originally been buried by the authorities. The 'Late Ramesside Letters' include mention of an order sent by Payankh to 'uncover a tomb amongst the foremost tombs [i.e. the royal tombs of the Valley of the Kings and elsewhere in Thebes] and preserve its seal until I return'. But, rather than striving to ensure this example of a royal tomb remained undisturbed, Payankh was doing the opposite – securing it until he could reclaim the wealth therein, either for the state, or perhaps to fund his own campaign against Panehsy, the former Viceroy of Kush, before it fell into the hands of robbers.[69] It is now understood that the entire re-caching process led by Butehamun and others was motivated at least in part by the opportunity to realize some of the value of the grave-goods, and that the policy partially amounted to an officially sanctioned stripping of the tombs, ostensibly to remove the incentive for robbery, but also to help prop up the ailing economy.[70]

That Herihor, with Butehamun's assistance, would stash away a hoard of New Kingdom treasures and furnish himself with a lavish burial therefore runs entirely counter to the state's efforts at this time to protect royal burials by stripping them of the kind of material the robbers would be interested in. It seems more likely that an important individual like Herihor, even if he received the richest burial allowed by the circumstances of his era, would have been buried with only a few precious and fine items, and very few by comparison with the thousands of items interred with Tutankhamun.

Indeed this would be in keeping with the practice of the 21st Dynasty, as in fact is suggested by the first of the interments in TT 320. The tomb seems originally to have been intended as a conventional tomb, the primary burial place of members of the family of the 21st Dynasty Chief Priests; it was only later that it was repurposed to conceal the cache of New Kingdom royal mummies. Such was recorded by a graffito inscribed to the right of the entrance, which sadly no longer survives. It records that in a Year 5, undoubtedly of the 21st Dynasty pharaoh Siamun, that the Chief Priest Pinudjem ɪɪ's niece and wife, and the daughter of the Chief Priest Smendes (ɪɪ), Nesikhons, was buried in the tomb. A second graffito, of a Year 10, now preserved in Carter House in Luxor, records the burial of Pinudjem ɪɪ himself.[71] Furthermore, the coffins of Pinudjem ɪɪ and several of his family members were found in the innermost part of the tomb, suggesting that they were deposited there first, before the mummies of the New Kingdom pharaohs and others, which were found closer to the entrance, had been brought in from elsewhere.

The coffined mummies of Pinudjem ɪɪ and Nesikhons were found along with those of some of their ancestors, including the Chief Priests Pinudjem ɪ and Masaharta, and also some of their descendants. It seems most likely that the earlier individuals were brought to TT 320 only after their own original tombs had been robbed. While Pinudjem and Nesikhons' coffined mummies were found with papyri, shabtis, shabti boxes and canopic equipment, the same cannot be said for the other individuals. While it is possible that their equipment was surreptitiously removed by the Abd er-Rassoul brothers, and may yet lie unrecognized in a museum or private collection, it is equally likely that these items originally accompanied the bodies in another location and had not survived by the time they joined Pinudjem ɪɪ and Nesikhons in TT 320.[72]

If this is correct, then we have something of a model for the kind of tomb we could expect the remaining Chief Priests to have had. Might Herihor and the others have received a relatively simple burial, comprising a coffined mummy, a modest set of burial equipment limited to the essential shabtis, shabti box, canopic jars and chest, and perhaps no more in an undecorated shaft tomb, perhaps sharing the space with other members of his family? In which case, the absence of any of Herihor's burial equipment is hardly surprising.

Possible traces of Herihor

That said, one very fine item that may well be from his tomb does in fact survive. In the collection of the Römer-Pelizaeus Museum in Hildesheim, Germany, there is a beautiful armband made of gold, decorated on the outside with turquoise – some of which is now missing – and an image of the serpent, apparently a *uraeus*-cobra symbolic of kingship. On the inner side, an inscription reads: 'The Chief Priest of Amun, King of Gods, Herihor, justified.'[73] This, undoubtedly, is 'our' Herihor, and the final element of the inscription, translated here as 'justified' but sometimes also rendered 'true of voice' or similar, was commonly used to signify that the individual had died – the epithet asserted that the deceased was morally righteous, and therefore fit to pass judgment and enter the afterlife. The conclusion that this object was likely buried with Herihor is inescapable, and its presence on the art market, where it emerged in the late 1970s before being acquired by the museum, suggests that his tomb cannot be intact. Further items of jewelry also reputedly from the tomb emerged at the same time, although information about them is sparse.[74]

And so the question of where he was buried remains. If Herihor's tomb was comprehensively plundered, and remained undecorated, as TT 320 was, it might well be entirely impossible to identify it among the numerous undecorated shaft tombs of the period. Based on the lack of solid evidence that his tomb was in the western wadis, it seems more likely that he would have been buried closer to the main part of the necropolis, and Professor Andrzej Niwinski, whose work in the cliffs behind the temples of Deir el-Bahri has led him to conclude that the tomb of Amenhotep I is in this area (see pp. 87–88), believes he may be close to finding the tomb of Herihor as well.

Like Romer, Niwinski believes that the absence of Herihor's grave-goods (besides the unprovenanced gold armlet) indicates that his tomb may still be intact. He draws attention in particular to the complete

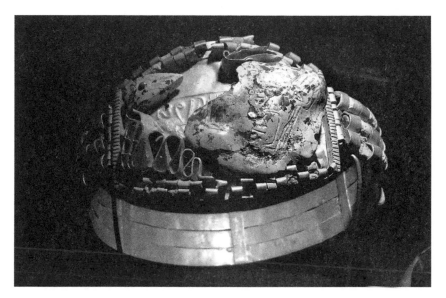

The armband of turquoise and gold inscribed with the name of Herihor.

absence of any of the shabtis,[75] which we would expect Herihor to have been buried with in significant numbers. Because shabtis were typically made of faience, they tend to survive well; unlike, for example, objects made of gold, which can be melted down and reused, making it easy for robbers to disguise what they have stolen. But modern-day plunderers know that they would be able to make a little money from the sale of faience shabtis on the antiquities market; it is therefore surprising that none has come to light. Then there is the presence at his site of seven graffiti of Butehamun. Niwinski argues that the graffiti must have been written immediately after the sealing of the (as-yet-undetected) tomb, and that the tomb can only therefore have belonged to one of two individuals whose tombs have so far not been identified: Herihor and his son Neferheres. But as in Romer's case, it is unclear why Niwinski would suggest that the graffiti of Butehamun would relate to the sealing of a tomb, rather than to an inspection.

Convinced of the presence of a royal tomb in the area of his excavations, Niwinski has built a case to suggest that it was originally that of Amenhotep I, and was later reused for Herihor, and/or perhaps his son or other family members: 'It seems not impossible, either, that the tomb may have been transformed into a very well-guarded cachette before the final closing.'[76] This is certainly not impossible, but it is supported by no evidence other than the absence of Herihor's grave-goods and the presence of the Butehamun graffiti. And this theory is followed by further, vague speculation that unfortunately, to my mind, detracts from the credibility of the theory: 'In such a situation a number of Sleeping Beauties lying there can be much higher....'[77]

Conclusions

What are the chances that the gold stripped from the New Kingdom tombs was simply diverted towards one greedy individual's burial? Very substantial quantities of gold were discovered in the tomb of Tutankhamun, but we must remember the possibility that this was the exception, not the rule even for the burial of the pharaohs of the New Kingdom, at the height of pharaonic prosperity. As we will see in the next chapter, a great deal of gold – and other precious materials – was also recovered from the royal tombs at Tanis, and it is clear that some of the material found there had originally formed part of the burials of earlier pharaohs in the Valley of the Kings.

Contrary to Romer and Niwinski's visions of a tomb full to bursting with glittering gold, Herihor may simply have been buried in an undecorated and/or pre-existing tomb, with minimal grave-goods – certainly relative to the treasures of Tutankhamun. It is by no means certain that he would have been buried amid such splendour, and indeed such treatment would seem exceptional given the apparent policy of deliberately reducing the quantity of precious materials with which individuals were buried so as to reduce the incentive for robbers and to protect the bodies of the deceased – the most important thing from the authorities' point of view but of no importance to plunderers – as well, of course, as recouping its value for the living.

And yet, the almost total absence of grave-goods securely connected with Herihor is puzzling, as is the absence of his body among the mummies of his contemporaries in the 'royal cache' tombs. There is still a puzzle here, which only future discoveries will resolve.

CHAPTER 5

A KINGDOM DIVIDED

The royal tombs of the Third

Intermediate Period

The collapse of the New Kingdom was brought about as the pharaohs of the 20th Dynasty gave way to competing centres of power in the north and south. The traditional royal house ruled in the north as the 21st Dynasty, and the priesthood based at the temple of Amun at Thebes accrued power in the south, splitting the country and signalling the beginning of what Egyptologists refer to as the Third Intermediate Period.

Many aspects of this transition remain obscure. What impact did it have on the way the king was perceived by his subjects, now that he had been effectively replaced in Thebes, the city of Amun, by a non-royal individual? What impact did this decentralization of power have on the judiciary, now that pharaoh was no longer the ultimate (earthly) authority in much of the country; on the economy, now that the land and trade routes within Egypt and beyond were controlled by two different authorities; and, most importantly for us, on decisions as to the proper way to bury the most revered dead, including the pharaohs of the 21st Dynasty in the north and their priestly counterparts in the south? The special significance of pharaoh was surely an important consideration in all aspects of the preparation for, and burial of, the kings of the New Kingdom. Now that the status of pharaoh himself had changed, and practical considerations dictated that the burial of the king in the Valley of the Kings would no longer be possible, things were going to have to change.

While attitudes surrounding high-status burials and historic royal burials at Thebes seem to have tended towards protection and austerity, as we have seen, the extraordinary discovery in the 1930s of the burials of the 21st and 22nd Dynasty pharaohs in the Nile Delta paints a different picture in the north. These tombs yielded a haul of treasure rivalling the 'wonderful things' of Tutankhamun's tomb. For a time Egyptologists believed that the 23rd Dynasty pharaohs might be buried in this northern region, too, as well as those of the 26th Dynasty, the last great native line of rulers, none of whom has ever been found.

Pierre Montet and the royal tombs of Tanis

In 1928, French archaeologist Pierre Montet began excavating the site of San el-Hagar, better known as Tanis, in the northeastern Delta. Montet had been attracted to the site by the possibility it seemed to offer of new evidence for relations between the ancient Egyptians and their Asiatic counterparts. He had previously excavated the site of Byblos, an important ancient harbour town in modern Lebanon, and was following the belief still held by some scholars that Tanis had been the site both of Avaris, the Second Intermediate Period base of the foreign Hyksos rulers, and subsequently Pi-Ramesse, the capital established by the 20th Dynasty Ramesside pharaohs at the end of the New Kingdom.[1] The most visible monuments at Tanis are the many fine and very large sculptures scattered about the area of the temple of Amun, which bear the name of Ramesses II, leading historians to the conclusion that this was his capital city. Now, however, we know that Pi-Ramesse originally lay some 20 miles (30 km) to the south of Tanis, at the modern village of Qantir, but was abandoned when the branch of the river on which it was located began to silt up. The site of Tanis was chosen for the relocation of the capital as it lay on a different branch of the river that was still entirely viable. When it was founded, the sculptures from Ramesses II's temple were transferred to the new site, rescuing his great monument and saving his successors the trouble of building their own from scratch, but also confusing archaeologists some three thousand years later.

Montet focused his efforts on the enclosure of the great temple of Amun, a northern counterpart to the great god's southern cult centre at

Karnak, and over the course of a decade greatly improved the history of the temple's development from the time of Ramesses II into the Ptolemaic Period, and uncovered a great deal of material apparently testifying to the site's Asiatic connections. The discoveries made were significant historically, helping to put flesh on the bones of our understanding of the Third Intermediate Period, but perhaps not of the most spectacular variety. This, however, was to change one day in February 1939.

Montet was working in the southwest corner of the Amun temple, just inside the inner enclosure wall, on what he characterized as a 'handsome pavement'.[2] When he removed one of the supposed paving stones, which he had noticed was jutting out, he found a gold cloisonné buckle, a small coffer and a group of shabtis naming a pharaoh called Sheshonq. His team had also found another intriguing arrangement of stones and, in keeping with a certain stereotype, they tested it by tapping it with a cane. It sounded hollow, and after a brief pause it was lifted, revealing, as quickly became apparent, a royal tomb. He wrote:

> I had the earth and stones blocking the entrance removed, and
> went down into a square chamber with walls covered with
> figures and hieroglyphics; this led into another chamber with
> a large sarcophagus emerging from the earth which filled
> three quarters of two rooms....Everyone is overjoyed. I had
> Hassanein's team come with all the carts so that we could clear
> this remarkable structure as quickly as possible.[3]

Montet had in fact entered the tomb via the roof.[4] They came down into a square chamber, one in a series of small rooms built of blocks of limestone and granite, the recycled remains of earlier Ramesside monuments. These compartments had been built into a cutting in the ground that was then filled in around them, effectively burying the chambers, so that access to them was subsequently provided via shafts.[5]

Although the blocks had first belonged to other buildings, and so still bore elements of their original decoration, the inner walls of the tomb had been decorated for the purpose. It was not long before Montet and his colleagues came across a cartouche, naming the pharaoh Osorkon, and realized that they had uncovered the final resting place of one of the kings of the Third Intermediate Period.

The tomb consisted of four chambers, of which three contained the remnants of at least one burial. Chamber 1 held an enormous but empty and anonymous sarcophagus, and inside Chamber 3 a sarcophagus of quartzite originally cut in the Middle Kingdom was found to have been re-inscribed for Hedjkheperre Setepenre Takeloth 1, the third king of the 22nd Dynasty.

The centrepiece of the tomb, however, was Chamber 4. Here Montet found the sarcophagus of Osorkon himself, specifically Usermaatre Setepenamun Osorkon II, Takeloth 1's successor. Behind this sarcophagus lay another of much smaller size, inscribed for a son of Osorkon named Hornakht. The tomb had clearly been ransacked, but a scatter of burial equipment, including shabtis, canopic jars and some jewelry, remained. To have discovered the burial place of at least two named pharaohs, a prince and a third anonymous, but likely royal, individual was sensational, and left Montet and his team overcome with emotion. Montet immediately diverted all resources to the complete clearance of the area above the tomb structure, which would lead to an even more spectacular discovery.

The tomb of Psusennes:
treasures to rival Tutankhamun's

Montet's team soon came upon another 'pavement' at the eastern end of the monument. The flagstones covering the entrance shaft were removed and a blocking stone that had been used to seal the chambers beyond was dismantled, revealing a small chamber decorated with inscriptions mentioning the name of Pasebkhanu I, better known by the Greek form of his name: Psusennes I. It seemed this second tomb was not that of further kings of the 22nd Dynasty, but of the third king of the preceding 21st Dynasty. Upon entering the chamber, the excavators could see in front of them an accumulation of shabti figures, alabaster jars and bronze ornaments, and over to the right, the astonishing sight of a falcon-headed coffin of solid silver, lying on a plinth in between two badly decomposed mummies. But to their surprise, this did not belong to Psusennes, but to a Hekakheperre Sheshonq, who ruled at some point in the sequence of 22nd Dynasty kings and is now given the ordinal number 'IIa'.[6] Inside the beautiful coffin, the mummy was by now little more than a skeleton,

thanks to the damp Delta environment, and was found to have been
placed inside a cartonnage casing,
which had also decomposed. But a
solid gold funerary mask had survived (see p. ix),[7] along with three
exceptionally fine pectorals of gold
and other precious materials, demonstrating that the burial had been
lavishly equipped. One of the pectorals incorporated a large greenstone
winged scarab, a second featured
a scarab of lapis lazuli flanked by
two rearing cobras, each wearing the white crown of Upper Egypt, and
a third was decorated with an elegant solar barque carrying a sun disc of
lapis lazuli beneath a starry sky.[8] He may not have left much of a mark
in the surviving historical record, but Hekakheperre Sheshonq was not
a king of modest means, and Montet spent the remainder of the 1939
season carefully removing the treasures from his tomb.

Montet inspecting the sarcophagus of
Psusennes I inside the tomb.

This discovery presented a puzzle: what had happened to the burial of
Psusennes himself? Montet was convinced that it would be found within
a granite building that lay immediately to the west of the chambers they
had just entered, realizing that the decorated western wall adjacent to the
coffin of Sheshonq concealed two entrances to further chambers beyond.

Though war was declared in Europe in September 1939, Montet was
able to return to the site in January 1940 to test his theory. His first task
was to define the outer extent of the monument. He removed the western
wall of the tomb of Osorkon II, which enabled him to extract the final
elements of the burial of Prince Hornakht. Working his way along the
western edge of the monument, he also uncovered a separate, single-
chambered tomb in which a beautiful quartzite sarcophagus inscribed
for Psusennes' successor, Amenemopet, was found, although it would
turn out to be empty.

On 16 February 1940, having defined the exterior of the building in
which he expected to find the burial of Psusennes, Montet had the right-
hand of the two concealed entrances removed. Progress was immediately

halted by the presence of a huge piece of granite, but closer inspection revealed that it had been set in place on bronze rollers, which, having been used three thousand years previously to roll the blocking stone into place, were now used to roll it away again.

Beyond, Montet found what he had been hoping for. Surrounded by shabtis, canopic jars and vessels of gold and silver lay a massive pink granite sarcophagus (see p. x). It took six days to clear the material from around the base of the sarcophagus before the lid could be lifted. Inside it, there lay an anthropoid black granite sarcophagus; inside that an anthropoid coffin of solid silver (see p. xiv); and inside *that* the mummy of Psusennes I, wearing a death mask of solid gold (see p. xii). Had Howard Carter not found King Tutankhamun eighteen years earlier, this might have become the 'face of Egypt'. Moreover, this was the only truly intact royal burial yet discovered, having lain completely untouched since it was sealed in the 22nd Dynasty until Montet rediscovered it (Tutankhamun's tomb had been entered by robbers at least once, even if they had not been able to take very much).

Pierre Montet examines the mummy of Psusennes I with the solid gold death mask still in place.

The ruins at Tanis with the royal tombs in the foreground and the remains of the entranceway to the temple of Amun, and the enclosure wall beyond.

The mummy was wrapped in almost unimaginable riches: twenty-two bracelets, two ankle bands, every finger and toe wearing a solid gold stall, thirty rings, two pectorals, four winged scarabs and a lavish collection of weapons, amulets and canes. It took two weeks to clear the tomb; it was not until the end of March that everything was securely packed up and ready for transfer to the safety of the Egyptian Museum in Cairo.

The full extent of the necropolis had still not been determined, but with a World War under way, Montet was in a race against time if he was to undertake any further work. King Farouk of Egypt, who had attended the opening of the coffin of Hekakheperre Sheshonq, persuaded Montet that he should not wait until the following year to enter the second sealed chamber. The decoration around the blocking included images of Pharaoh Amenemopet, whose empty sarcophagus Montet had found earlier in the season. When these walls were removed to allow entry to the chamber beyond, the team were again faced with a blocking stone, but as with the chamber of Psusennes this proved to be mounted on bronze rollers, allowing it to be moved easily. Within, Montet was again rewarded with the burial of a pharaoh – Amenemopet, as expected. The king had been buried in a sarcophagus originally made for Psusennes' wife, Mutnodjmet; presumably he had been buried in his own tomb and sarcophagus originally but was later moved, perhaps following the violation of his tomb by robbers. He possessed a burial assemblage rivalling that of Psusennes and Sheshonq, including an extremely fine mask of gold leaf that had formed an integral part of a coffin made of wood, itself largely perished.

Excavations were then suspended until just before the end of the Second World War. Further investigations led to the opening of another burial chamber leading off to the south of the Sheshonq chamber. This had been prepared for the burial of a son of Psusennes I named Ankhefenmut, but was found to be empty. The final surprise was a further chamber, completely concealed within the masonry of the tomb and only located when the team's architect, Alexandre Lézine, compared the full extent of the exterior of the tomb buildings with the layout of the rooms inside and realized that there was a space unaccounted for. His deduction led to the revelation of yet another untouched burial chamber, this time belonging not to a pharaoh, but a general favoured by Psusennes named Wendjebaendjed. Here a granite sarcophagus contained silver and wooden coffins and another gold mask, and an enchanting shallow libation bowl known as a *patera*, made of gold and silver and featuring a beautiful embossed scene of four young girls swimming in a pool amid fish, ducks and lotus flowers (see p. xv). The inscription tells us that it was given as a gift to the general by his king.[9]

Montet's work in the years following the war yielded much new information about the site of the temple of Amun at Tanis, including two subsidiary temples of Khonsu and Horus and the sacred lake, and evidence of continued activity at the site into the Ptolemaic Period. He did not find the further royal tombs that he had hoped to, but with his discoveries in 1939–40 he had already made an enormous contribution to our knowledge of the activities, and especially the burial practices, of the kings of the 21st and 22nd Dynasties.

Tanis during the excavation of the royal tombs.

Vast quantities of treasure and new light on burial practices, but gaps remain

Numerous items discovered within the royal tombs had evidently been reused from earlier burials. Takeloth 1 and Amenemopet were both found to have been buried in sarcophagi made about a thousand years earlier, in the Middle Kingdom; the latter was also buried with a jar inscribed for Sety 1 of the 19th Dynasty. Psusennes 1 had been interred in a sarcophagus originally made for Sety's grandson, Merenptah (now on display in the central atrium of Cairo's Egyptian Museum). Montet also found copious amounts of material purpose-made for the kings, of the finest quality and made using precious materials including gold and, most distinctively, silver in much greater quantities than had previously been present in royal burials.

Montet's discovery of the spectacular burials of Psusennes 1 and Amenemopet represented the first evidence for the location of the tombs of the 21st Dynasty pharaohs. Amenemopet had originally been buried in his own tomb and then subsequently moved into the tomb in

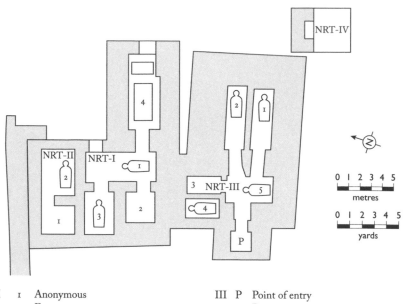

I   1   Anonymous
    2   Empty
    3   Takeloth II
    4   Osorkon II – Prince Hornakht

II 1   Empty
    2   Anonymous

III P   Point of entry
    1   Psusennes
    2   Amenemopet
    3   Empty sarcophagus of Ankhefenmut
    4   Wendjebaendjed
    5   Hekakheperre Sheshonq IIa

IV   Amenemopet's original tomb

Plan of the royal tombs at Tanis.

which he was found; this, it seemed, was the burial place of Psusennes I as intended from the outset. Curiously, Psusennes' monument seems to cut into the adjacent tomb, which contained at its centre the burial of the later king Osorkon II – as if the tomb containing the burial of the later pharaoh had been there first. It has been argued on this basis that in fact Osorkon was not its original occupant, but had made use of a previous pharaoh's monument, perhaps built for the first king of the 21st Dynasty, Nesubanebdjed (Smendes) I. Furthermore, careful analysis of the remains of the two mummies lying either side of the sarcophagus of Hekakheperre Sheshonq revealed them to be the remains of Siamun and Psusennes II.

This leaves only two pharaohs of the 21st Dynasty unaccounted for: Neferkare Amenemnisu, whose name appears alongside that of

The lid of the sarcophagus of Psusennes I, now in the central atrium of the Egyptian Museum, Cairo.

his successor Psusennes I on a bow-cover in NRT-III,[10] and Osorkon 'the Elder'. These kings may have been interred within the same tomb complex: it is clear that while some of the tombs were preserved intact, others were robbed, and that some chambers were reworked at certain points and certain bodies reburied. The empty chambers and anonymous sarcophagi might be connected with the burial of these two elusive kings, but conclusive evidence is lacking. Nonetheless, the necropolis provides a relatively complete record of the burial of the kings of this Dynasty.

The same cannot be said for the succeeding 22nd Dynasty, though Montet's work did advance our knowledge of the burial practices of this period. His excavations yielded the burials of two kings from the middle of the Dynasty: Hekakheperre Sheshonq, an otherwise ephemeral king who we now identify as Sheshonq 'IIa', one of the first of two sets of 'three other kings' of the period whose names were unknown to Manetho; and Osorkon II, who probably reigned slightly later on. Finally, although little of the burial remained, it is clear that Osorkon's father and predecessor Takeloth I was also buried in the tomb NRT-I; the prevalence of inscriptions of his son in this part of the tombs suggest that Osorkon had his father *re*buried here, Takeloth originally having been lain to rest elsewhere.[11]

When Montet first entered the tomb, he encountered a group of shabtis bearing the name 'Sheshonq', which led him initially to believe he had found the tomb of one of the kings of that name, but upon entering the tomb proper he read the cartouche of Osorkon on the walls. The large, anonymous sarcophagus in the antechamber may also relate to one of the kings of this name. It is unlikely to have been Osorkon II's successor Sheshonq III, or his successor, Sheshonq IV, as sarcophagi inscribed with the name of both kings were found in another tomb, NRT-V, a simple construction consisting of only an antechamber and burial chamber built slightly to the northwest of the others.[12] Finally NRT-II, an undecorated tomb next to and sharing a wall with NRT-I, housed a limestone sarcophagus, the remains of three coffins and the fragments of some canopic jars bearing the name Usermaatre-Setepenre, a prenomen used by more than one king of the period, but there is only one whose tomb has not been identified elsewhere – Sheshonq IV's successor, Pami.[13]

Some gaps remain, particularly at the beginning and end of the Dynasty. Although their reigns are well attested in the archaeological and textual record, the burials of the first two kings of the Dynasty, Sheshonq I and Osorkon I, are unknown. A canopic chest belonging to Sheshonq I exists, but appeared on the antiquities market without provenance.[14] Further burials may have been made at Tanis and it is possible therefore that the 22nd Dynasty burials represent an unbroken continuation of the 21st Dynasty tradition, and that there is simply a part of this royal necropolis that remains undiscovered.[15] But it is also possible that the tombs of these intervening pharaohs should be sought elsewhere.

A royal cemetery elsewhere in Lower Egypt?

Manetho held that the 22nd Dynasty pharaohs came originally from Tell Basta, the site of ancient Bubastis, another Delta city, approximately 40 miles (65 km) southwest of Tanis. It is clear that certain kings of the period, especially Osorkons I and II, were very active at this site.[16] However, Manetho's information was clearly flawed in certain cases, as for example his association of the 19th and 20th Dynasties with Thebes,

Faience fragments, perhaps from one or more shabtis, inscribed with the name 'Sheshonq Meryamun' and discovered by the Tell Basta Project led by Dr Eva Lange in 2009.

when it is generally accepted now that they were based primarily at Pi-Ramesse, in the eastern Delta, while the family also originated in this part of the country.[17]

Nonetheless, some very intriguing evidence that might help us in our search for tombs has come to light in recent years. Tell Basta has been under investigation by the Egyptian–German Tell Basta Project led by Dr Eva Lange. In March 2009, Lange and her team were excavating the previously unexplored area around the entrance to the great temple of Bastet, the famous cat-goddess, which dominated the site. Beneath a Roman-period pavement, the team discovered several fragments of faience that, despite their small size, preserved just enough of the original inscription to show that they had been decorated with a cartouche containing the royal name 'Sheshonq Meryamun'.[18] In all probability these fragments were originally part of shabti figurines; this and their location – in the area of a temple entrance, equivalent to the location of the royal tombs at Tanis – suggests that they may have come from a burial in the area. Several kings of the period were named Sheshonq and used the epithet 'Meryamun' ('beloved of Amun'); some of them, including, Hekakheperre

Sheshonq iia, Sheshonq iii and Sheshonq iv are known to have been buried at Tanis, but Sheshonqs i, iib, iic, v and vi are possible candidates for burial at this site. Though we cannot be certain which of these kings may have been buried here, the find supports the theory that the burials of some of the missing individuals should be sought outside Tanis.

Memphis has also been proposed as a possible site for the burial place of the missing 22nd Dynasty pharaohs. While there is little, if any, evidence that Sheshonq i was active at Tanis, he did build extensively, including at nearby Memphis.[19] Most intriguingly, there seems to have been a 'House of Millions of Years' of Sheshonq i 'that is in Hut-ka-Ptah' – the temple of Ptah at Memphis. The phrase 'house of millions of years' was used to describe a building or space dedicated to the funerary cult of a pharaoh, denoting the eternity of veneration, and thus life, the deceased pharaoh would find there, and in this case was probably a pylon and forecourt at the front of the Great Temple of Ptah, a parallel to a second 'house of millions of years' established by the same king at the front of the temple of Amun at Karnak. That the cult place in Memphis was still in use generations after Sheshonq's death is demonstrated by a stela in the Serapeum, set up some 150 years later, mentioning the personnel associated with it.[20] Again, the presence of a royal funerary monument of this period in the area of the temple entrance fits with the custom of the period, and strongly suggests that the tomb of Sheshonq i, and perhaps others of his line, might be found in this area. Strengthening the theory still further is the presence of the son of Osorkon ii, the High Priest of Ptah, Sheshonq, just to the west of the temple enclosure in an area known today as Kom al-Farikh. This rich burial, one of several of high-status individuals of the period, yielded some very fine jewelry worked in gold and other precious materials,[21] and provides incontrovertible evidence that Memphis was used as the burial place for members of the royal family during this time. Might it also have been the location of *the* royal cemetery for a time?

Theban Kings, unknown to Manetho?

As we have seen, reconstructing the Third Intermediate Period is a fraught business. The problems of reconciling the archaeological record with the textual accounts, including Manetho's, are severalfold. Evidence is less

Detail of a relief from the tomb of Prince Sheshonq, showing the
deceased before Anubis.

abundant relative to, for example, the preceding New Kingdom. Because
the country was fragmented, with the southern half of the country
controlled by the Chief Priests of Amun, and the northern half by the
pharaohs, the resources available to each group were diluted, perhaps
reducing building activities (and so leaving archaeologists less to find).
And the Delta, which made up a large part of the region in which the latter
group were active, is a wet environment that generally preserves materials,
particularly organic materials, much less well. Complicating things further,
certain royal names – including both the birth names (nomina) such as
Sheshonq, Osorkon and Takeloth, and the coronation names (prenomina),
which they were given on their accession to the throne – were used
over and over again by different kings, particularly in the period of two
and a half centuries or so following the end of the 21st Dynasty. As we

have already seen, the recovery of an object bearing the name Sheshonq Meryamun might relate to any one of eight different kings!

Finally, names such as Sheshonq show clearly that these individuals were not of Egyptian, but Libyan, origin, and it has been persuasively argued that these Libyans simply had a different way of doing things that altered Egyptian society, and has made them and their activities harder to detect in the evidence.[22] These Libyans were originally a series of nomadic tribes of various names including the Ma, the Meshwesh and the Libu. They began to arrive in Egypt no later than the 20th Dynasty, perhaps as voluntary settlers, or perhaps having been captured and forcibly settled by the Egyptian armies with which they fought, notably during the reign of Ramesses III. Slowly they began to exert an influence on Egyptian society and may have joined the ranks of the elite as early as the 21st Dynasty as the presence of the name Osorkon ('the Elder') among the name of the 21st Dynasty pharaohs suggests. They were unaccustomed to the idea of a central government controlling vast quantities of people and territory, preferring to govern in smaller units, and seem to have been a non-literate society. Although those who came to prominence in Egypt, including those who ruled as pharaoh, adopted the trappings of Egyptian kingship, including the standard titulary and use of the hieroglyphic script and cartouches, they may only have been following the local customs in order to ensure that their rule was accepted. The new custom of burying kings in relatively uncomplicated tombs within temple precincts may have been necessitated by a lack of access to an environment that allowed the cutting of rock tombs such as in the Valley of the Kings, but it may also reflect a different set of ideas brought to the country by foreigners.

In any case, constructing a coherent narrative of events of the kind that historians like, based on the idea of one king ruling for a while and then being succeeded by the next, usually a son, has proven to be more of a challenge in the case of the Third Intermediate Period than for some other chapters in Egyptian history.

In 1973, Kenneth Kitchen of the University of Liverpool published his attempt to rectify the problem. His book, *The Third Intermediate Period in Egypt (1100–650 BC)*, brought together the fragmentary but nonetheless vast body of evidence, and presented a coherent narrative history of the succession of pharaohs and the main events in the principal centres in Egypt and beyond. It is a classic, one of the greatest achievements of any historian of ancient Egypt. It remains indispensable for students of the period, partly as it became the established version of events for anyone interested in ancient Egypt, but also because no other overview of the period is so comprehensive in its reference to primary sources.

Kitchen's work is not without its shortcomings, however, and particularly contentious is his reconstruction of the sequence of kings ruling Egypt between the end of the 21st Dynasty and the time of the conquest of Egypt by another foreigner, the Kushite king Piye (or Piankhy). Piye travelled as far north as Athribis from his base in Nubia, and his eventual triumph signalled the beginning of the rule of the 25th Dynasty.

Piye's campaign was commemorated by a stela set up in the temple of Amun at Gebel Barkal, deep in the Kushites' home territory in modern-day Sudan and now kept in Cairo's Egyptian Museum. It provides a detailed description of the expedition, and also of the political 'anarchy' that supposedly triggered Piye's march northwards into Egypt. As he advanced, he encountered numerous local rulers, some of whom, crucially, were considered to be 'kings'. This helps to explain the number of different pharaohs attested in the archaeological record – at the time of Piye's campaign, there was more than one king ruling in Egypt.

Kitchen proposed that the situation in which there were as many as four kings, not including Piye, ruling at once was a relatively recent development at the time of Piye's invasion. According to Manetho, there was only one ruler of the 24th Dynasty, Bocchoris of Sais, whom Egyptologists agree should be equated with a Bakenranef who is known from a handful of stelae recovered from the Serapeum and a vase discovered in a tomb in Italy. He is thought to have been the successor of Tefnakht of Sais, the chief antagonist in the narrative of the Piye stela. On this Egyptologists are generally agreed.

The reconstruction of the preceding 22nd and 23rd Dynasties has generated much debate and argument, however, and has implications for our search for missing tombs.

Kitchen proposed that Manetho was right in that there were two dynasties of kings during this period, and that they ruled from different places – Bubastis and Tanis – but wrong in that he did not have all the names, and in not having realized that the two dynasties in fact overlapped chronologically. He proposed that more or less all the kings attested in the evidence should be fitted into either the 22nd Dynasty, which he believed was based at Bubastis, as per Manetho, or the 23rd Dynasty, based at Tanis. Kitchen made a persuasive case, and his theory went more or less unchallenged for more than a decade. Then, in a very concise article published in 1986, Patricia and Jeffrey Spencer noted that a number of the kings Kitchen believed to have been based in the Delta as part of these two dynasties were in fact only attested in Upper Egypt.[23] A short while later, building on this observation, Anthony Leahy published a new reconstruction that would radically alter our perception of the political geography of Egypt during this time.[24] He proposed that the rulers that Spencer and Spencer had identified at Thebes, not the Delta, were not part of the 22nd and 23rd Dynasties of Manetho at all; in fact, Manetho simply did not have any knowledge of the Upper Egyptian kings, because, Leahy argued, his sources were the archives of temples in the north and may not have included any record of the southern rulers whose influence was confined to that part of the country. Leahy claimed that Manetho was closer to being right about the number and names of the kings of the 22nd and 23rd Dynasties – that they did not overlap, as Kitchen had suggested, but rather one followed the other, in the usual Egyptian fashion.

In this new reconstruction, the situation in which Egypt was divided politically reached back much further before Piye's campaign, to the middle of the 22nd Dynasty, approximately a century earlier than Kitchen had allowed. In this new scheme, the line of southern kings, sometimes referred to as the 'Theban 23rd Dynasty', came to power at approximately the time that Osorkon II was buried at Tanis as ruler in the Delta, and would retain influence in the south of Egypt for the century leading up to Piye's invasion. And so a number of kings whose burials, prior to the new reconstruction, we might have expected to find at Tanis or elsewhere in the Delta, should now be sought elsewhere. And indeed, traces of some of these burials form part of the evidence that these southern rulers really did exist in parallel to the northern kings.

Kings of Thebes

Sometime between 1927 and 1933, during the great University of Chicago excavations of the temple complex of Medinet Habu in Luxor, a site dominated by the funerary temple of Ramesses III, the archaeologist Uvo Hölscher discovered the tomb of pharaoh Hedjkheperre Setepenamun Harsiesi Meryamun. Harsiesi reigned at the same time as Osorkon II in the north, and was an important figure as he seems to have been the first individual of this status in Thebes since the 21st Dynasty. The tomb, discovered beneath the Ptolemaic pavement surrounding the small Amun temple at Medinet Habu, was impressive. Any superstructure would have been deconstructed – perhaps mined for building material for other monuments – by the time the Ptolemaic pavement was laid, and all that was left for the excavators to investigate were the underground compartments. In contrast to the Tanis tombs, these were entered not via a shaft but a descending stairway approximately 11 m (36 ft) in length. This led to an antechamber and a burial chamber. All the subterranean elements were constructed of sandstone, the chambers being set into a pit that had been lined with mudbrick. Inside the burial chamber the excavators discovered a granite sarcophagus, the lid being of anthropoid shape but with a falcon head, in this regard recalling the Tanis burials. The sarcophagus basin was

View from inside the tomb of Harsiesi at Medinet Habu.

found to have originally belonged to a sister-wife of Ramesses II named Henutmire,[25] and was completely walled in so that its rim was at the level of the floor of the burial chamber, with the lid being slid into place after the mummy had been lain inside. Hölscher suggested this was a security measure, designed to ensure the sarcophagus would 'remain fixed and inviolate for all time'.[26] Like so many of such measures, however, it had failed: thieves had entered via a shaft and crack in the ceiling of the burial chamber. Despite this incursion, much of the burial equipment remained in the tomb, including four canopic jars of alabaster bearing the king's names and over two hundred shabtis, along with a skull and forearm thought by the excavators to belong to the mummy of the king himself.

There is no evidence that Harsiesi passed the kingship on to any of his descendants, but he did have a son (whose name is now lost) who is known to have become Chief Priest of Amun at Karnak,[27] which may have been something of a statement of intent on Harsiesi's

The sarcophagus of Harsiesi in the garden area outside the Egyptian Museum, Cairo.

part. This, of course, was the office that had been held by the southern rulers at the beginning of the 21st Dynasty, and various holders of the office in the succeeding decades would ultimately obtain the status of pharaoh, suggesting that it offered the potential for the individual Chief Priests to adopt the trappings of kingship and declare themselves pharaoh in their own right. Moreover, it was an office held by numerous sons of pharaoh, and seems to have been used as a means for the king to exert control over the temple and clergy of Amun, to serve as a step on the ladder towards those sons becoming pharaoh. That Harsiesi had a son who held the office suggests this may have been his tactic, but one that failed if his son never did become king.

It was at approximately the point of Harsiesi's demise that Takeloth II seems to have become king in Upper Egypt, and it may be that the two events were not unconnected. Takeloth's origins, family connections and seat of power have been much discussed. In Kitchen's reconstruction this individual was listed as part of the Bubastite 22nd Dynasty, as the direct successor of Osorkon II,[28] but it has since been noted that Takeloth II is only attested on monuments in Upper Egypt, including a number of inscriptions from Karnak, that his family reveals no connections to Lower Egypt and that genealogical evidence suggests that he flourished an entire generation after the death of Osorkon II.[29] Finally, he held the epithet *netjer heka Waset* – 'the divine ruler of Thebes'.

It seems, then, that his reign was a time of conflict between rival factions in Upper Egypt, which may explain the absence of any family connections between Harsiesi and Takeloth II. Like Harsiesi before him, Takeloth's son was also Chief Priest of Amun. The Chronicle of Prince Osorkon provides a detailed account of the struggle for supremacy in Thebes between two rival factions, each headed by a king and their chosen Chief Priest of Amun, over a thirty-year period in Upper Egypt. It begins in Takeloth's Year 11, when his son, Prince Osorkon, made a ceremonial visit to Karnak.[30] After a protracted struggle for power, ultimately it was Takeloth II's line that would emerge triumphant.

The events described in the Chronicle are dated by the reigns of Takeloth II and Sheshonq III. If they ruled in succession, as Kitchen proposed, there would be a twenty-year gap in the narrative during which no events are described. If, on the other hand, the two kings reigned not successively but concurrently, there would be no such gap – Year 1 of Sheshonq III would be equivalent to Year 4 of Takeloth II, and the change would be explained by the transfer of authority in Upper Egypt from the line of Sheshonq III to that of Takeloth II. Furthermore, Prince Osorkon B of the Chronicle, son of Takeloth II, has now been identified with king Usermaatre Setepenamun Osorkon III, so it seems that in this case the king's son did become first Chief Priest, and subsequently also pharaoh.

The tomb of Osorkon III

As we know that Harsiesi was buried at Thebes, and the line of Takeloth II and Osorkon III seems to have become well established in Thebes for a few decades, it seems reasonable to assume that their tombs might be found in the area. Three papyri, dating from the end of the 26th Dynasty (reigns of Necho II and Amasis) and the beginning of the 27th (Darius I), all dealing with the entirely quotidian matters of the transfer of land, mention a tomb of 'king Osorkon' on the west side of the river at Thebes.[31]

Of the four pharaohs who bore the name Osorkon, three of them (I, II and IV) seem to have been Delta-based pharaohs: Osorkon I and II were part of the early 22nd Dynasty line, the latter being buried at Tanis, as we have seen, and Osorkon IV was the king of Bubastis encountered by the Kushite king Piye during his conquest of Egypt. Osorkon III, whose influence most scholars would now agree was confined to Upper Egypt, and who had very strong associations with Thebes, would seem to be the only candidate.

Frustratingly, the reason the authors of these texts mentioned the tomb is that at that time it provided a useful marker in the landscape, a means of recording the location of other monuments. Although two centuries had passed by the time the last of the papyri was written, the tomb was obviously still very visible, and well known as Osorkon's place of burial. Frustratingly, no other landmarks that might help us to orient ourselves are mentioned, but it seems likely that the tomb was located within a temple precinct, in keeping with the royal tombs at Tanis, the tomb of Harsiesi within the temple precinct at Medinet Habu and the possible burial of a pharaoh Sheshonq at Tell Basta. Complicating matters in this instance, however, is the presence in western Thebes at the time of Osorkon III's death of numerous temples suitable to accept the burial of a king, most of them having been built as the mortuary temples for the pharaohs of the New Kingdom.

Other royals buried at Thebes

There is considerable evidence of cemeteries of the 8th and 9th centuries BC, the time of the Theban 23rd Dynasty, in the area of the Theban temple precincts. Fragments of cartonnage and a shabti box belonging to a granddaughter of Takeloth II, Nehemsybast, were found behind the Ramesseum by James Quibell in 1896.[32] Tamit, another granddaughter, was buried in the same area, as was her son, Ankhpakhrod II.

A further discovery of considerable significance for this period was recently made in the same area, but this time within the temple area itself. During the 19th century, some shabtis and other items of funerary equipment belonging to the 'Divine Adoratrice' Karomama had appeared on the antiquities market and were purchased by the great German Egyptologist and expedition leader, Karl Richard Lepsius. Subsequently, Quibell had found further shabtis belonging to the same individual during his excavations of the Ramesseum and surrounds. The French Archaeological Mission in Western Thebes and the Centre for the Study and Documentation of Ancient Egypt revisited the area in 2014, and discovered the tomb itself. It was located in the northern part of the small temple dedicated to the mother of Ramesses II, Queen Tuya, and consisted of a 5-m (16-ft) deep vertical shaft leading to a burial chamber, the lower courses of the blocking of which were found partially intact. Further shabti fragments recovered from inside the chamber confirmed the identity of the tomb owner. It has been suggested that this Karomama should be identified with a daughter of Osorkon II who had the same name, but this is little more than speculation and seems to sit uneasily with the division of the country between the line of Osorkon II in the north and the Upper Egyptian rulers who emerged at this time.

A number of descendants of Osorkon III's son and successor Takeloth III were buried in shafts cut into the floor of the temple of Hatshepsut at Deir el-Bahri,[33] but the burial of the king himself has proven elusive.

Takeloth III was probably succeeded by a Sheshonq 'VIa', and then by Rudamun. A daughter of the latter king, Nesterwy, was buried beneath the mortuary temple of Ramesses III at Medinet Habu,[34] and indeed this site was also the location of the most famous burial of any of the Upper Egyptian royals of this period: Shepenwepet I, daughter of Osorkon III

Chapels of the God's Wives at Medinet Habu.

and successor to Karomama as God's Wife of Amun. This title first appeared at the beginning of the 18th Dynasty, but its status seems to have been elevated at the time of Osorkon III. It was always held by a female member of the royal family, and from this time onwards always by a daughter of the king. Beginning with Shepenwepet I, the God's Wife became the most important member of the clergy of Amun, superseding even the Chief Priest. The God's Wife was accorded the same privileged access to the god as pharaoh and seems generally to have acted as his deputy within the domain of Amun at Karnak, preeminent both in spiritual and more practical terms: the God's Wife controlled the temple economy and was able to dedicate monuments, controlling manpower and resources through a substantial corps of officials in her service. As they were considered to be the consort of the god they did not marry and had no children – and no heirs, therefore, to whom they might pass on their role. Instead, the title passed from one pharaoh's daughter to the next, and successive pharaohs, beginning with Osorkon III, made use of the post as a means of establishing their control at Karnak by installing a daughter as God's Wife or, if the position was filled, as heiress to the God's Wife.

In front of the great temple of Ramesses III, slightly to the south of the main east–west axis leading through it, lie the chapels that mark the burial places not only of Shepenwepet I but of her successors as God's Wife: Amunirdis I, Shepenwepet II, Neitiqert (Nitocris) and Ankhnesneferibre. They were constructed in sequence, east to west, one next to the other, their doorways facing north towards the small cult temple of Amun that Ramesses had incorporated into his great temple complex five hundred years earlier. Shepenwepet I's chapel was, naturally, the first to be built. The superstructure had almost completely disappeared, its walls being preserved only slightly above the floor, but its underground burial chambers were much better preserved. They were faced with stone, and covered with a stone vault. The burial chamber had been robbed in antiquity and very little had been left behind by the plunderers. Traces of black, painted hieroglyphs on a yellow background are preserved on what was left of the chapel walls, but none is legible. There was in fact no clear evidence that this was the tomb chapel of Shepenwepet, but the excavators inferred as much on the basis that the next chapels in the sequence clearly belonged to her successors.

The chapels of Amunirdis I and Shepenwepet II were built of stone and are still standing today. Shepenwepet II's chapel was also used as the burial place of her successor Nitocris, and the latter's mother, Mehytenweshket. These ruins provide perhaps the clearest indication of the kind of structure we might expect for an Upper Egyptian royal tomb of this period. In essence, these were tomb-chapels, each fronted by an entrance pylon leading to a series of decorated cult chambers built above underground burial chambers with vaulted roofs (except that of Amunirdis I).[35] In all cases the sarcophagi were removed, two of the latter being reused in Ptolemaic tombs at Deir el-Medina – that of Nitocris is now in the Egyptian Museum in Cairo, and that of Ankhnesneferibre in the British Museum.[36]

Locating the lost Theban tombs

Given that the tombs of Harsiesi, the daughter of Rudamun, Nesterwyn, and daughter of Osorkon III, Shepenwepet, have all been found at Medinet Habu, one might propose that this was the likeliest spot for the burial of the kings of the period. However, that Osorkon III's tomb was used to orient the readers of the later papyrus texts suggests it was the most distinctive marker in its environs; it is difficult to imagine that this could have been the case if it was located within the massive temple precinct at Medinet Habu, which is not mentioned, and where there were so many other standing structures that the authors could have used as landmarks. Furthermore, the proposed house building mentioned in one of the texts, and the reference in another to the 'waste land in the tomb of the king Wsr-tn [Osorkon]', do not readily put one in mind of the sizeable but restricted and presumably highly valued land within the temple area. It seems more likely that the tomb lay in an area away from any other distinctive monuments.

In any case, Harsiesi's burial in the area should not be taken to mean that all Upper Egyptian kings would be buried at Medinet Habu – he was not of the same line as Osorkon III. It should also be borne in mind that the God's Wives of the 25th Dynasty were certainly not buried in the same place as their kings, who were interred in the royal cemeteries of their Napatan homeland.

The missing 26th Dynasty pharaohs

Despite Piye's apparent triumph over the various local rulers in Egypt, according to Manetho the rule of 25th Dynasty kings did not begin until the reign of Shabaqo. According to the inscription on a victory scarab, Shabaqo was forced to reassert Kushite control following a rebellion in Egypt,[37] indicating that the independent local rulers had not been entirely quashed. The Kushites' authority also came to be challenged by the Assyrian Empire, which, anxious not to lose any of its control of the territory and economy of the Levant to the Kushites, invaded Egypt on several occasions from the 670s BC onwards. There followed a period of a few years during which the two groups of foreigners – the Kushites acting as the legitimate pharaohs, the Assyrians with no interest in doing so – struggled for control of the country, before the Assyrians won a decisive victory in 664 BC, chasing the last pharaoh of the Kushite line, Tanwetamani, as far south as Thebes, and sacking the city.[38] Tanwetamani seems to have continued to rule his own territory in Kush, however, where the family line continued. The 25th Dynasty kings, and their predecessors and successors as kings of Kush, are all buried in the Napatan royal cemeteries, principally at el-Kurru and Nuri in modern Sudan.

The Assyrians pursued a policy of installing or confirming in office local rulers who would be loyal to them. One of the major centres of power lay at Sais in the western Delta, and here a puppet king named Necho was the Assyrians' favoured man. Necho was succeeded in 664 BC by Psamtek (Psammetichus) I. The influence of Sais began to grow during this time, and by his Year 9 in 656 BC Psamtek reached an agreement with the authorities in Thebes (notably no Kushite pharaoh was present by this time) for his daughter, Nitocris, to be adopted as heiress to the God's Wife of Amun. This signalled the transfer of power in Thebes to the Saite line. Egypt was by this point effectively reunified under the rule of the Saite kings, in contrast to the previous centuries of decentralization. And in keeping with earlier periods of centralized rule, the following century and a half of Saite rule seems to have seen something of a flourishing of the country's fortunes.

Despite this, very little of the ancient city of Sais remains, and none of the tombs of the pharaohs in question has been recovered. We know that these kings were buried in their capital city, thanks to a description provided to us by the Greek historian Herodotus, who was writing in

General view of Sa el-Hagar, site of the ancient city of Sais.

the 4th century BC. Of the fate of the fourth pharaoh of the line, Apries, whose nineteen-year reign was brought to an end when a contingent of his army mutinied and threw their support behind their general, Amasis, who declared himself pharaoh, Herodotus wrote:

> the Egyptians took him and strangled him, but having so done they buried him in the sepulchre of his fathers. This tomb is in the temple of Minerva, very near the sanctuary, on the left hand as one enters. The Saites buried all the kings who belonged to their canton inside this temple; and thus it even contains the tomb of Amasis, as well as that of Apries and his family. The latter is not so close to the sanctuary as the former, but still it is within the temple. It stands in the court, and is a spacious cloister built of stone and adorned with pillars carved so as to resemble palm trees, and with other sumptuous ornaments. Within the cloister is a chamber with folding doors, behind which lies the sepulchre of the king.[39]

The Roman goddess Minerva here can be equated with Neith, the patron deity of Sais, so the temple referred to here is presumably the city's principal sanctuary. During Hellenistic times the Ptolemaic administration pursued a deliberate policy of identifying particular Egyptian gods with Greek counterparts, sometimes creating hybrid versions incorporating aspects of both, such as Zeus-Amun – who became important in Alexander the Great's annexation of Egypt (see Chapter 6). This allowed the native Egyptians and incoming Greeks to live and worship harmoniously together, and to see their own gods and beliefs in one another's icons, and religious monuments. The practice of identifying Egyptian and Mediterranean deities continued into Roman times. Unfortunately, almost nothing of the temple of Neith/Minerva survives today, and therefore the chances of recovering the royal tombs, if Herodotus's account is correct, would seem to be very slim.

His description does seem, broadly, to fit what we know of the practices established over the preceding centuries at various sites throughout the

Right The solid gold funerary mask of Sheshonq IIa.

Opposite Decoration inside the burial chamber of Takeloth I, including cartouches of Usermaatre Setepenamun Osorkon II.

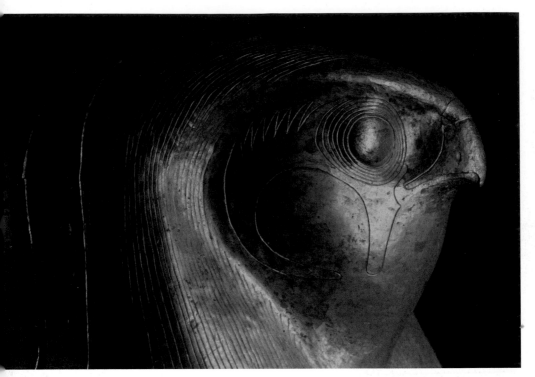

Above The silver falcon-headed coffin of Sheshonq IIa.

Right View looking into the tomb prepared for Sheshonq III.

The solid gold death mask of Psusennes I in the Egyptian Museum, Cairo.

The famous death mask of Tutankhamun.

Right The silver coffin
of Psusennes I.

Below The funerary mask
of Amenemopet.

Right The funerary mask of the general Wendjebaendjed.

Below Patera of gold and silver, with an embossed scene of four young girls swimming in a pool amid fish, ducks and lotus flowers.

Above Alexander as pharaoh of Egypt making
offerings to Amun, from the barque shrine
built in his name at the Luxor temple.

country, of royal individuals being buried within the temple precinct, with multiple individuals occupying a single structure, or series of structures lying close to one another. The 'spacious cloister built of stone and adorned with pillars' was presumably a chapel devoted to the Apries' mortuary cult (if any such was maintained following his usurpation by Amasis), while the burial itself was apparently to be found behind the folding doors of Herodotus's description, perhaps at a subterranean level, following the traditions elsewhere.[40]

When Jean-François Champollion, who famously won the race to make the breakthrough enabling the decipherment of the hieroglyphic script in 1822, visited the site in 1828, he recorded the presence of two enclosures; in the centre of that to the north of the village he observed a 'memnonium' or necropolis. He also noted two mounds, which he thought might have been the tombs of Amasis and Apries.[41]

The 'Great Pit' at the edge of the modern village of Sa el-Hagar was created by sebakhin, locals who dug out ancient mudbrick to use as fertilizer during the 19th century. This seems to have been the area of a suburb of the ancient city, while the 'northern enclosure' is now thought to have been the location of the main temple of Neith, and the royal tombs.[42]

In spite of its significance, Sais was largely neglected by archaeologists until the late 20th century, when the Egypt Exploration Society inaugurated a new mission to the site under the direction of Dr Penelope Wilson of the University of Durham. The lack of attention up to this point is perhaps explained by the site's appearance: at first glance little or nothing of ancient date survives, in stark contrast to some of the other Delta centres, such as Tanis, Bubastis or Behbeit el-Hagar. However, over the course of the last two decades Wilson and her team have investigated a vast area in and around the centre of the 26th Dynasty city, revealing evidence of human activity from the prehistoric down to Late Antique times. The original intention was that the project would reveal new information about the city's 26th Dynasty heyday and perhaps even about the royal tombs described by Herodotus. Several finds, made over several years, have helped improve the picture.

In April 2003, a large red granite fragment was discovered in the village of Ganag, less than 3 miles (5 km) north of Sa el-Hagar. It was decorated with images of the four sons of Horus – the deities whose heads typically

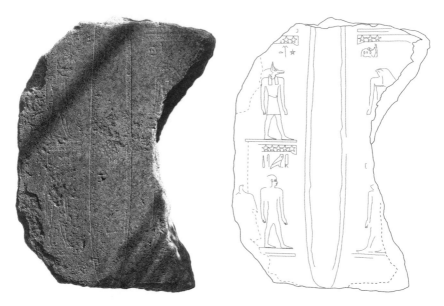

The granite block from Ganag, perhaps a part of a royal sarcophagus.

adorn canopic jars – suggesting that the object had a funerary function. Its material and size meant it must have come from a large object or a wall, and the convex shape of one side suggested that it might have come from some kind of container, such as a sarcophagus or its lid.[43]

Then, in 2007, a fine faience shabti of the 'King of Upper and Lower Egypt, Psamtek' was discovered to the east of the 'Great Pit' area of the site, to the south of the main enclosure. It was found in the fill used for the foundations of a Late Antique church and therefore not in its original context – the royal tomb – but not far away from the northern enclosure where it may originally have been placed.[44]

It is not clear which of the three kings named Psamtek this shabti belonged to, but it has been argued it was Psamtek I; as the first king of this name he would have had no need to distinguish himself from the others by using his coronation name, Wahibre.[45]

In fact, fourteen shabtis of king Psamtek are now known, along with two belonging to Necho (I or II), three of Apries and five of Amasis.[46] Many of these appear to have arrived in museum collections at a time corresponding to the intensive digging in the area of Sa el-Hagar by sebakhin in the late 19th century.[47] Agonizingly, it seems the tombs may

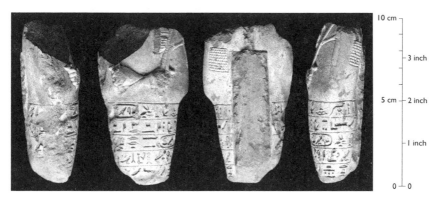

10 cm

3 inch

5 cm 2 inch

1 inch

0 0

The shabti of Psamtek discovered by Penelope Wilson in 2007.

indeed have been intact to an extent in Champollion's time but – having remained secure for 2,500 years – then disappeared. The provenance of most of the objects is unknown, but some of the shabtis were found entirely elsewhere, suggesting that some at least might have been made in Memphis and never even made it to Sais, or were brought from Sais to Memphis as *ex-voto* offerings.[48]

Further fragments of burial equipment have survived, including a fragment of a granite sarcophagus of Psamtek II now in Paris, a heart-scarab of Necho II, and two canopic jars of Apries. The jars were found in secondary contexts, reused as a container for a mummified falcon, and in an Etruscan tomb respectively, suggesting they were removed from the tomb in ancient times.[49]

One final discovery at Sais is worthy of note. Three granite palm capitals of half monumental size have also been found, recalling Herodotus's description of 'pillars carved so as to resemble palm trees'. They seem not to be in their original position, but might be the only identifiable fragments of the architecture of the tombs that have survived.[50] The shabti of Psamtek was found mixed in with other 26th Dynasty material used as the fill for later, Roman buildings: a bath house of the 1st century BC to 3rd century AD was made of crushed granite and orthoquartzite fragments probably of 26th Dynasty date, and elsewhere dumps of roman pottery have been found overlying dismantled pharaonic structures. Altogether the evidence suggests the major buildings of the Saite Period, including the temples and royal tombs, had been destroyed by Roman times.[51]

Further fragments may remain, and Wilson strikes a wryly optimistic note in a recent article on the subject: 'It is to be hoped that it will not be another century before the next fragment is found.'[52]

Hopes of a sensational discovery were briefly raised in 2014 when the Egyptian press reported that a mastaba tomb discovered at the site of Tell Tebilla in the Dakahlia province of the Delta was found to contain the burial of Psamtek I. These reports were premature, however. The excavations had revealed the burials of several individuals, along with some of their grave-goods, including a large number of faience shabtis and amulets, a very fine amulet of a bird in bronze and two anthropoid limestone sarcophagi. A badly decayed cartonnage mummy case had been gilded and among the inscriptions chased into the gold the cartouche of Psamtek had been read.[53] But this was simply a reference to the pharaoh, presumably the reigning king during the lifetime of the deceased or at the time of his death, and not the name of the owner of the tomb. While the headlines might have caused a few Egyptologists' hearts to skip a beat, the evidence presented clearly did not justify the claim that this was a royal burial, which had obviously been made in error. It is an interesting example of the misinformation that can arise when the news of a discovery circulates first through the news media, and not through more scholarly channels.

Conclusions

To some extent, the question of whether or not a discovery to rival that of the tomb of Tutankhamun could ever happen again underpins this book. The 'Gold of the Pharaohs' found by Montet at Tanis was, argu-ably, just such a discovery, but is almost unknown by comparison. This is at least in part because the attention of the media – which played such a huge part in bringing news of Carter's discovery to the world, and establishing Tutankhamun's name in the international conscious-ness – was focused on the escalating crisis that would lead to the Second World War, and because the excavations had to be cut short for the same reason.

It is true that the Tanis tombs yielded some extraordinary material, among the finest to have been recovered from Egypt and indeed anywhere in the ancient world. Even the most iconic of Tutankhamun's treasures, the solid gold death mask, is paralleled by a very similar example – that of Psusennes I (see p. xii). It does seem curious, and even *unfair*, that the latter has received so little public attention, but there are lots of reasons for this. A second solid gold death mask, extraordinary though it is, was by 1939 something that the world had already seen before. The assembly of treasure that Montet turned up does not quite match that from KV 62 – and, dare I say it, to my eyes at least, Psusennes' mask doesn't quite reach the same level of perfection in the image of the king's face in particular.

One's focus is also somewhat diluted by the whole tomb complex representing the burials of a series of pharaohs, rather than one individual who might entirely capture one's attention. The Tanis kings reigned at a time that was, and remains, less well established in the public's imagination – even though Tutankhamun was relatively little known and did not himself accomplish very much, his predecessors and successors were much better known; the Valley of the Kings itself was already famed as a royal cemetery and so well established as a likely spot for the discovery of new great treasures; and the media, but also the royals and other dignitaries who would grab the headlines when they visited the site, were traditionally well provided for in terms of hotels and so on. Tanis, far harder to get to, perhaps presented a less romantic vision as the setting for the discovery.

This chapter deals with the great number of pharaohs who ruled over those several centuries, many of them reigning only briefly and then only over much smaller areas than the kings of a united Egypt in previous times had done. The decoration and architecture of their tombs seem to have been less elaborate than those of the preceding New Kingdom, and the fact that many remain missing can perhaps be explained by some of the circumstances of the times and certain features of the burial practices adopted during the period. These kings may not have had access to the resources required to build more substantial monuments (although the grave-goods found at Tanis demonstrate access to considerable wealth, suggesting that the move to a different kind of tomb within the temple precinct was not motivated solely by economic pressures). Many of the pharaohs of this period were probably buried in the Delta, where conditions are far less favourable for the survival of archaeological material than in the desert cemeteries of the Nile Valley. The evidence also suggests that the missing tombs should be sought within temple precincts, but this makes their survival even less likely, because throughout Egyptian history the major cult temples were constantly in use and subject to a perpetual cycling of building, rebuilding, dismantling and renovation. The decaying superstructures of tombs built within a temple precinct were therefore doubtless often dismantled, and subterranean elements lost, as seems to have been the case with the Tanis tombs, and that of Harsiesi at Medinet Habu. Additionally, as is evident from Montet's excavations at Tanis, their superstructures were built of manoeuvrable stone blocks that would have been easily removed for reuse, an issue that would never have affected, for example, the rock-cut tombs of the New Kingdom. So we should perhaps not be surprised if tomb superstructures of the Third Intermediate Period and 26th Dynasty did not survive.

Nonetheless, the recent discoveries at the Ramesseum and in Dakahlia province show that tombs might still remain to be discovered. And as the complete revision of our understanding of the political geography of the Third Intermediate Period shows, any new discovery would have the potential to change our understanding of this confused period quite dramatically.

CHAPTER 6

BURIED THREE TIMES
IN EGYPT

The tombs of Alexander the Great

Alexander the Great is one of the most significant figures in history. The son of King Philip II of Macedon, Alexander had, by the time he was thirty years old, conquered North Africa as far west as the border with Greek Cyrenaica, in modern Libya, and territory far to the east into India and Pakistan, thereby establishing one of the largest empires of the ancient world. Alexander had been tutored by Aristotle in his youth and succeeded his father as king of Macedon in 336 BC at the age of twenty. He spent almost all of the rest of his life on a single continuous campaign of conquest, which began with the intention of defeating the Persian Empire but became a project to reach the 'ends of the world and the great outer sea'. He defeated the Persian emperor Darius III in a final decisive battle at Gaugamela (in modern Iraq) in 331 BC, having liberated Egypt from Persian rule, and would then advance to capture Babylon, Susa and Persepolis. Between 327 and 325 BC, Alexander attempted an ambitious campaign into the Indian subcontinent, enjoying a further series of victories and establishing new cities. He called a temporary halt to the expansion of his empire when his troops begged to be allowed to return home to see their loved ones, and returned to Babylon, where in 323 BC he died. During his reign he had founded some twenty cities, and sought to introduce elements of Greek culture into the territories he conquered, a process of Hellenization the effects of which could be seen as far from Greece as India and Afghanistan. His exploits inspired countless later rulers, particularly the Roman emperors, some of whom travelled to visit his final resting place, centuries after his death, to pay their respects.

Alexander in Egypt

In 343 BC, Artaxerxes III, the Persian emperor, invaded Egypt. The Persians had formerly ruled the country as the 27th Dynasty for just over a century, from 525 BC, but had been ousted in 404 BC by Amyrtaeus of Sais, an Egyptian and the only ruler of the 28th Dynasty. From this time the Persians considered Egypt to be a satrapy (a province led by a Persian-appointed satrap) in revolt, and their attempt to reconquer the country was inevitable. The reign of the incumbent pharaoh, Nectanebo II, had begun in 360 BC and saw something of a flourishing in art and building activity but was abruptly brought to an end by Artaxerxes' arrival. Nectanebo was forced to withdraw from his Delta stronghold, and fled from Memphis into Nubia were he may have sought refuge at the court of the Kushite king, Nastasen. The Persians were unpopular among the local population, apparently showing little respect for Egypt's ancient religion and traditions. A revolt was again led against their rule by a Saite king, Khababash, in the years 338–335 BC, but it ultimately failed.

Alexander the Great was to rid Egypt of the Persians for good. He arrived in Egypt in 332 BC, during the reign of Artaxerxes' successor as emperor, Darius III, having conquered the Persian naval bases along the coast of Asia Minor and Syria-Palestine. The Persian governor, Mazaces, had no choice but to surrender, enabling Alexander to journey unopposed across the Delta to Memphis, passing the cult centre of the sun god Ra at Heliopolis and the pyramids of Giza along the way. On his arrival in the capital he was proclaimed pharaoh by a population who despised the Persian regime. Alexander spent two months in Memphis, learning the beliefs and practices of a people whose devotion to their gods he much admired. He was devoutly religious himself, and adapted his own beliefs to those of the locals, seeing an equivalence between the deities of the Greek and Egyptian worlds, in particular between Zeus and Amun. It was during this time that he ordered new building works to be undertaken at

Egyptian temples, including that of Luxor, where a new shrine for the barque of Amun was built and covered with images of Alexander making offerings to the god (see p. xvi). Alexander's name appears throughout, written in hieroglyphs enclosed in a cartouche, alongside the traditional epithets and a new throne name: 'the King of Upper and Lower Egypt, Lord of the Two Lands, Meryamun Setepenra ("beloved of Amun, the chosen one of Ra"), the Son of Ra, the Lord of Arisings, Alexander'.

In search of a new Egyptian base of operations that was more suited to his Mediterranean operations, Alexander again journeyed north along the western edge of the Delta, settling on the small town of Rhakotis on the Mediterranean coast. He decided that his new city should be founded there. This was to become Alexandria, one of the great cities of the ancient world, famous for its lighthouse and library, and as a cosmopolitan centre for the arts and intellectual exchange, although it was little more than an idea under Alexander, the construction of its major buildings taking place only under his successors, Ptolemy I and II in particular. Alexander was seized by the desire to visit the oracle of Zeus-Amun at Siwa, and travelled along the coast, turning inland at Mara Matruh to follow the desert route leading across the Sahara to central Africa via a series of oases, the first of which, the Siwa Oasis, was home to the famous oracle. Despite the perilous and arduous desert journey he had just endured, Alexander visited the temple immediately upon arrival. He was met by a priest who, accidentally mangling a Greek phrase, greeted him as the 'son of god', pleasing Alexander greatly. Alexander would refuse to repeat the conversation he had with the oracle to anyone but his mother, Olympias (who, as it happened, he would never meet again before his death), but he revealed enough of its contents to suggest that it had been made clear to him that his father was not a mortal, and that he was himself the son of a god. Alexander subsequently journeyed back to Memphis, where he made further offerings to Zeus-Amun and made the final arrangements to assume the government of a country that had impressed him enormously. He left in 331 BC, never to return, although he continued to send offerings to the temple of Amun and Siwa for the rest of his life, and even asked the priests there for confirmation that they would set up a hero-cult for his close companion Hephaestion after his death.[1]

Alexander's death

Unlike all the other ancient figures whose tombs are the focus of this book, we know something of the circumstances of Alexander's death, which occurred in the palace of Nebuchadnezzar II in Babylon in 323 BC, when he was just thirty-two. The classical accounts vary in the details, but it seems that Alexander ate or drank something that led to him suffering over a number of days from a fever or pains of some kind, before dying in agony. Inevitably, theories that he was poisoned abounded. The chief suspect is Antipater, who had recently been removed as Alexander's viceroy in Macedon, although several of the classical sources express scepticism about the idea.

We also know something of the ensuing arguments about where to bury Alexander's body, and how he ultimately came to be laid to rest in Egypt. Alexander's death, but also the events that followed it, would, perhaps as much as his conquests, have a profound influence on the ancient world. Several of his generals, friends and rivals fought for control of his empire after his demise. Collectively they are known as the 'Diadochi', meaning the 'successors'. Of these Diadochi, two were particularly instrumental in determining the fate of Alexander's body.

Perdiccas was a friend of Alexander's who had risen through the ranks of his court, first as one of the royal bodyguards, then marshal, before finally being appointed Grand Vizier after the death of Alexander's favourite, Hephaestion. On Alexander's death, Perdiccas became the official protector of Alexander's wife, Roxanne, and their infant son, also called Alexander. When Alexander the Great died, it was agreed that his elder half-brother, Philip III Arrhidaeus, and his son, the newborn Alexander, would become co-sovereigns of Macedon, and by extension the rest of Alexander's territory (the child as Alexander IV of Macedon and II of Egypt). But as Arrhidaeus suffered from a learning disability and was deemed mentally unfit to rule, and Alexander was just a baby, Perdiccas became regent. With the support of several of Alexander's closest allies, including Seleucus, Perdiccas believed he could keep the empire together by wielding power over it in the names of Alexander and Arrhidaeus.[2]

The second of the Diadochi who is of interest to us here was another of Alexander's Macedonian generals, who rode at the emperor's side through Asia and shared his perilous journey across the Egyptian desert to the Siwa Oasis, where Alexander had consulted the great oracle of Amun. His name was Ptolemy.

In the weeks and months following Alexander's death, Perdiccas, Ptolemy and others discussed the fate of Alexander's body, each hoping to take charge of it for himself. This would be a decisive factor in the shaping of power in the empire: Alexander's resting place would quickly become a religious shrine, the deceased emperor being revered as a god in Asia and, as pharaoh, at least a semi-divine being in Egypt. Moreover, each of the Diadochi knew that assuming responsibility for the burial of the great emperor would bestow honour on the person responsible, and would also go a long way towards legitimizing any claims they might make for leadership in their own right. Winning custodianship of Alexander's body was perhaps the key to the question of who would succeed him.

At this stage, Egypt would not have been the obvious final destination for Alexander's body. He might have received a temporary burial in Babylon, where he had died and where his body was held, while the Diadochi continued to argue. Perhaps the most obvious final resting place would have been Aegae (modern Vergina) in Macedon, in the royal cemetery of his ancestors. But it is possible that Alexander himself wished to be buried in Siwa, close to the oracle of his 'father' Zeus-Amun.[3] In any case, from the beginning, his body was treated according to Egyptian traditions: rather than being cremated, as was the Macedonian custom, his corpse was embalmed – mummified – according to Egyptian procedures.[4] Whether this was undertaken for religious or practical reasons is uncertain. Perhaps some means of preservation was simply required while discussions over how and where he should be buried remained unresolved. In any case, the body was also subsequently laid to rest in a golden coffin, recalling another Egyptian tradition.[5]

In the autumn of 321 BC, after more than two years of uncertainty over the final destination of the body, events began to develop rapidly. At this time, Perdiccas had gone to Cappadocia to quell a rebellion. In Babylon, an elaborate catafalque had been constructed to carry Alexander's body, although its final destination remained uncertain, and Arrhidaeus had been waiting for Perdiccas to issue instructions as to how to proceed. In the preceding months, Perdiccas had received a number of proposals of alliance by marriage, as noble families around the empire sought to ensure they would survive and prosper as the new empire took shape. Meanwhile, Arrhidaeus decided to align himself with Ptolemy. At some point, with Perdiccas far away and unable to stop him, Arrhidaeus left Babylon with the body. Perdiccas was alerted and sent a squadron to intervene, but Arrhidaeus was joined by Ptolemy, under whose instructions he had been acting and who commanded a much larger army to ensure the funerary procession could continue.[6] Ptolemy now took charge and led the procession south into Egypt, to Memphis, where it arrived late in 321 BC.[7]

Here the classical sources might offer some insight into the motivations inspiring such events. In particular, the *Alexander Romance*, a collection of stories about Alexander, contains an account of the events immediately following the emperor's death, although we should treat the work with caution as it is attributed to Alexander's court historian, Callisthenes – who in fact died before Alexander himself. It is therefore now commonly referred to as a work of 'Pseudo-Callisthenes'. In any case, according to one of the legends it contains, Ptolemy had asked the oracle of Zeus at Siwa where the body should be taken, and he was told he should deliver it to Memphis.[8] Such an order would hardly have been inconvenient for Ptolemy: while Perdiccas aspired to control the entire empire, Ptolemy was only interested in ruling Egypt, and presiding over the burial of the great emperor in his adopted country would provide him with the legitimacy and authority he needed to fulfil his ambition.

The Memphite tomb of Alexander

Ptolemy's seizure of this moment was crucial. There had been no agreement about Alexander's burial, and he must have known that Perdiccas, and possibly others, would go to any lengths to retrieve the body before it could be buried. Perdiccas's advance on Egypt was predictable, and he was defeated, eventually being stabbed to death by his own troops, who were frustrated at their leader's diplomatic and military failures.[9] Ptolemy had apparently always intended to bury Alexander in Alexandria,

and now found himself unopposed, but could not carry out his ambitions until a suitable tomb – and indeed the city itself – had been built.
Here, the classical sources are vague and at times conflicting, but they
hint at the possibility that Ptolemy gave Alexander a temporary burial
at Memphis,[10] in order to establish Egypt as the country in which
Alexander's body was laid to rest and consolidate his own position as
its guardian, effectively curtailing any further movement of the body
by his rivals before he had the opportunity to remove it to Alexandria.
According to Pausanias's *Description of Greece*, this Memphite burial was
undertaken with Macedonian rites,[11] though the *Alexander Romance*
relates a different sequence of events:

> There is in Babylon an oracle of the Babylonian Zeus....The
> god's oracle was as follows:...'There is a city in Egypt named
> Memphis; let him [Alexander] be enthroned there.' No one
> spoke against the oracle's pronouncement. They gave Ptolemy
> the task of transporting the embalmed body to Memphis in
> a lead coffin. So Ptolemy placed the body on a wagon and
> began the journey from Babylon to Egypt. When the people
> of Memphis heard he was coming, they came out to meet the
> body of Alexander and escorted it to Memphis. But the chief
> priest of the temple in Memphis said, 'Do not bury him here
> but in the city he founded in Rhacotis [Alexandria]. Wherever
> his body rests, that city will be constantly troubled and shaken
> with wars and battles.'[12]

So was Alexander in fact denied burial at Memphis? The Roman historian
Curtius, who wrote the *Historiae Alexandri Magni* (Histories of Alexander
the Great), echoes Pseudo-Callisthenes' statement that Alexander's body
was taken first to Memphis and transferred a few years later to Alexandria,
but makes no comment on the treatment of the body while in Memphis.
In any case, eventually, according to Diodorus Siculus:

> He [Ptolemy] decided for the present not to send it [the body]
> to Ammon, but to entomb it in the city that had been founded
> by Alexander himself, which lacked little of being the most
> renowned city of the inhabited earth. There he prepared a

sacred enclosure worthy of the glory of Alexander in size and construction.[13]

Buried alongside the Apis bulls:
a tomb at the Serapeum?

No Memphite tomb of Alexander has ever been located, but the circumstances surrounding his burial have led some to theorize where it might have been located within the great city.

Having established himself as ruler of Egypt, Ptolemy now set about transforming it into a new hybrid Egyptian and Greek kingdom. As part of his effort, he endorsed the deification of Alexander, lending divine legitimacy to his own authority and that of his royal line, the Ptolemaic Dynasty. One of the most important cults in Memphis was that of the Apis bull, one form of which was a manifestation of Osiris, as Osiris-Apis, or Serapis in Greek. Alexander had made a sacrificial offering to the Apis bull during his visit to Memphis, and Ptolemy now created a new, typically classical, image for the god, as well as temples and shrines, a liturgy and a dedicated priesthood for his worship.[14] Serapis's temples would eventually include the Serapeum at Alexandria, built by Ptolemy III, but the older and better-known Serapeum is that at Saqqara – the labyrinthine network of catacombs that was used for the burial of the Apis bulls from the 18th Dynasty onwards (see pp. 36 and 46). This Serapeum is located in the heart of the Saqqara cemetery, a few hundred metres to the northwest of Djoser's Step Pyramid.

At first, the bulls were buried in individual tombs with decorated chapels above them, but in Year 55 of Ramesses II's reign the first of two main series of underground catacombs, now known as the 'Lesser Vaults', was inaugurated. Later, during the 26th Dynasty, it seems the entire complex was revamped. A new, larger sequence of catacombs, the 'Greater Vaults', was begun, and it was around this time that a ceremonial route to convey visitors from the cultivated land of the Nile Valley to the temple – the Serapeum Way – was created. During the 30th Dynasty, a new temple was constructed at the eastern extent of the main approach to the Vaults, built into a natural cliffside, perhaps replacing an earlier, 26th

Photograph taken in the 1940s during the excavations of Rizkallah Naguib Makramallah of the processional way leading to the Serapeum, with the hemicycle of philosophers in the foreground at left.

Dynasty building.[15] In addition, from this point, the ceremonial route leading eastwards, away from the Vaults, was lined on both sides with the sphinxes – 134 in total – uncovered by Auguste Mariette at the time of the Serapeum's rediscovery in 1850. Many were subsequently removed to the museums of Cairo, Berlin, Paris and elsewhere.[16]

Today, the only visible archaeological remains of this part of the Serapeum complex are those of a Hellenistic addition. During Ptolemaic times, visitors would have walked along the avenue of sphinxes, which takes a leftward turn (to the south), along one side of the funerary temple. At its end they would have encountered a semicircle ('hemicycle') of statues of some of the great Greek philosophers and poets, including Plato and Homer. This may have been set up as early as the reign of Ptolemy I, although a precise date has proven elusive.

Ptolemy's promotion of the cult of Serapis suggests that there would have been a considerable interest in the area of the Serapeum during the Ptolemaic Period, and the presence of the hemicycle of philosophers confirms it.

Perhaps most intriguingly, in the area of the Serapeum, Mariette also found several statues of peacocks being ridden by the god Dionysus. Some five hundred years after Alexander's death, the Roman author Aelian wrote that when the emperor was in Pakistan, he had been entranced by the first peacocks he saw and placed them under royal protection. Peacocks also featured in a grand procession of Ptolemy II that took place in Alexandria in 275–274 BC.[17]

Could the Serapeum, and specifically the Ptolemaic cult building, the entrance to which lay between the end of the avenue of sphinxes and the hemicycle of philosophers, have been used as a temporary tomb? They key may lie in the connection between Alexander, the new kingdom his successor Ptolemy was trying to create and their predecessor, the last native pharaoh of Egypt.

Alexander and the sarcophagus of his mythical father

According to Diodorus Siculus, Nectanebo II of the 30th Dynasty realized during his struggle against the Persian armies of Artaxerxes that resistance was futile and the kingship lost, and so he fled to Nubia.[18] However, Nectanebo's sarcophagus was discovered in Alexandria, entering

The sarcophagus of Nectanebo II in the British Museum, London.

the collections of the British Museum as a gift from King George III in 1803.[19] Perhaps, therefore, Diodorus was wrong, and Nectanebo did not flee Egypt; or perhaps he returned and was buried, though it seems somewhat unlikely that he would have been buried with the status of a pharaoh after his defeat at the hands of the Persians. Indeed, it seems more probable that the sarcophagus had been prepared for him earlier in his reign, in which case we have no reason to doubt Diodorus's account – Nectanebo did indeed flee, his sarcophagus never to be used, at least not for its original purpose. Intriguingly, at the time of its removal, local legend had it that it had been repurposed for the burial of Alexander.

Diodorus tells us that Nectanebo was in Memphis up to the moment of his capitulation, and it seems most likely that this was his capital city, and also perhaps the place where he would have intended to have been buried, although he may have favoured his home city of Sebennytos in the Delta. The *Alexander Romance* also recounts the period after Nectanebo's defeat, but with a key twist: that Nectanebo fled not to Nubia, but to the Macedonian court of Philip II, Alexander's father, in the guise of an Egyptian magician. In this form he convinced Philip's wife Olympias that he was the Egyptian god Amun, and that they would have a child together. That child was Alexander.[20]

For Ptolemy, attempting to create a myth around Alexander and his connection to Egypt, this could not have been more convenient, and indeed it has been suggested that he instigated stories and legends such as this one.[21] Whatever its origins, a powerful connection between Alexander and Nectanebo became established. Could this connection have extended to the fate of their mortal remains? Perhaps Ptolemy, burying Alexander in Memphis to further his own political agenda, seized the opportunity to inter Alexander in the unused sarcophagus originally made for Alexander's immediate predecessor as legitimate pharaoh of Egypt and his mythical father, and then transported Alexander's body inside this sarcophagus to Alexandria when the second tomb was finally ready.[22]

If true, we can only really speculate as to where the sarcophagus, with Alexander's body inside it, might have lain during its time at Memphis, but Saqqara – and specifically the area of the Serapeum – would seem a reasonable suggestion. It has been argued that the entrance to the cult temple built by Nectanebo II may have led not only to the main sanctuary area, but also to a side chamber to the south that might have housed the sarcophagus. A second entrance leading to this additional chamber was guarded by four statues in the shape of lions of Greek style, a symbol of Macedonian royalty.[23]

While no evidence of activity that can be attributed with certainty to the reign of Ptolemy I has yet come to light in the confines of the Serapeum, which has been comprehensively cleared, there are areas just beyond it that have not yet been thoroughly excavated (see Chapter 1). One might not expect a tomb that had been abandoned to have survived to the same extent as one that was intended to house the remains of the deceased for all eternity; there is a slim chance that something might remain, but given all the archaeological activity in the area in the last century and more, it is very unlikely that any conclusive evidence will be found.

The body is transferred to Alexandria

In the years following Perdiccas's defeat, Ptolemy's position had been strengthened even further by events unfolding elsewhere in the empire. In 317 BC, Alexander the Great's half-brother, Philip III Arrhidaeus, was murdered by their mother. The following year, his mother, Olympias, was herself murdered, stoned to death on the orders of Cassander, another of the Diadochi and governor of Macedon following Alexander's death. Seven years later, Alexander's wife, Roxanne, and their young son, Alexander IV, were poisoned, again by Cassander. Finally, Alexander's sister, Cleopatra, was set upon and murdered by a group of women – under Perdiccas's instructions – while she was travelling to meet Ptolemy, with whom she had begun corresponding, possibly in an attempt to protect herself through alliance with him. And so, a little more than a decade after his death, Alexander's immediate family had all been removed from the race for succession.[24] Of Ptolemy's other rivals, Antigonus 'the One-eyed', a general whom Alexander had left in control of Asia Minor, had declared himself *basileus* – king – in 306 believing himself to be the rightful heir to all Alexander's territory. The empire no longer existed as a single unity, however: along with Ptolemy, who had taken control of Egypt, Cassander became king of the Macedonians; Seleucus, king in Babylon; and Lysimachus, king in Thrace. In 305 BC, having restrained himself from

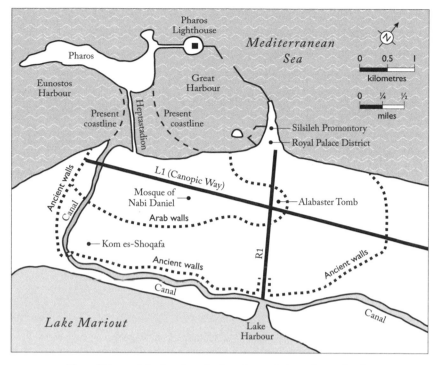

Map of Alexandria showing the locations of: the palaces district; the Alabaster Tomb; the mosque of Nabi Daniel; and the intersection of the main north–south and east–west streets.

doing so previously, Ptolemy crowned himself pharaoh and quickly set about establishing Alexandria, which Alexander had founded, but not developed, as his new capital.

The city came to be built on a rocky strip of land bounded to the south by Lake Mariout and to the north by the Mediterranean Sea. The former provided access to the Nile and therefore to the whole of Egypt, while the latter connected the city to the rest of the Hellenistic world, one of the great centres of which Alexandria would become. An island lying approximately half a mile (1 km) offshore, named Pharos by the Greeks, offered some natural protection against seafaring invaders; it was on this island that the famous lighthouse was built. It was connected to the mainland by a 1,200-m (3,940-ft) long artificial causeway, or Heptastadion, probably built on the orders of Ptolemy I and II. The Heptastadion divided the area between Pharos and the Alexandrian coast into two harbours:

the Eunostos, mainly used for commercial purposes, to the west, and the Portus Magnus, the 'Great' or 'Royal' Harbour, to the east.

The best contemporary description we have of the city is provided by the Greek geographer, Strabo:

> the city contains most beautiful public precincts and also the royal palaces, which constitute one-fourth or even one-third of the whole circuit of the city; for just as each of the kings, from love of splendour, was wont to add some adornment to the public monuments, so also he would invest himself at his own expense with a residence, in addition to those already built, so that now, to quote the words of the poet, 'there is building upon building'....The Sema also, as it is called, is a part of the royal palaces. This was the enclosure that contained the burial places of the kings and that of Alexander.[25]

That Alexander's body did eventually arrive in Alexandria, and that his mausoleum and cult would become central to the growing city, is clear.[26]

Sometime between 311 BC, when Alexandria officially became Egypt's capital, and 283–282 BC, when Ptolemy I died and was succeeded by his son Ptolemy II Philadelphus, a cult of Alexander was established with a priesthood.[27] But we do not know when or how the body arrived or was buried; the classical sources are silent on this part of the story. Whether Ptolemy I finally realized his ambition to bury his king in the city he founded, or allowed his son and heir to take responsibility for the matter is unclear; having strengthened his own grip on Egypt, he may have seen greater advantage in bestowing legitimacy upon his successor and, he presumably hoped, a long line of his descendants stretching many years into the future. If this was the case, and it was Philadelphus who brought Alexander's body to Alexandria, it may have been as part of the Ptolemaia celebrations in 275–274 BC. The Ptolemaia was a festival inaugurated by Philadelphus to honour his father, who would become known as Ptolemy Soter, 'the saviour', and was deified on his death. The celebrations glorified the Ptolemies and their connection to Alexander and involved athletic, musical and drama competitions, and parades in which men, women and animals accompanied by lavish quantities of gold, jewels and fine cloth would appear before Philadelphus and his sister-wife Arsinoe II, themselves amid dozens of guests and canopies and couches adorned with more precious materials. In keeping with the Olympic Games, which the Ptolemaia were intended to rival, the festival was celebrated every four years and dignitaries from all around the world were invited to marvel at the ostentatious displays designed to demonstrate the wealth, power and mythical signifance of the Ptolemaic royal house.[28]

Had the inaugural Ptolemaia incorporated the ceremonial arrival of Alexander's body in Alexandria, it may have lain in Memphis for as much as half a century.[29] We know almost nothing about the circumstances of Alexander's burial in Alexandria, but in any case the sources suggest this may only have been the first of two burials.

A second Alexandrian tomb: the 'Sema'

According to the Greek geographer, Strabo, writing in 30 BC:

> The Sema also, as it is called, is a part of the royal palaces. This was the enclosure which contained the burial-places of the kings and that of Alexander...the body of Alexander was carried off by Ptolemy and given scpulture in Alexandria, where it still now lies.[30]

So, at around the time of Octavian's conquest – almost three centuries after Alexander's body first arrived in Alexandria – Alexander was kept, along with 'the kings' (presumably the Ptolemies), in a mausoleum called the Sema. This name comes from a Greek word meaning 'tomb', but the mausoleum was sometimes also referred to as the 'Soma', meaning 'body', and the two terms came to be used interchangeably in the classical sources.[31] If this was the case, then either Alexander's tomb was enlarged to receive the burials of his successors, or his body was transferred from its original tomb to a larger monument designed to house the burial of multiple royals. The second possibility in fact seems more likely: that the Sema was not the tomb in which Alexander was originally laid by Ptolemy (or perhaps by his successor, Philadelphus) is revealed by another writer, Zenobius:

> Ptolemy (Philopator) built in the middle of the city a *mnema*, which is now called the Sema, and he laid there all his

forefathers together with his mother, and also Alexander the Macedonian.[32]

Ptolemy IV Philopator reigned from 221 to 204 BC, over a century after the end of the reign of Ptolemy I, and Zenobius's words suggest that the new tomb he built – the *mnema* or Sema – was not in the same place as the original one, precluding the possibility that Philopator simply enlarged the pre-existing tomb.[33]

We have no way of knowing when Philopator created this new burial place, but it has been suggested that it may have been around 215 or 214 BC, when he survived an assassination attempt and shortly afterwards defeated Antiochus III, the advancing Seleucid king, in a battle at Raphia, near modern Gaza. According to this theory, Philopator saw the opportunity to create a new burial place for the kings of his Ptolemaic line, combined with that of Alexander, renewing the connection between the two and thereby his own legitimacy and that of his Dynasty. This would also have coincided with the celebration of the quadrennial Ptolemaia in 215–214 BC.[34]

An ancient tourist attraction?

The Sema seems to have attracted a number of high-profile visitors. The Roman Lucan's unfinished epic poem, *Pharsalia*, tells of Julius Caesar's visit to Alexandria:

> ...in eager haste he went down into the grotto hewn out for
> a tomb. There lies the mad son of Philip of Pella....the dead
> Ptolemies and their unworthy dynasty are covered by indignant
> pyramids and mausoleums.[35]

Caesar was followed later by Octavian, as recounted by two of the classical writers. Suetonius relates that:

> About this time he [Octavian] had the sarcophagus and body
> of Alexander the Great brought forth from its shrine, and after
> gazing on it, showed his respect by placing upon it a golden
> crown and strewing it with flowers; and being then asked
> whether he wished to see the tomb of the Ptolemies as well, he
> replied, 'My wish was to see a king, not corpses.'[36]

The account of Cassius Dio mirrors this chain of events, and adds the somewhat ghoulish detail that in touching the face of Alexander, Octavian accidentally broke off his nose.[37]

Lucan's reference to a 'grotto' and Suetonius's to the body being 'brought forth' suggest that the body may have lain in a chamber cut into the ground. Further descriptions of the Sema are very thin on the ground. Octavian's comment about not wanting to see corpses implies that the other Ptolemies were mummified, as Alexander had been. Philadelphus and his co-ruler and sister-wife Arsinoe II are known to have been cremated in accordance with the Macedonian tradition,[38] but we have no such information about the other Ptolemies, and the idea that they would have wished for a burial in keeping with that of Alexander himself seems very plausible.

Further ancient accounts furnish a few further details about Alexander's body itself. Strabo tells us that it lay:

> ...not, however, in the same sarcophagus as before, for the present one is made of glass, whereas the one wherein Ptolemy laid was made of gold. The latter was plundered by the Ptolemy nicknamed 'Cocces' and 'Pareisactus',[39] who came over from Syria but was immediately expelled, so that his plunder proved unprofitable to him.[40]

We are told also that Cleopatra VII took gold from the Sema to finance her battle against Octavian;[41] and when Caligula, who reigned as Roman emperor from AD 37 to 41, visited he apparently carried off Alexander's breastplate.[42] And so it seems the burial was gradually stripped of its treasures. The record of later visits suggests it had become clear that action needed to be taken to restore the burial. The next recorded visit of an emperor was that of Septimius Severus, who had the tomb locked up;[43] Septimius's son Caracalla also visited. The historian Herodian tells us that he:

> went to the tomb of Alexander where he took off and laid upon the grave the purple cloak that he was wearing and the rings of precious stones and his belts and anything else of value that he was carrying.[44]

Several emperors had, naturally, been inspired by Alexander and sought to see similarities between themselves and the great Macedonian emperor. Caracalla convinced himself that he was a living incarnation of Alexander, but was ridiculed by the Alexandrians, and took revenge by sending his soldiers on a rampage through the streets and murdering their young men. Following this, he protected the palace district within an enclosure called the Brucheum, which may have included the Sema.[45]

The Sema disappears

The Brucheum housed the Roman imperial administration and was therefore at the centre of the action during times of unrest. It was put under siege between AD 262 and 264 during a war between Marcus Julius Aemilianus and Theodotus, rival claimants to the title of emperor. Then in 269 it was again attacked, this time by the invading armies of Palmyra under Queen Zenobia. Her son, Wahballath, assumed control of the city, but was soon expelled by the armies of the new Roman emperor Aurelian. Zenobia's ally, Firmus, subsequently took charge of the city, but he too was defeated by Aurelian, whose troops devastated the Brucheum in the process. The city was sacked by Diocletian in 298 in response to an Alexandrian rebellion against Roman rule. It was at this time that Diocletian erected the massive, 25-m (80-ft) high red granite column at Alexandria's Serapeum. It still stands today, although it is better known colloquially (and erroneously) as 'Pompey's Pillar'.[46]

No mention is made of the Sema in any of the records of these events. It has been suggested that its destruction would have pleased the Romans, who idolized Alexander but despised the Ptolemies and Alexandrians and their possession of his body,[47] but it may simply have disappeared from both view and memory by this point.

On 21 July AD 365, a catastrophic tsunami hit Alexandria, and it may be then that the entire area of the royal quarter was lost beneath the coastal waters.[48] Despite this destruction, the memory of Alexander's tomb seems to have survived among the local population for many centuries, and European travellers from the 17th century onwards recorded the various claims they heard that this or that site had been the location of the great hero's body.

The Attarine Mosque

Leo Africanus, a 16th-century diplomat and traveller who published his *Descrittione dell'Africa* (Description of Africa) in 1550, wrote of his visit to Egypt that:

> In the midst of the ruins of Alexandria, there still remains a small edifice, built like a chapel, worthy of notice on account of a remarkable tomb held in high honor by the Mahometans; in which sepulchre, they assert, is preserved the body of Alexander the Great....An immense crowd of strangers come thither, even from distant countries, for the sake of worshipping and doing homage to the tomb, on which they likewise frequently bestow considerable donations.[49]

Africanus did not provide any precise information about the whereabouts of this edifice, but a similar story was recorded by the English traveller George Sandys, who visited Alexandria in 1610. He located the chapel within the courtyard of the Attarine Mosque, built on the site of the former church of St Athanasius. The Ottoman explorer Evliya Çelebi visited Alexandria at some point between 1670 and 1682 as part of a forty-year tour around the Ottoman Empire that he published in a ten-part 'Book of Journeys', in which he described 'Alexander's tomb' decoration as involving men, animals and supernatural beings. He also observed that it had been used for ritual purification, as a kind of bath or similar.[50]

What Çelebi had seen was a pharaonic Egyptian sarcophagus. Further details were provided by Dominique Vivant Denon, who was among the savants who accompanied Napoleon's expedition to Egypt at the end of the 18th century. He visited the Attarine Mosque in 1798 and provided the following description:

> In the centre of this court, a little octagon temple encloses a cistern of Egyptian workmanship, and incomparable beauty, both on account of its form, and of the innumerable hieroglyphics with which it is covered, inside and out. This monument...appears to be a sarcophagus.[51]

The savants were probably aware of the stories connecting the sarcophagus with the tomb of Alexander, and they removed it to a French ship. However, by summer 1801 the French had been defeated by the British in Egypt, and as part of the armistice negotiations the British insisted that their opponents surrender the antiquities they had gathered, among which perhaps the most famous is the Rosetta Stone, and which also included the Attarine Mosque sarcophagus.[52] The Rosetta Stone is now the single most visited object in the collections of the British Museum. The sarcophagus, displayed only a short distance away in the Egyptian sculpture galleries, attracts much less attention, but is of considerable historic importance, at least as far as our quest is concerned. Despite the discovery of the Rosetta Stone and the potential its inscription – copied in two forms of Egyptian and also in ancient Greek – offered for the decipherment of the hieroglyphic script, it would be another two decades before Jean-François Champollion cracked the code, allowing scholars to read Egyptian for the first time, so the decoration on the sarcophagus remained largely impenetrable. A British agent, Edward Daniel Clarke, had been dispatched to Alexandria to establish what antiquities the French possessed, and what should be taken for Britain. He had heard that among them was a great stone sarcophagus, but it was only when he arrived and began to speak to locals that he was told they included 'the tomb of Alexander'. Clarke, naturally, was keen to endorse this idea and to emphasize that the sarcophagus had been venerated as such by the local population, to demonstrate what a coup this was for the British,[53] but he also seems to have been genuinely convinced that the Mosque lay on the site of the Sema.[54]

It is unclear whether Denon believed the sarcophagus had any genuine connection to Alexander. It is certainly an extremely fine piece of work. Cut from a single piece of conglomerate, it is over 3 m (10 ft) in length and 1 m (3 ft) in depth, and is decorated with detailed scenes of Ra, Osiris and texts from the Book of Amduat on the outside, and the four sons of Horus, Anubis and other funerary deities on the inside. It was pointed out in 1806 by one Richard Ramsden that it was strange that the Macedonian emperor should be buried in a sarcophagus decorated with such traditional Egyptian vignettes and hieroglyphs (and also that any sarcophagus of such importance ought to have a lid),[55] and the British

Museum's description did not mention the alleged link between the sarcophagus and Alexander. This must have seemed very prudent when Champollion's monumental breakthrough allowed the inscriptions to be read and it transpired that the sarcophagus was in fact that of Nectanebo II. It is, however, a very fine example of monumental stone sculpture of the Late Period, and it is not difficult to imagine that it would have been considered a most suitable monument in which to place the body of Alexander while it awaited proper burial in Memphis.

The Mosque of Nabi Daniel

A second mosque in Alexandria, that of Nabi Daniel, has also come to be connected with the tomb of Alexander. The prophet Daniel, whom the mosque commemorates, was identified by two Arab astronomers, Abu Ma'shar and Mohammed ibn Kathir al-Farghani, with Alexander. The Daniel of their story conquered Asia, founded Alexandria and was buried there, initially in a golden sarcophagus and subsequently in a second made of stone.[56] The present-day mosque was built at the end of the 18th century, but lies on the site of an older building. It overlies a crypt in which the body of Daniel himself is supposed to rest, along with his companion Sidi Lokman el Hakim, a religious storyteller.[57]

The mosque of Nabi Daniel, Alexandria. Taken in 1905.

The crypt within the mosque of Nabi Daniel, Alexandria.

In 1850, Ambroise Schilizzi, a dragoman (interpreter and guide) of Greek origin in the service of the Russian consulate, announced that he had found a secret crypt beneath the mosque and had seen within it a crystal sarcophagus containing a mummy wearing a golden crown. All attempts to verify his claim have failed, however; it seems that this is simply one of the many tall tales that have been spun in relation to the famous emperor.[58]

Mahmoud Bey el-Falaki's map

In 1865, the court astronomer to the Ottoman Viceroy of Egypt, Mahmoud Bey el-Falaki, made a map of Alexandria. He did so at a crucial moment: the city was expanding rapidly, eastwards of the old Tulunid city walls into areas that had been occupied in Ptolemaic, Roman and Byzantine times, and much of what el-Falaki observed would soon disappear. The following year he began excavating in an attempt to describe the ancient city in its various incarnations.

By the time el-Falaki was making his map, Alexandria was over two thousand years old. The city had shrunk considerably since its heyday in the Ptolemaic and Roman periods, when at times it was eclipsed only by Rome itself in terms of its size and wealth.

Following the Muslim conquest of Egypt in AD 641, a new capital city was created at Fustat, now part of modern Cairo, which brought about a dramatic decline in Alexandria's fortunes. Much of the stone used to construct the buildings of Alexander's city became part of the early medieval fortifications of the city, and a great deal more was removed altogether to be used in the construction of the new capital and other cities as far away as Samarra (Iraq) and Istanbul.[59] The city therefore shrank, and in early medieval times occupied only a small area at the base of the Heptastadion. The causeway had silted up and was built upon extensively, with defensive walls erected in AD 881 by Ahmad ibn Tulun. The centre of the city shifted entirely to the Heptastadion during the Ottoman Period, and the ancient areas were largely abandoned.

The modern city of Alexandria sprawls across the areas occupied throughout history, but prior to the beginning of its modern revival in the second half of the 19th century, far more of the ancient city was visible than can be seen now. The remains of the ancient street plan, city walls, cisterns, cemeteries and monumental buildings were still in evidence, and some of the columns that lined the main east–west and north–south streets were still standing. The location of the city's two main temples were marked by surviving monuments: the Serapeum by Diocletian's column, and the Caesareum by two obelisks – Cleopatra's 'needles' – that would subsequently be carried off overseas, to London and New York respectively.[60]

El-Falaki was unable to excavate thoroughly, only making soundings where the modern constructions allowed it – the archaeological equivalent of keyhole surgery. Untangling the dense stratigraphy, and establishing the difference between the Ptolemaic, Roman and Arab phases of the city, particularly its street plan and outer walls, at a time when scientific archaeology had yet to be invented, would have been beyond him, and so the plan he developed has been called into question. And yet he was aware of and honest about his limitations, and more recent excavations have generally confirmed his findings.[61]

El-Falaki was able to articulate the grid-outline of the city, identifying the main east–west street, the Canopic Way, as 'L1', and the main

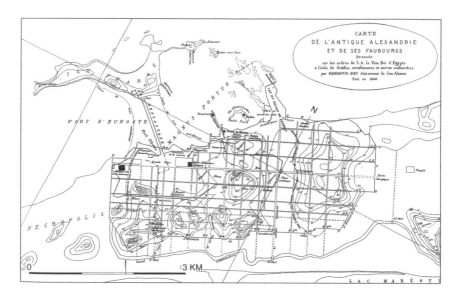

Mahmoud Bey el-Falaki's map of Alexandria.

north–south street, which ran inland from the base of the ancient Lochias Peninsula to Lake Mariout in the south, as 'R1'. The Sema was thought to have been built at the point where these two intersected. The Canopic Way, it seems, runs beneath the modern Shariya el-Horreya (Freedom Street), but the route of the north–south thoroughfare is much harder to discern.

Along with R1, El-Falaki identified Street 'R5' as a major intersection along the Canopic Way, and as the mosque of Nabi Daniel was located in the same area, he became convinced that it had been constructed on the site of the Sema.[62] He investigated, as, later, did Evaristo Breccia, the Italian archaeologist and second Director of the Graeco-Roman Museum in Alexandria, but neither was able to reveal any evidence of an ancient royal burial.[63] Breccia, his predecessor Giuseppe Botti and successor Achille Adriani conducted a first wave of scientific excavations in the city and revealed Ptolemaic and Roman cemeteries at various locations, including Anfushi, Shatby, Kom es-Shoqafa, Hadra and Mostafa Pasha.[64]

In 1907, Breccia discovered a series of slabs of alabaster on the surface in the Roman Catholic Terra Santa cemetery in the el-Ibrahimya district, a short way inland from the coast and to the east of the Silsileh promontory. He made no announcement of this until seven years later, when he mentioned it in a guide to Alexandria's ancient sites, but otherwise seemed not to think it worthy of further investigation. His successor, Adriani, thought otherwise, and in 1936 he resumed the excavations.

Adriani uncovered a large rectangular well, and proposed that the massive and highly polished alabaster slabs formed its monumental floor. Eventually, Adriani reassembled a tomb in the Macedonian style, which he suggested had two rooms and a temple façade. If it had been constructed at the beginning of the Ptolemaic Period as its style suggested it was, it would have lain in the area of the city's eastern walls – possibly even outside them – a little further east than the 'middle of the city' where Zenobius located the Sema. It would seem most likely to have been the tomb of a high-status Macedonian individual at the beginning of the Ptolemaic Period.[65] Could this have been the tomb constructed for Alexander by Ptolemy I or II? Adriani was convinced that he had identified the site of the Sema, but this seems unlikely, not only because the location does not seem quite right – at the eastern extent of the city rather than in the middle and closer to the Lochias Peninsula – but also because by the time

The principal tomb compartments within the catacombs of Kom es-Shoqafa. The architecture and decoration combine Egyptian and Hellenistic styles and may provide some clues as to the appearance of the first Alexandrian tomb of Alexander.

The Alabaster Tomb.

Philopator had built the Sema, a Macedonian tomb of this type would have been a little old-fashioned. In fact, the tomb is unique in Alexandria, but then one would perhaps not expect Alexander's tomb to be anything other than unique. Further investigations in the area as recently as the 1990s and early 2000s failed to add any evidence to Adriani's hypothesis, but this and other high-status Hellenistic tombs found in the city, such as the principal tomb within the catacombs of Kom es-Shoqafa, might provide clues as to the form of the tomb of Alexander. No evidence has so far come to light to suggest that any of them, however, are either the first of his tombs or the Sema.

A tomb at Siwa?

The claims made by Schilizzi, el-Falaki and Adriani are of varying credibility, and ultimately none of them stands up to scrutiny. These three men have one thing in common, however, and that is a somewhat unscientific desire to identify what they had discovered as Alexander's tomb, prioritizing this bold claim over more cautious, considered statements about what they had found. Schilizzi was no scholar, of course, but the others were, and engaged in serious scientific work. Sometimes it can seem as though archaeologists are working backwards, looking for the evidence only after deciding on their conclusion – that what it is they are looking for is in a certain place, even when there is already good evidence to suggest otherwise. An ill-conceived project to look for the tomb at a third location in Egypt is another example of this phenomenon.

In the early 1990s, a Greek archaeologist named Liana Souvaltzi described the excavations she had been directing at the Siwa Oasis – with official permission from the Antiquities Service – at the International Congress of Egyptologists in Turin.

According to the classical authors Curtius and Justin, just before Alexander's death he signalled that he wanted to be buried in the temple of Zeus-Amun at Siwa, where he had famously consulted the Oracle of Amun.[66] According to Diodorus, Ptolemy had originally intended to carry out these wishes but then decided against it.[67] Siwa is therefore a part of the story of Alexander's death and burial, but there is no suggestion that he was buried there; on the contrary, it is stated that despite his wishes, he was not.

Souvaltzi announced that she was investigating the hypothesis that, contrary to these accounts, Alexander was in fact buried at Siwa. The site she was digging was a 1st-century AD Greco-Roman temple, and a series of finds she produced, including images of carved symbols associated with Alexander, a text apparently written by Ptolemy explaining that he brought the body to Siwa, and a mummified Macedonian head, to justify her claims variously turned out to have been misinterpreted or even faked. By the time it was reported that she was being guided in her search by a pair of talking snakes, any credibility she might once have claimed had run out. Her permit to work in Egypt was not renewed after her 1996 season, but she nonetheless published a book entitled *The Tomb of Alexander the Great at the Oasis of Siwa* in 2002, and seems never to have admitted defeat.[68]

The Souvaltzi episode is nothing more than a red herring in the search for the tomb of Alexander, yet it is useful as an illustration of the extent to which archaeology and the wider public can be misled when there exists the possibility that a sensational discovery might be made. It is difficult to see what justification Souvaltzi had for any hypothesis that Alexander was buried in Siwa in the first place, but she was nonetheless granted the concession to carry out potentially damaging work at an important archaeological site, and by making sensational claims before producing any evidence for them – the opposite of a scientific approach – she was able to continue her work for a number of years before her luck ran out. One wonders to what extent her claims have been taken seriously in some quarters, and whether anyone happening across a copy of her book might yet be similarly misled. Such fantastical ideas are not rare in the search for Alexander's tomb, and will perhaps, regrettably, continue to form a part of the character of the quest to discover tombs such as this.

Conclusions

Ultimately, the tombs discussed in this chapter are a little different from those of the preceding chapters in several ways. The celebrated deceased was not Egyptian, but Macedonian. Both the first and second Alexandrian tombs were probably not of traditional Egyptian style, and the chances of their having survived when Alexandria was a such bustling centre of activity of all kinds, particularly building and rebuilding, but also periodically subject to violent sieges, are perhaps slimmer than for tombs that were built in more remote areas, or at cemetery sites that generally have never been occupied to the same extent. The textual sources provide more information than we have for the other tombs discussed in this book, but they are imprecise and often of dubious reliability.

It is not impossible that the remains of one, or even both, of the Alexandrian tombs may yet await discovery, but it is unlikely that we would find them intact: we know the first of the tombs built for Alexander in his capital city was abandoned, and the likelihood of the second having survived untouched is very small indeed. If any remains survived the waves of rebuilding in ancient times, the sieges, the earthquake and tsunami of AD 365, the gradual abandonment of large parts of the city in medieval times and its more recent redevelopment, they now lie deeply buried beneath the streets of an overcrowded 21st-century *al-Iskandaria*, which has other things on its mind.

CHAPTER 7

THE LOST TOMB OF CLEOPATRA

A mausoleum lost underwater or a secret

burial awaiting discovery?

Of all the characters of the ancient world, few have achieved the enduring fame of Cleopatra. As Queen of Egypt, she was celebrated in her lifetime, of course, but her memory seems never to have faded into obscurity, thanks to the classical authors of the late 1st and early 2nd centuries AD, most notably Plutarch and Suetonius, who ensured her story was not lost. In more recent times, William Shakespeare, George Bernard Shaw and other authors and playwrights have cemented her popularity in the Western mind.

Cleopatra was the last ruler of the Ptolemaic Dynasty, the line of pharaohs descended from Ptolemy I Soter. She was therefore Macedonian Greek in heritage, not Egyptian. Cleopatra ruled Egypt from 51 to 30 BC, ascending the throne just over 250 years after Ptolemy I had claimed it for himself, and was perhaps more Egyptianized than any of her fore-bears. The Ptolemaic Period is fascinating for its fusion of Egyptian and Hellenistic culture, and distinct in the artistic and architectural styles, language, script and religious practices that developed during the three centuries from the accession of Ptolemy I to the absorption of Egypt into the Roman Empire at the end of Cleopatra's reign. Following Alexander's death, Ptolemy I established a Greek colony in Upper Egypt at Ptolemais Hermiou (modern Minsha in Sohag province), and during the reigns of his successors, Ptolemy II Philadelphus and Ptolemy III Euergetes, Macedonian veterans were rewarded with gifts of land and began settling in the Nile Valley. Some of the settlers married Egyptians, and so created a substantial Greco-Egyptian elite. But this cultural fusion had its limits: the Greeks continued to live under Greek law and receive a Greek education and were tried in Greek courts as citizens of Greek cities. They remained a privileged minority.

Because of the series of wars over the division of Alexander the Great's empire following his death, Ptolemy I was limited in his ability to initiate great building projects in his chosen kingdom. His son, Ptolemy II, had the luxury of being able to pursue more cultural ambitions, and during his reign Alexandria, and the library that Ptolemy I had founded, reached something of a peak as a centre of scientific endeavour, learning and the arts. Ptolemy III took the kingdom back into war with Syria and succeeded in marching triumphantly into Babylonia, expanding the territory over which the Dynasty ruled to its greatest extent. After this great victory, Ptolemy III concentrated on domestic affairs, in which he was also very influential. He invested heavily in Egypt's temples and cults, leaving a more substantial mark than his predecessors in the country's great religious sanctuaries, thus accelerating the 'Egyptianizing' of the royal house.

From here the Dynasty went into decline. Ptolemy IV Philopator's reign saw further military triumph, but he gave two of his ministers, Sosibios and Agathokles, sweeping powers in running Egypt and was much influenced by the latter's sister, Agathokleia, who had become his mistress. His successor, Ptolemy V Epiphanes, who succeeded the throne as a child, found himself facing a revolt of the indigenous population not only in the southern part of the country under successive local rulers, but also in the Delta, where the Rosetta Stone records that he was able to put down a rebellion. These episodes of protest by the local population show that the royal line was losing its grip over very substantial parts of the country by this time. Ptolemy V was succeeded by his infant son Ptolemy VI Philometor, but after ten years Philometor was defeated by Antiochus IV, the ruler of the Seleucid kingdom, thus beginning years of successional struggling between and within these two lines. Several more Ptolemies, and a few Cleopatras, followed, against a backdrop of the increasing power of the Roman Empire. By the reign of Ptolemy XII, Egypt had become a de facto protectorate of Rome. This king was ousted by an Alexandrian mob in 58 BC, was restored by the Romans three years later, then died in 51 BC, leaving the throne to his son, the ten-year-old Ptolemy XIII Theos Philopator, who ruled with his sister and wife, Cleopatra VII – *the* Cleopatra.

Her reign thus began at a time when Egypt and the rest of the Ptolemaic kingdom was already perilously close to becoming the property of Rome, and at the same time was threatened from the East by the Macedonian Seleucid Empire.

Pompey, general and consul of the Roman Republic, offered protection to the Pharaoh Ptolemy XIII until his defeat by Julius Caesar in 48 BC at the Battle of Pharsalus. Pompey attempted to flee to Egypt, but was assassinated on his way to shore in Alexandria, and Ptolemy XIII and his counsellors were aware that Caesar was not far behind. At this time Cleopatra was vying for power with both Ptolemy XIII and another sister, Arsinoë IV, and saw an opportunity to turn the crisis to her advantage. When Julius Caesar arrived she lost no time in visiting him (arriving wrapped in a rug, according to Plutarch) and securing his allegiance against Ptolemy XIII. The young pharaoh was subsequently defeated, soon thereafter drowned in the Nile, and Cleopatra became undisputed Pharaoh of Egypt.

Two classic stories: one of love, one of death

The rest of the story is well known. Cleopatra would marry, and name her younger brother, Ptolemy XIV, her co-regent. But she and Caesar became lovers and had a child, Caesarion, together. She, Ptolemy XIV and her son visited Rome, where they were accommodated in lavish surrounds by Caesar, who also erected a golden statue of her in the form of Isis at the temple of Venus Genetrix in the Forum Julium in Rome. Caesar was assassinated in 44 BC. Ptolemy XIV died shortly afterwards, probably having been poisoned by Cleopatra who then named Caesarion as her successor. In 41 BC Cleopatra allied with Mark Antony, and persuaded him to have Arsinoë, her sister and former rival, killed. Cleopatra also famously took him as her lover and they had twins, Alexander Helios and

Cleopatra Selene II, in 40 BC. Four years later Antony returned to Egypt, married Cleopatra and fathered another child, Ptolemy Philadelphus, by her. He subsequently granted territory to their children: Alexander Helios became king of Armenia, Media and Parthia; his twin sister Cleopatra Selene II was given Cyrenaica and Libya; Ptolemy Philadelphus became ruler of Syria and Cilicia – while Cleopatra was made Queen of Kings and Queen of Egypt, and her son Caesarion, King of Kings and King of Egypt, was proclaimed the son and heir of the now-deified Julius Caesar. Mark Antony's rival Octavian, however, had been named Caesar's adopted son and heir in the latter's will and could not accept this. Antony sent a dispatch announcing the 'Donations of Alexandria' to the Senate but they refused to confirm them. His subsequent marriage to Cleopatra, and, moreover, his declaration that he would wish to be buried in Alexandria rather than Rome further enraged the Senate. In 33 BC, Octavian declared war. In 31 BC his forces defeated Mark Antony's navy in the Ionian Sea, near the promontory of Actium on the west coast of modern Greece. A year later, he journeyed to Egypt and again defeated Mark Antony, just outside Alexandria. Knowing that his time had come, Mark Antony fell on his sword. There would be no new alliance for Cleopatra to strike this time and she, too, took her own life; the means remain uncertain, but it is generally believed that she poisoned herself, probably by inducing an asp to bite her. At least, this is how the legend goes.

The tomb in the classical sources

Although the classical sources can at times be frustratingly vague on what we might regard as archaeological information, and must be treated with caution, they can provide us with a useful picture of what we might expect to find. Plutarch, a Greek historian and Roman citizen who wrote a series of biographies entitled *Parallel Lives*, described Cleopatra's tomb and the dramatic episode it served as the stage for at

Left Relief of Cleopatra VII and Caesarion on the rear wall of the temple of Hathor at Dendera.

length in his book on Mark Antony.[1] He writes that towards the end of Cleopatra's life, when it had become clear that she and Mark Antony would not be able to resist Octavian's advance, 'she herself, now that she had a tomb and monument built surpassingly lofty and beautiful, which she had erected near the temple of Isis, collected there the most valuable of the royal treasures, gold, silver, emeralds, pearls, ebony, ivory and cinnamon'. Following Mark Antony's defeat, Cleopatra, 'fearing his [Mark Antony's] anger and his madness, fled for refuge into her tomb and let fall the drop-doors, which were made strong with bolts and bars'.[2] When Mark Antony attempted suicide, apparently believing that Cleopatra had already done so herself, he was carried 'to the doors of her tomb. Cleopatra, however, would not open the doors, but showed herself at a window, from which she let down ropes and cords. To these Antony was fastened, and she drew him up herself', taking him into the tomb with her.[3] When Octavian's efforts to persuade her to give herself up failed, he sent his agent, Proculeius, to negotiate with her. Proculeius 'stationed himself outside [the tomb] at a door which was on a level with the ground. The door was strongly fastened with bolts and bars, but allowed a passage for the voice.'[4] But Cleopatra still refused the leave the tomb, and so Proculeius arranged for another agent of Octavian's to speak to Cleopatra at the door while he 'applied a ladder and went in through the window by which the women had taken Antony inside'.[5]

Cassius Dio, who lived almost a century later than Plutarch, provides a similar account. He wrote of Cleopatra that 'she herself rushed suddenly into the mausoleum…as an invitation to Antony to enter there also',[6] and that when Mark Antony tried to kill himself, 'Cleopatra, hearing it, peered out over the top of the tomb. By a certain contrivance its doors, once closed, could not be opened again, but the upper part of it next to the roof was not yet fully completed. Now when some of them saw her peering out at this point, they raised a shout so that even Antony heard. So he, learning that she survived, stood up, as if he had still the power to live; but, as he had lost much blood, he despaired of his life and besought the bystanders to carry him to the monument and to hoist him up by the ropes that were hanging there to lift the stone blocks.'[7]

Taken together, these two accounts suggest clearly that Cleopatra had had a mausoleum built for herself and Mark Antony, of considerable size, on two floors and with a massive door, 'near the temple of Isis'. But was this mausoleum really used for the burial of either Antony of Cleopatra? After all, it was apparently not finished, and in any case, they were perhaps no longer in complete control of their own affairs once Octavian had seized power in Alexandria. The same sources shed some light on the fates of Antony and Cleopatra after their tragic demise: 'as for Antony, though many generals and kings asked for his body that they might give it burial, Caesar [Octavian] would not take it away from Cleopatra, and it was buried by her hands in sumptuous and royal fashion, such things being granted her for the purpose as she desired,' says Plutarch.[8] Furthermore, Cleopatra 'had herself carried to the tomb, and embracing the urn which held his ashes, in company with the women usually about her, she said: "Dear Antony, I buried thee but lately with hands still free".'[9] Of her own death and burial, Plutarch explained that Octavian, 'although vexed at the death of the woman, admired her lofty spirit; and he gave orders that her body should be buried with that of Antony in splendid and regal fashion'.[10]

The account of Suetonius, another Roman historian writing in AD 121, agrees, stating that Octavian 'allowed them honourable burial in the same tomb' and, significantly, that he 'gave orders that the mausoleum that they had begun to build should be completed'.[11]

Similarly, according to Cassius Dio, Cleopatra expressed to Octavian her wish to die, and to do so alongside Mark Antony: 'send me to Antony; grudge me not burial with him, in order that, as it is because of him I die, so I may dwell with him even in Hades'.[12] Despite her best efforts and fine track record, Cleopatra appears to have been unable to seduce the young emperor, and instead was forced to deceive him into thinking that she would go willingly to Rome as his trophy before seizing her opportunity to commit suicide. Cassius Dio states that initially she remained 'in the building' – the mausoleum – and for a time was 'occupied in embalming Antony's body'.[13] Although she was subsequently taken to the palace, Dio also states that Antony and Cleopatra 'were both embalmed in the same fashion and buried in the same tomb'.[14]

A mausoleum in Alexandria

The grand mausoleum that the classical sources describe would be entirely fitting for a royal couple of the Hellenistic world. Alexander the Great and some other members of the Ptolemaic Royal family had been buried in the Sema in the centre of Alexandria (see pp. 213–16), and Cleopatra's sister and daughter would be buried in similar monuments, albeit not in Egypt: Arsinoë iv in the Octagon at Ephesus, and Cleopatra Selene in the mausoleum built to receive the body of her husband, Juba ii of Numidia, at Tipaza, Algeria. Even without the historical accounts, our best guess would be that Cleopatra was buried in such a monument in or around Alexandria. This was the capital city after all, and it would retain this status even under Roman rule. It was also the place of Cleopatra's death. There is no good reason to suppose that she would have been moved any great distance, unless Octavian, who Suetonius tells us was 'anxious to save Cleopatra as an ornament for his triumph',[15] wished to celebrate his victory in Rome. What are the chances that this would *not* have been recorded in the classical sources, however? Very slim, one suspects.

How have the ruins of such a sizeable and significant building eluded archaeologists? Perhaps Alexandria's coastal location is responsible. Strabo describes the various waterside and island features of the city:

> In the Great Harbour [Portus Magnus] at the entrance, on the right hand, are the island and the tower Pharos, and on the other hand are the reefs and also the promontory Lochias, with a royal palace upon it; and on sailing into the harbour one comes, on the left, to the inner royal palaces, which are continuous with those on Lochias and have groves and numerous lodges painted in various colours. Below these lies the harbour that was dug by the hand of man and is hidden from view, the private property of the kings, and also Antirhodos, an isle lying off the artificial harbour, which has both a royal palace and a small harbour. They so called it as being a rival of Rhodes. Above the artificial harbour lies the theatre; then the Poseidium – an elbow, as it were, projecting from the Emporium, as it is

called, and containing a temple of Poseidon. To this elbow
of land Antony added a mole projecting still farther, into the
middle of a harbour, and on the extremity of it built a royal
lodge which he called Timonium. This was his last act, when,
forsaken by his friends, he sailed away to Alexandria after his
misfortune at Actium, having chosen to live the life of a Timon
to the end of his days, which he intended to spend in solitude
from all those friends.[16]

Evidently there was a royal palace on Cape Lochias – which broadly
corresponds to modern Cape Silsileh – that stood distinct from, but was
in some way connected to, the 'inner' royal palaces. A palace also lay on
Antirhodos, an island in the eastern harbour, Portus Magnus, with the
Timonium, built by Mark Antony, very close by. This monument was
named after Timon of Athens, who used his inherited wealth to lavish gifts
on friends he wished to flatter, only to find that they turned their backs
on him when his money ran out. Following his defeat at Actium, Mark
Antony also considered himself to have been abandoned by those close
to him and sought to spend the rest of his days alone in the Timonium.

This royal quarter is now lost beneath the coastal waters. We know
that the sea level around Alexandria has risen by 1–1.5 m (3–5 ft) since
ancient times. More significantly, however, the land level has sunk by
6–8 m (20–26 ft). This part of the Mediterranean seafloor is also prone
to earthquakes, as it lies at the boundaries of the African and Anatolian
tectonic plates. We know that on 21 July AD 365, a catastrophic tsunami
hit Alexandria and this may have been the moment when the royal
complex was entirely submerged.[17] The seafloor has continued to move
since that time, and large quantities of sediment have settled over many
of the areas of the ancient city, further obscuring what once was there.

As a result, there was very little archaeological evidence of the great
buildings and monuments of the harbour until much more recent times.
In 1961, a statue of Isis was discovered in the eastern harbour by Kamel
Abul-Saadat, Egypt's first underwater archaeologist, along with a number
of other pharaonic artefacts, but no further investigations were carried
out until the 1990s. In 1993, in response to concerns that coastal erosion
was destabilizing the base of the Citadel of Qaitbay, approximately 180

concrete blocks, weighing between 7 and 20 tons each, were placed 30 m (100 ft) offshore as a barrage against the tides. These were found to have been placed on top of some ancient remains, however, and as a result the Supreme Council of Antiquities commissioned a more thorough investigation. This mission started its work in the autumn of 1995 and eventually discovered 2,500 fragments of ancient monuments scattered over an area of 2.5 hectares (6 acres), demonstrating that many of the monuments of the ancient island of Pharos had survived, albeit in ruins.

Two Frenchmen have come to dominate this relatively new chapter in Egyptian archaeology: one, Jean-Yves Empereur, is a scholar with a doctorate in classical literature from Paris's Sorbonne; the other, Franck Goddio, was originally an economist who came to underwater archaeology a little later in life. He is visiting senior lecturer at Oxford University's Centre for Maritime Archaeology.

Empereur founded the Centre d'Études Alexandrines in 1990 and has worked at various sites within the modern city of Alexandria in addition to his work offshore. His underwater explorations have focused on the area around the entrance to the eastern harbour, in and around the promontory at the end of which the Citadel of Qaitbay stands. In 1993, a dyke was to be built by the Egyptian authorities in this area, which was already believed to be the location of the famous Lighthouse of Alexandria, one of the seven wonders of the ancient world. In 1994, Empereur set to work to rescue what archaeological material he could before it was destroyed by the modern construction project. In the course of this now famous excavation, numerous fragments of colossal statues and monumental buildings dramatically emerged from the sea-bed. Among them were the remains of the lighthouse itself, against which some of the immense statues of Ptolemaic kings and queens are thought to have stood. This was clearly an area of great significance for the Ptolemaic court.

Goddio's excavations, however, would be even more far-reaching, and reveal something of Cleopatra's final resting place. In 1992, his Institut Européen d'Archéologie Sous-Marine (IEASM, or European Institute for Underwater Archaeology) was granted permission to investigate the seafloor of the eastern harbour at Alexandria. The area under scrutiny was too large for systematic removal of the sediments that cover the ancient remains, but various geophysical techniques have allowed a more comprehensive map of the subsurface features to be built up. Goddio and his team have identified various features known from the classical texts, including Antirhodos, the Timonium and Caesarium. Goddio's team have also identified the present Cape Silsileh, a promontory extending out into the ocean from the area of the Bibliotheca Alexandrina, as corresponding to the ancient Cape Lochias.

Acra Lochias: the submerged royal quarter

A third underwater mission may perhaps be the most interesting of all to us. In 1997, The Hellenic Institute of Ancient and Mediaeval Alexandrian Studies in Athens obtained permission from Egypt's Supreme Council of Antiquities to conduct a survey to a distance of up to 900 m (2,950 ft) from the coast, along a 3-mile (5-km) stretch of coastline immediately to the east of Cape Silsileh, between the districts of Shatby in the west and Roushdy in the east. This was subsequently extended by a further 3 miles (5 km) to the east. According to the project director, Harry Tzalas, his 'sub-site Chatby 1' corresponds to the Acra Lochias, the royal quarters of the Ptolemaic Period where we might expect to find a royal palace, the temple of Isis Lochias and even perhaps the mausoleum of Cleopatra VII:[18]

> Some 400 architectural elements: large granite and quartzite – bare or inscribed – blocks and slabs, broken columns, capitals, together with broken granite seats, catapult projectiles as well as several unidentified pieces lie on the sea floor. The largest are: a monumental granite base of over 2 m [6 ft] in height, the tower of a monolithic diminutive pylon weighing over 7 tons, and the threshold of a monumental door of an estimated weight of 11 tons. Because of their weight and their important distance from the shores our assumption is that each of these elements mark the site of specific building and are not part of the transported material dumped in the sea as a buttress to the action of the waves. Nor can these heavy pieces be moved by the action of the waves and the swell, so they can be considered as being more or less in situ.[19]

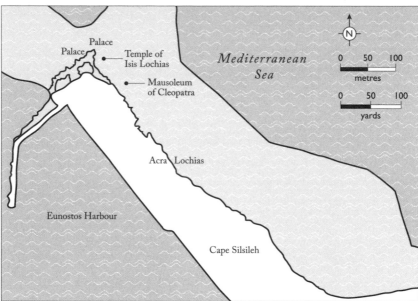

Top: Granite pylon-shaped block, supposedly from the Ptolemaic royal quarters, discovered in the harbour of Alexandria by Harry Tzalas.

Above: Map of the Silsileh promontory as reconstructed by Harry Tzalas. 'Acra Lochias' was the ancient name for the promontory, which is now partly submerged, while 'Cape Silsileh' refers only to the modern above-water area.

Tzalas believes the 'tower of the pylon', which was made from a single piece of red granite, was a part of the temple of Isis Lochias, which may be the temple of Isis close to which Plutarch tells us Cleopatra built her mausoleum. Perhaps of greatest interest is the threshold, which would have stood beneath a monumental door of perhaps 6 m (20 ft) in height.[20] The evidence of a monumental doorway, corresponding to the descriptions of Cleopatra's mausoleum, apparently in situ and close to the archaeological evidence for the temple of Isis Lochias, is intriguing to say the least.

It would seem that the classical sources and archaeological evidence align very nicely here. The former tell us what we should expect, and their reliability seems to be confirmed by the latter. If, indeed, this is the evidence of the tomb as described in the classical sources, it seems it must have been destroyed by earthquakes, tsunamis and flooding.

But there remains the possibility that Cleopatra was not buried in her grand mausoleum; perhaps, contrary to the written evidence, she was refused a 'proper' burial by a spiteful Octavian, or factions loyal to the queen resisted his control and took charge of the funerary arrangements themselves. One current expedition in Egypt has taken this slim possibility as the basis for a quest to find the tomb at a remote site a little to the west of Alexandria.

Taposiris Magna

Taposiris Magna lies 28 miles (45 km) to the west of Alexandria. During Hellenistic and Roman times it was a substantial city, strategically placed on the edge of Lake Mariout, which provided access to the Canopic branch of the Nile and possibly also to the Red Sea via the canal supposedly built by Darius I, the great Persian king of the Achaemenid Empire. It was also just a short distance from the Mediterranean coast. Its harbour was of sufficient size to accommodate a fleet of warships, while the environment provided fertile land for farming and an abundance of fish and birds for that archetypal ancient Egyptian pastime, fishing and fowling.

The majority of the remains of the ancient town lie to the south of a long narrow elevation of land called the Taenia Ridge, on top of which the two most visible archaeological features can be found. The first of these

View of the temple and necropolis area at Taposiris Magna.

is a monument rising some 127 m (417 ft) above the ridge. The main part of this cylindrical tower sits on an octagonal stage: the tower is thought possibly to have been a kind of watchtower to warn ships approaching from the Mediterranean of the coastline, and has formed the model for reconstructions of the more famous Alexandrian lighthouse. It has been noted that it may not have been ideally placed to perform such a function, being some way inland,[21] and it may alternatively have been some kind of funerary monument, perhaps attached to rock-cut tombs nearby. The second monument, the main feature of the site, is the temple enclosure.

The Greek name of the site, according to Plutarch, in fact means 'the tomb of Osiris', and its modern name, Abusir, deriving from the ancient *bw Wsir* or *pr Wsir*, the 'place' or 'house' of Osiris, also suggests a close association with that god. This designation gives the site clear funerary connotations, and it seems also to have been a focus for the festival of Khoiak.[22] This was an annual celebration revolving around the myth of Osiris, Isis, Horus and Seth. Osiris, king of the gods, was murdered by his brother Seth, who wished to take the throne. He was briefly revived by his sister-wife Isis and they conceived a son, Horus, who would

Rock-cut tombs next to the remains of the supposed lighthouse
at Taposiris Magna.

grow up to avenge his father's murder by killing Seth. The origins of the
festival can be traced back to the Middle Kingdom and it survived into
Christian times, Khoiak being the Coptic name of the fourth month of
the inundation season, when the festival was held. Osiris's revivification
was identified with the emergence of the fertile land – a kind of rebirth

View looking out across the temple area at Taposiris Magna, taken from the top of the entrance pylon.

– after the Nile floodwaters had receded. Celebration of the festival at Taposiris is depicted on a mosaic in the town of Palestrina, east of Rome, part of a wider scene of life along the river Nile.

Since 2005, an archaeological project led by Kathleen Martínez of the Dominican Republic has been searching for Cleopatra at the site. As we have seen, both the classical sources and the archaeological evidence – albeit by no means conclusively – suggest that Cleopatra's tomb was located in Alexandria. However, Martínez has formulated a theory that Cleopatra and Mark Antony were buried inside the temple dedicated to Isis and Osiris at Taposiris Magna.[23]

Cleopatra and Isis of Taposiris Magna

Martínez draws attention to the association of Cleopatra with Isis and Mark Antony with Osiris because Taposiris Magna was a place of worship of both Egyptian deities. It is certainly true that Cleopatra sought to portray herself as an incarnation of Isis, both at home and abroad. She was known as Nea Isis, the 'new Isis', and dressed as the goddess on arriving in Tarsus to meet Mark Antony,[24] and again at a festival in Alexandria celebrating the latter's victory over the King of Armenia.[25] Julius Caesar had erected a statue of her in the guise of Isis at the temple of Venus Genetrix in Rome, and Cleopatra herself erected a similar statue on the Acropolis in Athens when she visited in the summer of 32 BC.[26] The existence of a cult of Isis of Taposiris after her death is attested by a 2nd-century AD statue of the goddess that was discovered at Fiesole in Italy naming her as 'Isidi Taposiri', Isis of Taposiris, and she was also worshipped on the Greek island of Delos.[27] This was not entirely unprecedented: several queens in the Ptolemaic royal family had sought to associate themselves with Isis, including Arsinoë II, Berenice I and Cleopatra III, prior to *our* Cleopatra (VII),[28] and possibly her daughter, Cleopatra Selene, afterwards.[29] It could be argued, however, that this association was extended further in Cleopatra's case by the association of Mark Antony with Osiris, and the identification of her son Caesarion with Horus.

A rectangular structure within the Taposiris Magna temple enclosure has been identified as a 'sanctuary' of Isis. From 1998 to 2004 the site was excavated by a Hungarian team led by Dr Győző Vörös. The project revealed what he believed to be the ground plan of the main sanctuary of the temple, aligned east–west in the centre of the temple enclosure. It was here that the team discovered the head of what they believed to be the cult statue of Isis, her head tilted to the right.[30] The style and pose of this statue has been taken to be the same as that in Fiesole, and both are understood to depict Isis in mourning for her husband, the deceased Osiris. While this interpretation may be somewhat fanciful, there is an underlying logic, given the site's apparent association with the death of the mythical king of Egypt.

Ms Martínez's research thus led her to believe that this temple would have had a particular significance for Cleopatra, given its association with Isis, with whom Cleopatra sought to identify herself. Martínez argues that the temple at Taposiris Magna would also have provided a secure place for the burial of a pharaoh at the end of the Ptolemaic Period because of a complex of hidden tunnels inside and outside the enclosure walls.[31]

Whether or not the theory has any credibility, it has certainly captured the attention of the media and the wider public, creating the perception that the theory and the work is very plausible. It therefore demands our attention.

Statue fragment, the face of a male individual, possibly Mark Antony.
Discovered at Taposiris Magna.

The project does not fit the mould of the traditional archaeological expedition in Egypt. The project director has no prior track record of success in this field; Ms Martínez is something of an outsider, in that she trained originally as a lawyer. Her unusual credentials and old-school approach to her archaeology – the sensational quest for the lost tomb of an ancient celebrity – have gained her a reputation as a maverick among academics. She has been assisted during the excavations by Dr Zahi Hawass, who at the outset of the project was the head of Egypt's Supreme Council of Antiquities and subsequently became Minister of Antiquities. Though he has since retired from his formal role within the Ministry, he remains active as an archaeologist, scholar, writer and broadcaster, and his involvement in the project lends it much credibility. However, in over ten years of active excavation, very few archaeological data or interpretations arising from the project have been made available in published form, and there is therefore very little allowing the archaeological community to assess the claims of the excavators. None of this should be taken to mean that the project or the theory is not plausible, and it does not mean that the tomb of Cleopatra will not be found at Taposiris Magna.

We must, however, ask ourselves whether or not there is any good reason to think that the tomb might be at the site. Scrutinizing the project and the rationale behind it is difficult given the paucity of scientific publications arising from it, alongside the many, but generally vague, descriptions of the project circulated by the mainstream media. In 2011, Ms Martínez was quoted as saying:

> What brought me to the conclusion that Taposiris Magna was a possible place for Cleopatra's hidden tomb was the idea that her death was a ritual act of deep religious significance carried out in a very strict, spiritualized ceremony....Cleopatra negotiated with Octavian to allow her to bury Mark Antony in Egypt. She wanted to be buried with him because she wanted to reenact the legend of Isis and Osiris. The true meaning of the cult of Osiris is that it grants immortality. After their deaths, the gods would allow Cleopatra to live with Antony in another form of existence, so they would have eternal life together.[32]

Tombs at Taposiris

Naturally, a settlement of this size and significance had a cemetery attached to it, in this case extending to the east and west of the temple. The expedition has apparently uncovered twenty-seven tombs, typically cut into the ground with a staircase leading to one or more simple burial compartments, exhibiting *loculi* (niches cut into the walls) to receive the bodies of the deceased. Ten mummies have been recovered from these tombs, of which two were gilded. Dr Hawass has argued that: 'The discovery of this cemetery indicates that an important person, likely of royal status, could be buried inside the temple. It was common for officials and other high-status individuals in Egypt to construct their tombs close to those of their rulers throughout the pharaonic period.'[33] The logic here is flawed, however. It is true that throughout ancient Egyptian history, individuals of lower status wished to be buried close to those of high status, including their pharaoh; one might argue that wherever the burial of a high-status individual is present, one might also expect to find burials of lower-status people. But this does not necessarily work the other way; Taposiris Magna was clearly a substantial settlement, and its community must have needed somewhere to bury its dead. The presence of a cemetery dedicated to ordinary citizens does not tell us much more than that people died; it does not follow that we should expect the burial of a high-status individual in the vicinity.

Perhaps more intriguingly, Dr Hawass has reported that 'the mummies were buried with their faces turned towards the temple, which means it is likely the temple contained the burial of a significant royal personality, possibly Cleopatra VII'.[34] This is certainly interesting and may reflect a desire on the part of the deceased to show a reverence towards the temple or a part of it, but one might explain this in numerous ways without recourse to the suggestion that there is any tomb within the temple; most obviously, a reverence of Osiris and/or Isis, to whom the monument was dedicated and whose myth was fundamentally associated with funerary beliefs and practices.

The mysterious shafts

More unusually, a number of shafts leading to a network of underground tunnels have been found in the area of the temple enclosure. One in the northwest corner of the temple was found by Martínez and Hawass to contain two bodies, one of which had apparently been buried with gold jewelry and a snake-handled staff, while the other appeared to have fallen or been thrown down the shaft. The shaft continued beyond 34 m (110 ft) beneath the surface, at which point the excavations met the water table and could proceed no further.[35] In another shaft just outside the southeast corner of the temple enclosure, the lower part of a fine black basalt statue of a woman in the striding pose holding an ankh in one hand and a roll of cloth in the other was found. At the bottom of this shaft, 24 m (78 ft) below the surface, a chamber was found to contain the alabaster head of another statue, this time a male figure.

There is evidence therefore of burials having been made within the temple enclosure. However, there is nothing to suggest the presence of the remains of anyone of royal status, nor even that these were burials made according to proper custom and practice, rather than hurried or even covert or secondary burials. In any case, we know the temple enclosure was converted into a fortified settlement at some point, as happened elsewhere, for example in Luxor and at Medinet Habu; temple enclosures provided ready, easily defensible walls within which to defend against one's enemies, so it would not be unexpected to find human remains within the temple enclosure. The important thing here is that there is nothing to suggest the presence of a deliberately constructed tomb rather than simply the deposition of the remains of deceased individuals.

Conclusions

The critical question is whether or not all of this is enough to persuade us either that Cleopatra never had a mausoleum in the Portus Magnus in Alexandria, or that she did but was never buried there (with or without Mark Antony). On the first, Harry Tzalas's work uncovered good evidence to suggest that there was precisely such a monument, and the remains are exactly where the classical sources suggest they should be. These same sources are also unambiguous in saying that this *is* where the lovers were buried. While we should be aware that these sources are not necessarily reliable, that is not the same as considering them to be wrong; moreover, in this case, the archaeological evidence seems to corroborate them, and the theory that Cleopatra and Mark Antony were not buried in Alexandria, but in secret elsewhere so that the Romans could not desecrate the bodies is in any case somewhat suspect, as the Romans were generally respectful of the wishes of those who would be buried. [36]

In other words, there seems little justification for the hypothesis that led Kathleen Martínez to search for the tomb of Cleopatra at Taposiris Magna, and little evidence recovered in the course of her excavations to support it. Nonetheless, this is a theory that has captured the public imagination, helped raise awareness of the importance of the site and has no doubt had people thinking about and reading up on Cleopatra's story, and that can only be a good thing. And it seems likely that the present expedition will continue to generate such interest while the case remains open. However, it is much more probable that the evidence of the final resting place of this great queen has already been brought to light from beneath the surface of the ocean just beyond the present shoreline of Alexandria.

FINAL THOUGHTS

This book was prompted by a question I have often been asked over the years: *is* there anything left to find?

I always reply that yes, there is plenty more to find. There are dozens of archaeological teams working in Egypt every year, and they are all finding things, all the time. The Egypt Exploration Society publishes a 'Digging Diary' of the work of archaeological projects in Egypt every six months in its magazine *Egyptian Archaeology*, and the quantity of new material being uncovered is staggering. The remains of Egypt's ancient past are scattered throughout the country, and despite two centuries of archaeological work, some areas have never been thoroughly investigated, and even those that have been well studied before are worth revisiting because of advances in the technologies and historical interpretations that can be brought to the material.

In the last few years there has been a regular supply of newly dis-covered tombs, some intact, with their grave-goods in place, exactly as they had been left in ancient times. To find, in particular, a mummy still surrounded by the accoutrements accorded to the deceased upon burial is a remarkable experience. In the early 2000s a Japanese team led by Masahiro Baba and Sakuji Yoshimura uncovered a series of intact burials of the Middle Kingdom in the area of the tomb-chapel of a man called Ta, and inside one of the many shafts that litter the area, they found the coffin of an individual named Senu, inside which his mummy still lay, wearing a beautiful cartonnage mask with a painted feathered head-dress.[1] In 2007, an expedition of the Katholieke Universiteit Leuven led by Harco Willems was investigating the tomb of a man named Uky in

The mask of Senu after conservation.

Deir el-Bersha, approximately 150 miles (245 km) south of Cairo, when they unexpectedly uncovered the burial of another man. After clearing Uky's – evidently plundered – shaft, a second was opened and discovered to be intact. At the bottom, beyond an unmoved blocking stone, the team found the late First Intermediate Period coffin of a man called Henu. The photographs taken at the time of the discovery show the coffin in place in the burial chamber, carefully laid on top of which was a pair of sandals and two charming funerary models, one of three women grinding grain, and a second of four mudbrick makers. A wooden statue of the deceased had been standing next to the coffin for almost four thousand years, and his mummy was found within it.[2] These are the kinds of discoveries that make Egyptian archaeology so exciting, and headlines proclaiming the discoveries of new mummies[3] appear with surprising frequency. There is still plenty more to find.

Will we find them?

So which of our missing tombs might we expect to make headlines in the near future? It seems very possible that Emery had, in fact, uncovered the tomb of Imhotep in either mastaba 3508, or, perhaps more likely, 3518, simply lacking the clinching piece of evidence he needed in either case: Imhotep's name. The two enormous tombs identified by Ian Mathieson may yet be contenders, but even if neither of them is anything to do with Imhotep, it is difficult to imagine that excavating them would not yield previously unknown ancient material of some kind. Although Emery and Mathieson have made compelling cases, in considering these candidates it is important to acknowledge that much of the evidence for a tomb of Imhotep comes from a time when he had already passed into legend. To what extent those centuries-later pilgrims who came to North Saqqara to appeal to him for guidance or healing really believed that they were in the presence of his tomb is unknowable. One wonders to what extent visitors to the supposed birthplace or tomb(s) of Jesus Christ believe they

The undisturbed burial chamber in the tomb of Henu at Deir el-Bersha, the sandals, tomb-models and statue of the owner still in place.

are genuinely in the exact place, or simply happy at the idea that they might be closer than they would normally be to the divine?

The discovery in 2017 of a previously unknown 13th Dynasty pyramid belonging, probably, to a princess, is a good indication of the possibility that there may still be sizeable tombs to be found. The wide area over which the known 12th and 13th Dynasty royal burials were scattered – from Saqqara in the north to Abydos in the south – at sites that have never been comprehensively investigated, suggests that some of the gaps in the record of royal tombs of the period will yet be filled.

The chances that Amenhotep I's tomb may yet be found intact are zero, as the king's mummy was among those found in the 'royal cache', TT 320. It seems probable that one of the three tombs variously identified as the king's is the tomb in question, but Andrzej Niwinski's conviction that the tomb remains to be found and is at Deir el-Bahri is intriguing, as is his argument that the clifftop location he is investigating provides the best fit with the description of its location given in the Abbott Papyrus.

Until the Valley of the Kings really is 'exhausted', as Theodore Davis once famously, and mistakenly, proclaimed it to be, speculation that further intact tombs may be revealed will continue. That it is the central area of the Valley that we know to have been in use during the late 18th Dynasty, and that we also know was inundated with the flash flood that prevented anyone from finding KV 62, 63 and possibly 55, only fuels the fire. There are no doubt those who are tired of the endless intrigue around the possibility of further burials of Amarna royals turning up, but the constant scrutiny of the material recovered from KVs 55 and 62 has led to some significant improvements in our understanding of the history of the period recently, not least as the mysterious pharaoh Ankhkheperure-mery-Neferkheperure Neferneferuaten, whose grave-goods were reworked for use in Tutankhamun's tomb, has gradually come into focus. The discovery of any further material of this period in the Valley could send the specialists back to their desks to rewrite the history of the period yet again.

The argument that Herihor's tomb might be found in the western wadis first identified as a region of interest by Howard Carter, far from the main part of the Theban necropolis, seems unfounded, sadly, and there is little evidence with which to construct an alternative hypothesis, notwithstanding Professor Niwinski's assertion that 'his' tomb, if and when it is found, will prove to be that of Amenhotep I, reused by Herihor. The trail otherwise seems to have gone cold. And yet, the absence of any evidence of Herihor himself – besides the gold armlet of unknown provenance – when so many of the other high-ranking individuals of his era were safely relocated to the cache tombs, remains puzzling.

Although the Valley of the Kings was abandoned by the royals at this time due to the threats of robbery and economic instability, it is clear that later kings of the Third Intermediate Period resumed the tradition of burial at Thebes. Harsiesi built his tomb within the confines of Medinet Habu, while the references to the tomb of Osorkon III in contemporary legal records show unambiguously that he, too, was laid to rest in the area, even if they fall short of giving enough detail to furnish us with its precise location. The evidence of his tomb may yet materialize, along with those of the other Upper Egyptian kings, including Osorkon's son and successor Takeloth III, whose burial places have yet to be identified.

The classical writers provide a richer kind of evidence of the tombs of Alexander and Cleopatra than we have for the earlier tombs discussed here. These sources, as far as we can trust their narratives, provide certain clues as to the nature and location of the tombs, but aligning their descriptions with the archaeology on the ground – or seafloor – is no straightforward endeavour.

While various underwater missions, and that led by Harry Tzalas in particular, have uncovered tantalizing clues that may constitute evidence of Cleopatra's mausoleum, there is still too little for conclusions about her final resting place to be drawn. And though the Taposiris Magna project, based largely on a modern interpretation of an ancient mythology, is imaginative and intriguing, it is yet to reveal any substantial evidence to justify the hypothesis that Cleopatra was buried there.

Of course, it is quite possible that none of the tombs in question has survived, at least not intact, and that in that sense the potential spec-tacular discoveries we have considered will never materialize. But the likelihood that nothing further of these individuals and their tombs will turn up also seems slim. Could there really be nothing more to find of the tomb of Imhotep, when we know vast swathes of the North Saqqara plateau remain unexcavated? Or of the tombs of Amenhotep I, Herihor,

Osorkon III and others who were almost certainly buried at Thebes when archaeological projects continue to find new material in the necropolis, season after season, and even the Valley of the Kings itself has yet to be fully explored? Of Alexander and Cleopatra's tomb, when so much of ancient Alexandria may still be lying underneath the modern city, or beneath the waves just beyond the shoreline?

Sifting through the sources

The subject of 'missing tombs' is inherently populist – sensationalist, even – and by no means every Egyptologist's favourite part of our subject. But this has always been a tension that is central to Egyptology, and central to the stories of those who have sought to find such missing tombs as the ones we have considered here. Sensational claims undeniably have their place in our field, but they can be problematic when they are made without the justification provided by credible scientific research. Bryan Emery's work in search of the tomb of Imhotep was thorough, well documented and published (even if he could be criticized for excavating far more than could be thoroughly published within a reasonable timeframe, which has led to much of the material recovered from North Saqqara remaining unpublished even to this day). In 2015, Nicholas Reeves made sensational claims about KV 62 that were extensively covered in the media, but his ideas were also comprehensively and scientifically articulated in a paper made freely available online from the outset. I cannot think of a better example of scholarly research in Egyptology made accessible to the public. Other projects, sadly, have made sensational claims but have not published their findings adequately, leaving specialists unable to critique their ideas and leaving the public unaware that the claims might be unsubstantiated or even false.

This book deals with a number of projects and hypotheses that have not yet been published in scientific form. I wanted nonetheless to include them so they could be examined critically, and also because some may never, for one reason or another, be published through academic channels. The ease with which material can be 'published' online and the recent trend for announcing the discovery of new archaeological material via the press before any scientific publication has been possible, coupled with the challenge of publishing *everything* scientifically when archaeological material is so abundant in Egypt – there is simply too much for the community of scholars to deal with – has provided me with a wealth of material that is only available in non-scientific form. I have chosen to draw together and balance the arguments for and against the various groundbreaking research projects and ideas presented in these pages, rather than ignore them because they do not conform to the established rules for scientific publication, so that the reader might approach them critically. I have presented my own conclusions while trying to leave the reader plenty of scope to draw their own. If nothing else, my intention is to encourage readers to be critical of what they see and read.

A subject like this – the search for missing tombs – lends itself well to an unorthodox balance of less-scientific over more scientific publication: tomb-hunting generates much public and media interest, which may run counter to the academic aspirations of the discipline, but remains a part of Egyptology nonetheless – and a vital part at that. Egyptology survives, and thrives, because of the special lure it holds for so many people, academics or not. Collected in these pages are just a few of the myriad stories that make ancient Egypt so compelling for so many, both for its ancient cast of characters and for the extraordinary nature of the discoveries that have revealed them to the modern world. As we have seen, from the first days of the pharaohs to the classical era, and from the glittering waves of Alexandria to the dusty wadis of the Valley of the Kings, surely there remains more beneath the surface that will bring us closer to the personalities that shaped this remarkable ancient civilization. There surely *is* more digging to do, and more to find – more evidence of the tombs discussed in this book, but also undoubtedly of other ancient people and monuments who so far have eluded us.

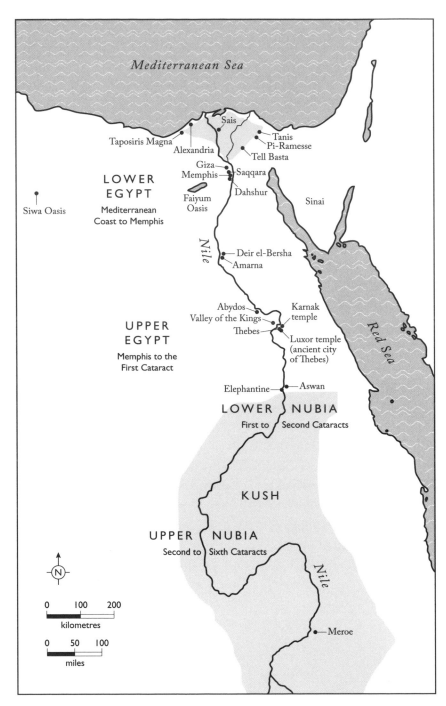

Map of Egypt, Nubia and the Levant showing the principal sites
discussed in the text.

KING LIST

PREDYNASTIC

'Dynasty 0' *c*. 3000 BC–*c*. 2950 BC

Existence Uncertain

Iryhor (?) / Ro (?) / Ka (?) /
Scorpion (?)

EARLY DYNASTIC /
OLD KINGDOM

(1 line of kings, 800+ years)

1st Dynasty *c*. 2950 BC–*c*. 2750 BC

Narmer
Aha
Djer
Djet
Den
Anedjib
Semerkhet
Qa'a

2nd Dynasty *c*. 2750–*c*. 2650

Hetepsekhemwy
Raneb
Ninetjer
Weneg (?)
Sened (?)
Peribsen
Khasekhemwy

(1 line of kings, 500+ years)

3rd Dynasty *c*. 2650–*c*. 2550

Netjerikhet (Djoser)
Sekhemkhet
Khaba
Zanakht
Huni

4th Dynasty *c*. 2550–*c*. 2400

Sneferu
Khufu
Radjedef
Khafra
Menkaura
Shepseskaf

5th Dynasty *c*. 2400–*c*. 2300

Userkaf
Sahura
Neferirkara Kakai
Shepseskara Izi
Raneferef
Nyuserra Ini
Menkauhor
Izezi
Unas

6th Dynasty *c*. 2300–*c*. 2150

Teti
Userkara
Pepy I
Nemtyemzaf I
Pepy II

FIRST INTERMEDIATE PERIOD

(eventually 2 lines of kings, *c*. 150 years)

7th/8th Dynasty *c*. 2150–*c*. 2100

Nemtyemzaf II (?), then
Numerous ephemeral kings

9th/10th Dynasty *c*. 2100–*c*. 2000

Several kings, including

Khety (Akhtoy) I–V
Merykara

11th Dynasty (Thebes only) *c*. 2075–*c*. 2020

Inyotef I–III
Inyotef II
Inyotef III

MIDDLE KINGDOM

(1 line of kings, *c.* 250 years)

11th Dynasty (all Egypt) *c.* 2020–*c.* 1950

Mentuhotep II *c.* 2020–*c.* 1970
Mentuhotep III *c.* 1970–*c.* 1960
Mentuhotep IV *c.* 1960–*c.* 1950

12th Dynasty *c.* 1950–*c.* 1750

Amenemhat I *c.* 1950–*c.* 1920
Senusret I *c.* 1920–*c.* 1875
Amenemhat II *c.* 1875–*c.* 1845
Senusret II *c.* 1845–*c.* 1840
Senusret III *c.* 1840–*c.* 1805
Amenemhat III *c.* 1805–*c.* 1760
Amenemhat IV *c.* 1760–*c.* 1755
Neferusobek *c.* 1755–*c.* 1750

SECOND INTERMEDIATE PERIOD

(eventually many lines of kings, 200+
years)

13th Dynasty *c.* 1750–*c.* 1630

Traditionally sixty kings, including (order
uncertain)

Sobekhotep I
Amenemhat V
Ameny Qemau
Sahorunedjheryotef
Sobekhotep II
Horu
Amenemhat VII
Wegaf
Khendjer
Sobekhotep III
Neferhotep I
Sahathor
Sobekhotep IV
Sobekhotep V
Sobekhotep VI
Ay
Sobekhotep VII
Neferhotep II

14th Dynasty

Numerous ephemeral kings, wholly
contemporary with other dynasties

15th Dynasty (Avaris only) *c.* 1630–*c.* 1521

Six kings, wholly contemporary with other
dynasties, including:

Sekerher (Salitis?)
Sheshi
Khyan
Apophis *c.* 1570–*c.* 1530
Khamudy *c.* 1530–*c.* 1521

16th Dynasty

Numerous ephemeral kings, wholly
contemporary with other dynasties

17th Dynasty (Upper Egypt only)
c. 1630–1539

Numerous kings, wholly contemporary
with other dynasties, probably ending

Intef V
Intef VI
Intef VII
Sobekemsaf II
Senakhtenre Ahmose
Seqenenre Taa
Kamose *c.* 1541–*c.* 1539

NEW KINGDOM

(1 line of kings, *c.* 450 years)

18th Dynasty *c.* 1539–*c.* 1292

Ahmose I *c.* 1539–*c.* 1514
Amenhotep I *c.* 1514–*c.* 1493
Tuthmosis I *c.* 1493–*c.* 1481
Tuthmosis II *c.* 1481–*c.* 1479
Tuthmosis III *c.* 1479–*c.* 1425 with
Hatshepsut *c.* 1475–*c.* 1458
Amenhotep II *c.* 1426–*c.* 1400
Tuthmosis IV *c.* 1400–*c.* 1390
Amenhotep III *c.* 1390–*c.* 1353
Amenhotep IV (Akhenaten)
c. 1353–*c.* 1336
Smenkhkare *c.* 1340–*c.* 1337
Ankhkheperure Neferneferuaten
(Nefertiti) *c.* 1336–*c.* 1332
Tutankhamun *c.* 1332–*c.* 1323
Ay (II) *c.* 1323–*c.* 1320
Horemheb *c.* 1320–*c.* 1292

19th Dynasty c. 1292–c. 1190

Ramesses I c. 1292–c. 1290
Sety I c. 1290–c. 1279
Ramesses II c. 1279–c. 1213
Merenptah c. 1213–c. 1203
Sety II c. 1203–c. 1197 (in dispute,
    Amenmesse c. 1203–c. 1200)
Siptah c. 1197–c. 1192
Tausret c. 1192–c. 1190

20th Dynasty c. 1190–c. 1069

Sethnakht c. 1190–c. 1187
Ramesses III c. 1187–c. 1156
Ramesses IV c. 1156–c. 1150
Ramesses V c. 1150–c. 1145
Ramesses VI c. 1145–c. 1137
Ramesses VII c. 1137–c. 1130
Ramesses VIII c. 1130–c. 1126
Ramesses IX c. 1126–c. 1108
Ramesses X c. 1108–c. 1099
Ramesses XI c. 1099–c. 1069

THIRD INTERMEDIATE PERIOD

(1 line of kings for c. 200 years, then several
lines for c. 200 years)

21st Dynasty c. 1069–c. 945

Smendes c. 1069–c. 1045
Amenemnisu c. 1045–c. 1040
Psusennes I c. 1040–c. 990
Amenemopet c. 990–c. 980
Osorkon 'the Elder' c. 980–c. 975
Siamun c. 975–c. 955
Psusennes II c. 955–c. 945

22nd Dynasty c. 945–c. 715

Sheshonq I c. 945–c. 925
Osorkon I c. 925–c. 890 with
    Hekakheperre Sheshonq IIa c. 890
    Tutkheperre Sheshonq IIb c. 890
    Maakheperre Sheshonq IIc c. 890
Takeloth I c. 890–c. 875
Osorkon II c. 875–c. 835
Sheshonq III c. 835–c. 795
Sheshonq IV c. 795–c. 785
Pami c. 785–c. 775
Sheshonq V c. 775–c. 735

23rd Dynasty c. 735–c. 715

Osorkon IV c. 735–c. 715

Upper Egyptian kings c. 840–c. 715

Details uncertain, wholly contemporary
with other dynasties

Harsiesi –840?
Takeloth II c. 840–c. 820
Pedubast I c. 820–c. 800 with Iuput I
    c. 800
Sheshonq IV/VI c. 800–c. 780
Osorkon III c. 780–c. 760
Takeloth III c. 760–c. 745
Rudamun c. 745–c. 725
Peftjauawybast c. 725–c. 715

24th Dynasty (Sais only) c. 730–c. 715

Details uncertain, wholly contemporary
with other dynasties

Tefnakht c. 730–c. 720
Bocchoris c. 720–c. 715

25th Dynasty (Kingdom of Kush) c. 800–664

Alara
Kashta
Piye c. 747–c. 715
Shabaqo c. 715–c. 702
Shebitku c. 702–c. 690
Taharqa c. 690–664
Tanwetamani 664–656

26th Dynasty (Sais only) c. 672–664

Necho I c. 672–664

LATE PERIOD

(1 line of kings, subject–foreign
domination, 332 years)

26th Dynasty (all Egypt) 664–525

Psamtek I 664–610
Necho II 610–595
Psamtek II 595–589
Apries 589–570
Amasis (Ahmose III) 570–526
Psamtek III 526–525

27th Dynasty (First Persian Regime) 525–404

Cambyses 525–522
Darius I 522–486
Xerxes 486–465
Artaxerxes I 465–424
Darius II 424–404
Artaxerxes II 404 (in Egypt)

28th Dynasty 404–399

Amyrtaeus 404–399

29th Dynasty 399–380

Nepherites I 399–393
(Psammuthis 393?)
Achoris 393–380
(or Psammuthis 380?)
Nepherites II 380

30th Dynasty 380–343

Nectanebo I 380–362
Teos 362–360
Nectanebo II 360–343

31st Dynasty (Second Persian Regime) 343–332

Artaxerxes III 343–338 (in Egypt)
Artaxerxes IV (Arses) 338–336
Darius III 336–332

GREEK PERIOD

(1 line of kings, 302 years)

Macedonian (Argaeid) Regime 332–310
Alexander III (the Great) 332–323
Philip III Arrhidaeus 323–317
Alexander IV 317–310
Ptolemaic Dynasty 310–30 BC
Ptolemy I Soter 305 (as pharaoh)–282/3
Ptolemy II Philadelphus 282/3–246
Ptolemy III Euergetes 246–221
Ptolemy IV Philopator 221–204
Ptolemy V Epiphanes 205–180
Ptolemy VI Philometor 180–145
Ptolemy VII Neos Philopator 145
Ptolemy VIII Euergetes with
      Cleopatra II 145–116
Ptolemy IX Soter 116–110
Ptolemy X Alexander with Cleopatra
      III 110–109
Ptolemy IX (restored) with
      Cleopatra III 109–107
Ptolemy X (restored) 107–88
Ptolemy IX (restored) 88–80
Ptolemy XI Alexander with
      Berenice III 80
Ptolemy XII Auletes 80–58
Berenice IV (queen regent) 58–55
Ptolemy XII (restored) 55–51

Cleopatra VII (queen regent)
      with Ptolemy XIII Theos Philopator
      51–47
      with Ptolemy XIV 47–44
      with Ptolemy XV Caesarion 44–30

ROMAN EMPIRE

(succession of foreign rulers, 670 years)

Augustus Caesar 30 BC–AD 14
Tiberius (Tiberius Caesar Augustus)
      AD 14–37
Caligula (Gaius Caesar Augustus
      Germanicus) AD 37–41
Claudius (Tiberius Claudius Caesar
      Augustus Germanicus) 41–54
Nero (Nero Claudius Caesar Augustus
      Germanicus) 54–68
Galba / Otho / Vitellius 68–69
Vespasian (Caesar Vespasianus
      Augustus) 69–79
Titus (Titus Caesar Vespasianus
      Augustus) 79–81
Domitian (Caesar Domitianus
      Augustus) 81–96
Nerva (Nerva Augustus) 96–98
Trajan (Nerva Traianus Augustus)
      98–117
Hadrian (Traianus Hadrianus
      Augustus) 117–138
Antoninus Pius (Titus Fulvus Aelius
      Hadrianus Antoninus Augustus
      Pius) 138–161
Marcus Aurelius (Marcus Aurelius
      Antoninus Augustus) 161–180
      with Lucius Verus (Lucius Aurelius
      Verus Augustus) 161–169
Commodus (Marcus Aurelius
      Commodus Antoninus Augustus)
      180–192
Pertinax / Didius Julianus / Clodius
      Albinus / Pescennius Niger 193
Septimius Severus (Lucius Septimius
      Severus Pertinax Augustus) 193–211
      with Caracalla 198–211
Caracalla (Marcus Aurelius Antoninus
      Augustus) 198–217
      with Geta (Publius Septimius Geta
      Augustus) 209–211
Macrinus / Diadumenian 217–218
Elagabalus (Marcus Aurelius
      Antoninus Augustus) 218–222

Severus Alexander (Marcus Aurelius
Severus Alexander Augustus)
222–235
Maximinus ii (Gaius Julius Verus
Maximinus Augustus) 235–238
Gordian i & Gordian ii /Balbinus &
Pupienus 238
Gordian iii (Marcus Antonius
Gordianus Augustus) 238–244
Philip (Marcus Julius Philippus
Augustus) 244–249
Decius (Gaius Messius Quintus
Traianus Decius Augustus) 249–251
Trebonianus Gallus & Volusianus
251–253
Aemilianus (Marcus Aemilius
Aemilianus Augustus) 253
Valerian (Publius Licinius Valerianus
Augustus) 253–260
with Gallienus 253–260
Gallienus (Publius Licinius Egnatius
Gallienus Augustus) 260–268
Claudius ii Gothicus (Marcus Aurelius
Claudius Augustus) 268–270

Quintillus (Marcus Aurelius Claudius
Quintillus Augustus) 270
Aurelian (Domitius Aurelianus
Augustus) 270–275
Tacitus / Florianus (Marcus Claudius
Tacitus Augustus) 275–276
Probus (Marcus Aurelius Probus
Augustus) 276–282
Carus (Marcus Aurelius Carus
Augustus) 282–283
Carinus & Numerian 283–284
Diocletian (Gaius Aurelius Valerius
Diocletianus Augustus) 284–305
with Maximian (Marcus Aurelius
Valerius Maximianus Augustus)
286–305
Galerius (Gaius Galerius Valerius
Maximianus Augustus) 305–311
with Constantius i (Flavius Valerius
Constantius Augustus) 305–306
Constantine i (Flavius Valerius
Constantinus Augustus) 306–337

NOTES

INTRODUCTION

1 TT 279.
2 Emery 1965: 8.

CHAPTER 1

1 Waddell 1940: 41–43.
2 JE 49889. The initials here stand for 'Journal d'Entrée', the French name given to the register in which all objects entering the museum were recorded. Objects in the collection that have been published in the museum's own series of catalogues are also assigned a second number beginning 'CG', for 'Catalogue général des antiquités égyptiennes du Musée du Caire'. Furthermore, some objects have also been given temporary numbers, usually with the prefix 'T/N' or similar, all of which can lead to confusion when the same objects are referred to by different numbers in the literature.
3 Gunn 1926: 194.
4 Lauer 1996: 496.
5 Gunn 1926: 177.
6 Wildung 1977: 32–33.
7 Wilkinson 1999: 99.
8 Wildung 1977: 35–43.
9 Wildung 1977: 47 ff.
10 S3507.
11 Designated S2405.
12 3035.
13 In tomb no. 3111.
14 Emery 1965: 3–4.
15 3510.
16 Emery 1965: 6.
17 Emery 1965: 6.
18 Emery 1965: 8.

19 Emery 1967: 145.
20 Emery 1970: 6.
21 Emery 1970: 7.
22 Emery 1970: 11.
23 Emery 1971: 3.
24 Emery 1971: 4.
25 Smith 1974: 48.
26 Smith 1971: 201.
27 Kawai 2012: 41–43.
28 Myśliwiec 2005: 161.
29 Myśliwiec 2005: 164.
30 Mathieson 2007a: 82.
31 Mathieson 2007b: 93.
32 Mathieson 2006: 18–21.

CHAPTER 2

1 Dodson 2003, 49, 54.
2 Dodson 2003, 88–9.
3 Dodson 2003, 89–91.
4 Wegner 2014: 25.
5 Wegner 2014: 22.
6 CT 777–785.
7 Wegner and Cahail 2015: 149–62.
8 British Museum EA 10221,1. See the database record (with bibliography) at https://goo.gl/fnpxpC; last accessed 18 May 2018.
9 In fact, ten are listed but the sixth and seventh entries seem to name the same individual, 'Taa', who we identify as Seqenenre Tao, the penultimate ruler of the 17th Dynasty. Dodson 2016: 59, n. 19.
10 Polz 1995: 14.
11 The numbering of these kings as Intef VI and V follows Dodson 2016: 58–59.
12 Louvre E3019.
13 Louvre E 3020.
14 British Museum EA 6652.

15 Peet 1930: 3738.

16 Weigall 1911.

17 Buckley *et al.* 2005: 74.

18 Buckley 2005: 23.

19 Buckley 2005: 22.

20 Buckley 2005: 23, 25.

21 Polz 1995: 11.

22 James 1992: 93.

23 Polz *et al.* 2012: 115.

24 Willockx 2010.

25 Rummel 2013: 14–17.

26 Polz 1995: 18.

27 Niwinski 2007: 1391, 1393.

28 Niwinski 2007: 1393, 1395.

29 Niwinski 2007: 1398.

30 Niwinski 2007: 1398–99.

31 Niwinski 2007: 1393.

32 Niwinski does not use the word 'immediately', saying, 'He left his graffiti after the tomb closing operation had been accomplished, which limits its date to his lifetime. There were two royal persons living in Thebes in those days, whose tombs still remain unknown to us. The first of these was Herihor, the second – his son, early co-regent of Psusennes I, the King Neferheres…' The use of the word 'after' suggests the tomb might have been closed at any point prior to the graffiti having been written but Niwinski's subsequent emphasis on individuals of this time implies that he means *immediately* afterwards. Niwinski 2007: 1395–96.

33 Niwinski 2000: 222.

34 Vandersleyen 1967: 123–59.

35 Niwinski 2007: 1397. http://www.britishmuseum.org/research/collection_online/collection_object_details.aspx?objectId=111442&partId=1&searchText=amenhotep+sandstone&page=1; last accessed 18 May 2018.

36 http://www.britishmuseum.org/research/collection_online/collection_object_details.aspx?objectId=121230&partId=1&searchText=690+amenhotep&page=1; last accessed 18 May 2018.

37 Arnold 1994: 159; Arnold 1988: 140.

38 Niwinski 2007: 1397.

39 Niwinski 2007: 1397.

40 Niwinski 2007: 1398.

41 Niwinski 2007: 1391. In a subsequent report published after several further seasons of excavation, Niwinski remained 'more than optimistic', although he was still not able to draw firm conclusions. Niwinski 2015: 383.

CHAPTER 3

1 A leading candidate would be tomb WV 25 in the western branch of the Valley of the Kings. Dodson 2016: 73.

2 Davies 1908: 30.

3 Martin 1974: 4.

4 Martin 1974: 1.

5 The Amarna Project, 'Guide book: Royal Tomb'.

6 Martin 1989: pl. 25, 26.

7 Dodson 2009a: 24–25.

8 Dodson 2009a: 18–26.

9 Martin and el-Khouli.

10 Gabolde and Dunsmore 2004.

11 Martin 1974: 36–37.

12 Martin 1974: 37, n. 1.

13 Gabolde and Dunsmore 2004: 33.

14 Davis 1907: 1.

15 Ayrton 1907: 7–8.

16 Ayrton 1907: 8.

17 Ayrton 1907: 9.

18 Davis 1907: 2–3.

19 Bell 1990: 135–37.

20 Bell 1990: 136.

21 Gabolde 2009: 111.

22 Gabolde 2009: 114.

23 Forbes 2016: 18–21.

24 Dodson 2009b: 29.

25 Dodson 2009b: 29.

26 Allen 1988: 117–21.

27 Hornung 2006: 206.

28 Van der Perre 2012: 195–97.

29 Reeves suggests the lobes of the ears, which now exhibit depressions to indicate pierced ears, originally had

holes right through them to allow for earrings to be attached. He argues that while it is well known that, from the reign of Akhenaten onwards, pharaoh was often shown with pierced ears, the presence of earrings is much less commonly attested and only in instances where pharaoh is depicted as a child. While it is not impossible that the death mask was originally intended to depict Tutankhamun as a child, and was then reworked to depict the same individual as an adult, it is more likely that the reworking was the result of its originally having been designed for a woman. Reeves 2015c: 517–19.

30 Reeves 2015c: 519.

31 Reeves 2015b: 77–79.

32 It is worth pointing out at this point that it seems strange that the supposed storage chamber (if indeed that is how it should be interpreted) in the west wall was concealed, when no such attempt was made to conceal the Treasury.

33 A false wall of rubble and plaster was constructed between the two but this was removed by Howard Carter – necessarily, as it would have been impossible to remove the gilded shrines and other large items from the burial chamber intact otherwise; this also demonstrates that it would have been impossible for those larger items to have been put in place had a smaller doorway been present.

34 Reeves 2015a. Available at https://www.academia.edu/14406398/The_Burial_of_Nefertiti_2015_ Accessed 18 May 2018. At that time the paper had been viewed over 246,000 times, which is a staggering number for a scholarly paper in Egyptology.

35 Reeves and Wilkinson 1996: 130–31.

36 Reeves 2015a: 10.

37 Reeves 2015a: 4, n. 32.

38 Bickerstaffe (undated, no pagination).

39 Hardwick 2015.

40 In this scenario the Hwt of Ankhkheperure, which was certainly in Thebes and was a place of Amun-worship, can only have belonged to her, and was as Allen suggests probably the mortuary temple that would have accompanied a tomb in the Valley of the Kings, according to the pattern of the New Kingdom before and after the Amarna Period. Allen 2016: 11.

41 Reeves 2015a: 5.

42 Dodson 2009b: 32.

43 Dodson 2009a: 36–38. Allen 2016: 11–12.

44 Smith 1912: 38.

45 Harris, Wente et al. 1978: 1149–51.

46 Hawass and Saleem 2016: 123.

47 Hawass, Gad et al: 2010.

48 Hawass and Saleem 2016: 123.

49 Hawass and Saleem 2016: 123.

50 See e.g. Smith, himself exercising caution: 'this skeleton is of a man about 25 or 26 years of age', Smith 1912: 38; and Joyce Filer: 'It is clear from the evidence that this was a man between the ages of twenty and twenty-five years and veering towards the lower end of this range', Filer 2000: 13–14.

51 Gabolde 2009: 116.

52 Gabolde 2009: 111–14.

53 Hawass and Saleem 2016: 123.

54 Hawass and Saleem 2016: 131–32.

55 See e.g. Dodson 2009a: 13–17; Gabolde 2002: 32–48.

56 The 'Younger Lady' cannot have been any of Akhenaten's daughters if the conclusion from the DNA study that her parents were Amenhotep III and the 'Elder Lady' is correct.

57 Hessler 2015.

58 Hessler 2015.

59 Hessler 2016a.

60 Hessler 2016b.

61 Cross 2016: 520.

62 Dodson and Cross 2016: 4.

63 Cross 2008: 303–10.

64 Cross 2016: 518.

65 http://www.thebanmappingproject.
     com/atlas/index_kv.asp; last accessed
     18 May 2018.

66 Cross 2016: 520–21.

67 Cross 2016: 521.

68 Dodson and Cross 2016: 7.

69 Hawass 2016: 248.

70 Hawass 2016: 249.

CHAPTER 4

1 Van Dijk 2000: 301.

2 Van Dijk 2000: 308–9. The general
    was presumably the later successor of
    Amenhotep as Chief Priest of Amun,
    however, there is as yet not universal
    agreement as to whether this was
    Payankh or Herihor.

3 See e.g. Kitchen 1986: 248. The term is
    not used here, however, as 'renaissance'
    in the English language refers almost
    exclusively to the revival in art and
    literature during the 14th–16th
    centuries AD. The meaning in the
    context of the late New Kingdom
    is quite different; 'rebirth' is a more
    neutral term but the Egyptian *wehem
    mesut* is preferred here.

4 Kitchen 1996: 250.

5 Payankh's descendants held the office
    of Chief Priest of Amun for a further
    four generations. Scholars had at
    one stage concluded that the Chief
    Priest Herihor was the predecessor
    of Payankh, the office having then
    passed to Payankh and then directly
    from Payankh to his son Pinudjem (1)
    (Kitchen 1986: 252–53). However this
    has now been challenged (Jansen-
    Winkeln 1992: 22–37, and 2006: 225;
    and refuted by Kitchen 2009: 192–94,
    Jansen-Winkeln 2006: 225). Although
    the dated documents relating to these
    individuals suggest Herihor was the
    predecessor of Payankh, as does the
    fact that every other Chief Priest of
    Amun thereafter to the beginning of
    the 22nd Dynasty was a descendant
    of Payankh's, there are several reasons
    for concluding that the order of these
    two individuals should be reversed.

The titles of Payankh do not fit well
with those of his successors, whereas
Herihor's do. Payankh's are more
detailed, showing his rise through the
military ranks, and they are closer to
those of Panehsy, who was in charge
of Nubia from the beginning of the
period of *wehem mesut*. Payankh's titles
refer to a pharaoh as in Ramesside
times, whereas Herihor's do not.
Payankh also never assumed any
royal attributes, whereas Herihor and
his successors did. Finally, Herihor
and Pinudjem I were both builders
in Thebes, and Pinudjem succeeded
Herihor directly in decorating the
temple of Khonsu. Jansen-Winkeln
2006: 225.

6 von Beckerath 1999: 176–77.

7 von Beckerath 1999: 182–83.

8 von Beckerath 1999: 176–77, 182–83.

9 Peden 1994b: 21.

10 Wente and Van Siclen 1976: 261.

11 Bierbrier 1982: 41.

12 A good list is published in Reeves and
     Wilkinson 1996: 192.

13 Papyrus Salt 124.

14 The 'Turin Strike Papyrus'.

15 Papyrus Mayer B. Reeves 1990: 273.

16 Reeves 1990: 275.

17 Reeves and Wilkinson 1996: 191.

18 A date of summer 1871 was apparently
     given separately by three of the
     Abd er-Rassoul brothers and this is
     the date most commonly given in
     Egyptological literature. However,
     various different dates have been
     suggested, including one as early as
     1859. Bickerstaffe 2010: 32–36.

19 Bickerstaffe 2010: 14–15.

20 Bickerstaffe 2010: 16–17.

21 Graefe and Belova 2010: plans 02–06.

22 Graefe and Belova 2010: plan 08.

23 Bickerstaffe 2010: 21.

24 Cited by Bickerstaffe 2010: 19.

25 Bickerstaffe 2010: 22.

26 Freely accessible online
     via the Internet Archive:
     https://archive.org/details/

The_Night_of_Counting_the_Years; last accessed 18 May 2018.

27 Bickerstaffe 2010: 23.

28 See the complete list in Reeves and Wilkinson 1996: 196.

29 Reeves and Wilkinson 1996: 195.

30 Reeves 1990: 277.

31 Taylor 2016: location 7856.

32 Reeves 1990: 277. Taylor 2016: location 7860.

33 Taylor 2016: location 7881.

34 Taylor 2016: location 7881.

35 Bickerstaffe 2010: 21.

36 Taylor 2016: location 7903.

37 Romer 1984: 196–97.

38 Carter and Mace 1923: 79.

39 Carter and Mace 1923: 80.

40 Carter 1917: 115.

41 James 1992: 187.

42 Carter 1917: 107–8.

43 Litherland 2014: 21.

44 Carter 1917: 108. In 1921 Émile Baraize published a report on the discovery of a further cliff-tomb in the area (Baraize 1921), which is now known by his name.

45 Carter 1917: 109.

46 PM I.2, 591–92. See also Lilyquist 2004.

47 Romer 1984: 197.

48 Carter 1917: 110–11.

49 Carter 1917: 111.

50 Carter 1917: 109–10.

51 Carter 1917: 107.

52 Peden 2001: 232.

53 Romer 1984: 197.

54 Romer 1984: 197.

55 Romer 1984: 197.

56 Romer 1984: 199.

57 Carter 1917: 111.

58 Romer 1984: x, 198.

59 Romer 1984: 196.

60 Peden 1994a: 279.

61 Reeves 1990: 130 (cited by Peden 1994a: 280).

62 Litherland 2014: 56.

63 Litherland has noted that these graffiti take the form of signs that have been interpreted as 'tomb' signs, but offers no alternative explanation. Litherland 2014: 24.

64 Litherland 2014: 57.

65 Litherland 2014: 58.

66 Litherland 2014: 59. He considers wadis 'A', 'C' and 'D' more likely candidates for the discovery of further tombs.

67 Carter 1917: 111–12.

68 Litherland 2014: 73–80.

69 Reeves 1990: 277.

70 Taylor 1992: 202–3.

71 Graefe and Belova 2010: 46.

72 Graefe and Belova 2010: 50–52.

73 Eggebrecht 1993: 76.

74 Aston 2014: 46.

75 Noted in a lecture given at the Museo Arqueológico Nacional de España in Madrid in October 2016 and available via YouTube at https://youtu.be/i9y1SiRULXY; last accessed 18 May 2018.

76 Niwinski 2007: 1396.

77 Niwinski 2007: 1396.

CHAPTER 5

1 He was wrong on both counts (although he remained convinced he was excavating Pi-Ramesse until his death): excavations carried out by an Austrian team at the site of Tell el-Daba since the 1960s have confirmed that this was the location of Avaris, while Qantir has now been identified as the site of Pi-Ramesse.

2 Coutts 1988: 19.

3 Reeves 2000: 191.

4 Reeves 2000: 191.

5 Reeves 2000: 190.

6 Holwerda et al. 2009: 445.

7 Coutts 1988: 20–21.

8 Yoyotte 1999: 328–30.

9 Yoyotte 1999: 325.

10 Kitchen 1996: 261.

11 Dodson 2016: 111.

12 Dodson 2016: 110.

13 Dodson 2016: 110.

14 Dodson 2016: 110.

15 Dodson 1988: 229–33.

16 Bard 1999: 947.

17 Sagrillo 2009: 349.

18 Lange 2010: 20.

19 Sagrillo 2009: 357.

20 Sagrillo 2009: 357–58.

21 Reeves 2000: 194.

22 See especially Leahy 1985: 51–65.

23 Spencer and Spencer 1986: 198–201.

24 Leahy 1990: 155–200.

25 Dodson 2012: 108.

26 Hölscher 1954: 9.

27 Dodson 2012: 107.

28 Kitchen 1996: 107.

29 Aston 1989: 139–53.

30 Caminos 1958: 17.

31 E. 7858 (Necho II): 'Peteesi confirms to a woman 6 *aruras* [a measurement of land] in the domain of Amun in Tshetres, which had been given to his wife and which her brother had confirmed to him (Peteesi), near the tomb of king Userton'. Turin 231.2 (Amasis): 'Pshenesi given to Tsenenhor half of a vacant house-site, on which he proposes to build, on the west of Thebes near the tomb of king Userton'. E. 7128 (Darius I): 'You made me happy with the price of this land that is in the waste land in the tomb of the king Wsr-tn on the west of Thebes'.

32 Aston 2014: 23 24.

33 Aston 2014: 28ff.

34 Aston 2014: 38.

35 Dodson 2016: 111.

36 Dodson 2016: 111.

37 Ritner 2009: 496.

38 Kahn 2006.

39 Rawlinson 1909.

40 Dodson 2016: 118.

41 Wilson 2016: 75.

42 Wilson 2016: 88.

43 Wilson 2016: 76–77.

44 Wilson 2016: 76.

45 Wilson 2016: 81.

46 Wilson 2016: 81.

47 Wilson 2016: 84.

48 Wilson 2016: 86.

49 Dodson 2016: 118.

50 Wilson 2016: 89–90.

51 Wilson 2016: 86.

52 Wilson 2016: 90.

53 El-Aref 2014.

CHAPTER 6

1 Brunt 1983: 285.

2 Saunders 2006: 34.

3 Saunders 2006: 35.

4 Saunders 2006: 30.

5 Saunders 2006: 30.

6 Saunders 2006: 37–39.

7 Saunders 2006: 40.

8 Saunders 2006: 35.

9 Saunders 2006: 41–42.

10 Chugg 2004/5: 49. Also the Parian Marble: 'Alexander was laid to rest in Memphis'.

11 Chugg 2004/5: 47.

12 Chugg 2004/5: 48.

13 Chugg 2004/5: 46–47.

14 Saunders 2006: 45–46.

15 Jones 1999: 714–15.

16 Jones 1999: 714. PM III2.2: 778.

17 Saunders 2006: 160–61.

18 Oldfather 1952: 383.

19 It was given the accession number EA 10 and remains there to this day.

20 Wolohojian 1969: 24–33.

21 Saunders 2006: 47.

22 Chugg 2004/5: 182. It has also been noted that the sarcophagus might never have been at Memphis and might equally have come from Sebnnytos, home city of the 30th Dynasty (Saunders 2006: 194).

23 Chugg 2004/5: 183–85.

24 Saunders 2006: 54–55.

25 Strabo, *Geography, XVII.8.* Jones 1932: 33–37.
26 Saunders 2006: 52.
27 Saunders 2006: 52.
28 Saunders 2006: 56–59.
29 Saunders 2006: 61.
30 Strabo, *Geography, XVII.8.* Jones 1932: 37.
31 Saunders 2006: 67
32 Proverbia III.94. Cited by Jones 1932: 35.
33 Fraser 1972: 16.
34 Saunders 2006: 69.
35 Saunders 2006: x, 81. Chugg, 2004/5: 105–6.
36 Suetonius, *'The Deified Augustus' XVIII.* Rolfe 1913: 149.
37 Dio, *Roman History VI.LI.* Cary 1917: 45–47.
38 Saunders 2006: 81.
39 Ptolemy X.
40 Strabo, *Geography, XVII.8.* Jones 1932: 37.
41 Saunders 2006: 82.
42 Saunders 2006: 83.
43 Saunders 2006: 85.
44 Herodian, *History of the Empire, 4.8.7-7.* Quoted in Saunders 2006: 88.
45 Saunders 2006: 89.
46 Saunders 2006: 90–91.
47 Saunders 2006: 92.
48 Mirsky 2010.
49 Saunders 2006: 121.
50 Saunders 2006: 121–22.
51 Saunders 2006: 131–22.
52 Saunders 2006: 136–37.
53 Saunders 2006: 137–40.
54 Saunders 2006: 140–41.
55 Saunders 2006: 142.
56 Saunders 2006: 125.
57 Fraser 1972: 16–17.
58 Saunders 2006: 148.
59 McKenzie 2007: 9–10.
60 McKenzie 2007: 12–15.
61 McKenzie 2007: 19.
62 Saunders 2006: 153.
63 Saunders 2006: 153–54.
64 Saunders 2006: 163.
65 Saunders 2006: 164–65.
66 O'Connor 2009: 39
67 O'Connor 2009: 42
68 Saunders 2006: 179–83.

CHAPTER 7

1 Plutarch, *Lives, Antony LXXIV-LXXXVI.* Perrin 1920: 307.
2 Plutarch, *Lives, Antony LXXVI.* Perrin 1920: 311.
3 Plutarch, *Lives, Antony LXXVII.* Perrin 1920: 313.
4 Plutarch, *Lives, Antony LXXVIII.* Perrin 1920: 315.
5 Plutarch, *Lives, Antony LXXIX.* Perrin 1920: 317.
6 Dio, *Roman History VI.LI.* Cary 1917: 29.
7 Dio, *Roman History VI.LI.* Cary 1917: 31.
8 Plutarch, *Lives, Antony LXXXII.* Perrin 1920: 321.
9 Plutarch, *Lives, Antony LXXXIV.* Perrin 1920: 325.
10 Plutarch, *Lives, Antony LXXVI.* Perrin 1920: 331.
11 Suetonius, *'The Deified Augustus' XVII.* Rolfe 1913: 147.
12 Dio, *Roman History VI.LI.* Cary 1917: 37.
13 Dio, *Roman History VI.LI.* Cary 1917: 33.
14 Dio, *Roman History VI.LI.* Cary 1917: 43.
15 Graves 1957: locations 1462–63.
16 Strabo, *Geography, XVII.9.* Jones 1932: 37–39.
17 Mirsky 2010.
18 Tzalas 2015: 347–49.
19 Tzalas 2015: 349.
20 Tzalas 2015: 350.
21 Vörös 2001: 65.
22 Vörös 2001: 88.
23 Hawass 2010: 200.

24 Plutarch, *Lives, Antony LIV*. Perrin 1920: 263.

25 Plutarch, *Lives, Antony LIV*. Perrin 1920: 263.

26 Weill Goudchaux 2001: 139–40.

27 Vörös 2004: 49.

28 Bricault and Versluys 2014: 9.

29 Bricault and Versluys 2014: 12.

30 Hawass and Martínez 2013: 239. Vörös 2001: 148ff.

31 Hawass and Martínez 2013: 235.

32 https://www.nationalgeographic.com/magazine/2011/07/Cleopatra/; last accessed 18 May 2018.

33 Archaeology News Network 2011.

34 Archaeology News Network 2011.

35 Hawass and Martínez 2013: 240.

36 Meadows 2010.

FINAL THOUGHTS

1 Baba and Yoshimura 2010: 9–12.

2 De Meyer 2007: 20–24.

3 BBC News 2017.

BIBLIOGRAPHY

Abbreviations

ASAE	*Annales du Service des Antiquités de l'Egypte*, Cairo
BES	*Bulletin of the Egyptological Seminar*, New York
BSFE	*Bulletin de la Société Française d'Égyptologie*, Paris
CdE	*Chronique d'Égypte*, Brussels
EA	*Egyptian Archaeology. The Bulletin of the Egypt Exploration Society*, London
GM	*Göttinger Miszellen*, Göttingen
JAMA	*Journal of the American Medical Association*, Chicago
JARCE	*Journal of the American Research Center in Egypt*, Cairo
JEA	*Journal of Egyptian Archaeology*, London
KMT	*Kmt Magazine: A Modern Journal of Ancient Egypt*, Sebastopol
MDAIK	*Mitteilungen des Deutschen Archäologischen Instituts*, Cairo
PAM	*Polish Archaeology in the Mediterranean, Reports*, Warsaw
PM	*Topographical Bibliography of Ancient Egyptian Hieroglyphic Texts, Reliefs and Paintings*, Oxford
SAK	*Studien zur Altägyptischen Kultur*, Hamburg

Allen J. P. 1988. 'Two Altered Inscriptions of the Late Amarna Period' *JARCE* 25: 117–21.

Allen J. P. 2016. 'The Amarna Succession Revised' *GM* 249: 9–13.

Archaeology News Network. 2011. 'Search for the tomb of Antony and Cleopatra continues'. https://archaeologynews-network.blogspot.co.uk/2011/07/search-for-tomb-of-antony-and-cleoptra.html; last accessed 18 May 2018.

Arnold D. 1994. *Lexikon der Ägyptischen Baukunst*. Zurich.

Arnold D. 1988. *Die Tempel Ägyptens. Götterwohnungen, Baudenkmäler, Kultstätten*. Zurich.

Aston D. A. 1989. 'Takeloth II: A King of the "Theban Twenty-Third Dynasty"?' *JEA* 75: 139–53.

Aston D. A. 2014. 'Royal Burials at Thebes during the First Millennium BC' in Pischikova E., Budka J. and Griffin K. (eds), *Thebes in the First Millennium BC*. Cambridge. 23–24.

Ayrton E. 1907. 'The Excavation of the Tomb of Queen Tiyi, 1907' in Davis T. M., *The Tomb of Queen Tiyi*. London. 7–10.

Baba M. and Yoshimura S. 2010. 'Dahshur North: Intact Middle and New Kingdom coffins' *EA* 37: 9–12.

Baraize E. 1921. 'Rapport sur la decouverte d'un tombeau de la XVIIIe dynastie à Sikket Taqet Zayed' *ASAE* 21: 183–7.

Bard K. A. 1999. *Encyclopedia of the Archaeology of Ancient Egypt*. Abingdon and New York.

BBC News. 2017. 'New mummies discovered in tomb near Luxor, Egypt'. http://www.bbc.co.uk/news/world-middle-east-41213024; last accessed 18 May 2018.

Bell M. R. 1990. 'An Armchair Excavation of KV 55' *JARCE* 27: 97–137.

Bernand E. 1998. 'Testimonia selecta de portu magno et palatiis Alexandriae ad aegyptum e scriptoribus antiquis excerpta' in Goddio F. (ed.), *Alexandria. The Submerged Royal Quarters*. London. 59–142.

Bickel S. and Paulin-Grothe E. 2012. 'The Valley of the Kings: two burials in KV 64' *EA* 41: 36–40.

Bickerstaffe D. 2010. 'History of the discovery of the cache' in Graefe E. and Bellova G. (eds), *The Royal Cache TT 320: a re-examination*. Cairo. 32–36.

Bickerstaffe D. Undated. 'Did Tutankhamun Conceal Nefertiti? What is the Secret of KV62?'. https://www.academia.edu/18188424/Did_Tutankhamun_Conceal_Nefertiti_in_KV62; last accessed 18 May 2018.

Bierbrier M. L. 1982. *The Tomb Builders of the Pharaohs*. London.

Bricault L. and Versluys M. J. 2014. 'Isis and Empires' in *Power, Politics and the Cults of Isis: Proceedings of the Vth International Conference of Isis Studies, Boulogne-sur-Mer, October 13–15, 2011*.

The British Museum Collection Online: http://www.britishmuseum.org/research/collection_online/search.aspx; last accessed 18 May 2018.

Brunt P. A. (trans.) 1983. *Arrian. Anabasis of Alexander, Volume II: Books 5–7. Indica*. Loeb Classical Library 269. Cambridge, MA.

Buckley I. 2005. 'Excavations at Theban Tomb KV 39' in Cooke A. and Simpson F., *Current Research in Egyptology II*. Oxford. 21–28.

Buckley I. M., Buckley P. and Cooke A. 2005. 'Fieldwork in Theban Tomb KV 39: The 2002 Season' *JEA* 91: 71–82.

Caminos R. 1958. *The Chronicle of Prince Osorkon*. Rome.

Carter H. 1917. 'A Tomb Prepared for Queen Hatshepsuit and Other Recent Discoveries in Thebes' *JEA* 4: 107–18.

Carter H. and Mace A. 1923. *The Tomb of Tut-Ankh-Amen* vol. I. London, New York, Toronto and Melbourne.

Cary E. 1917. *Dio's Roman History VI, Books LI–LV*. Translated by Earnest Cary. Loeb Classical Library 83. London and Cambridge, Massachusetts.

Chugg A. M. 2004/5. *The Lost Tomb of Alexander the Great*. London.

Coutts H. 1988. *Gold of the Pharaohs*. Edinburgh.

Cross S. W. 2008. 'The Hydrology of the Valley of the Kings' *JEA* 94: 303–12.

Cross S. W. 2016. 'The Search for Other Tombs' in Wilkinson R. and Weeks K. (eds), *The Oxford Handbook of the Valley of the Kings*. New York.

Davies N. de G. 1908. *The Rock Tombs of El Amarna. Part V. —Smaller Tombs and Boundary Stelae*. London.

Davis T. M. 1907. *The Tomb of Queen Tiyi*. London.

De Meyer M. 2007. 'The tomb of Henu at Deir el-Barsha' *EA* 31: 20–24.

Dodson A. 1988. 'Some Notes Concerning the Royal Tombs at Tanis' *CdE* 63: 221–33.

Dodson A. 2003. *The Pyramids of Egypt*. London.

Dodson A. 2009a. *Amarna Sunset. Nefertiti, Tutankhamun, Ay, Horemheb and the Egyptian Counter-Reformation*. Cairo.

Dodson A. 2009b. 'Amarna Sunset: the late-Amarna succession revisited' in Ikram S. and Dodson A. (eds), *Beyond the Horizon: Studies in Egyptian Art, Archaeology and History in Honour of Barry J. Kemp*. Cairo. 29–43.

Dodson A. 2012. *Afterglow of Empire. Egypt from the fall of the New Kingdom to the Saite Renaissance*. Cairo.

Dodson A. 2016. *The Royal Tombs of Ancient Egypt*. Barnsley.

Dodson A. and Cross S. 2016. 'The Valley of the Kings in the reign of Tutankhamun' *EA* 48: 3–8.

Eggebrecht A. 1993. *Roemer- und Pelizaeus Museum*. Hildesheim.

El-Aref N. 2014. 'More ancient discoveries in Egypt's Dakahliya: Gallery'. http://english.ahram.org.eg/NewsContent/9/40/93814/Heritage/Ancient-Egypt/More-ancient-discoveries-in-Egypts-Dakahliya-Galle.aspx; last accessed 18 May 2018.

El-Khouly A. and Martin G. T. 1987. *Excavations in The Royal Necropolis at El-'Amarna, 1984*. Cairo.

Emery W. B. 1965. 'Preliminary Report on the Excavations at North Saqqâra 1964–5' *JEA* 51: 3–8.

Emery W. B. 1967. 'Preliminary Report on the Excavations at North Saqqâra, 1966–7' *JEA* 53: 141–45.

Emery W. B. 1970. 'Preliminary Report on the Excavations at North Saqqâra, 1968–9' *JEA* 56: 5–11.

Emery W. B. 1971. 'Preliminary Report on the Excavations at North Saqqâra, 1969–70' *JEA* 57: 3–13.

Filer J. 2000. 'The KV 55 body: the facts' *EA* 17: 13–14.

Forbes D. 2016. 'The KV 55 Gold Again' *KMT* 27, 3: 18–21.

Fraser P. M. 1972. *Ptolemaic Alexandria*. Oxford.

Gabolde M. 2002. 'La parenté de Toutânkhamon' *BSFE* 155: 32–48.

Gabolde M. 2009. 'Under a Deep Blue Starry Sky' in Brand P. J. and Cooper L. (eds), *Causing His Name to Live: studies in Egyptian history and epigraphy in memory of William J. Murnane*. Leiden. 109–20.

Gabolde M. and Dunsmore A. 2004. 'The royal necropolis at Tell el-Amarna' *EA* 25: 30–33.

Goddio F. (ed.) 1998. *Alexandria. The Submerged Royal Quarters*. London.

Goddio F. and Fabre D. 2010. 'The Development and Operation of the Portus Magnus in Alexandria – An Overview' in Robinson D. and Wilson A. (eds), *Alexandria and the North-Western Delta. Joint Conference Proceedings of Alexandria: City and Harbour (Oxford 2004) and The Trade and Topography of Egypt's North-West Delta (Berlin 2006)*. Oxford. 53–74.

Goudchaux G. W. 2001. 'Cleopatra's Subtle Religious Strategy' in Walker S. and Higgs P. (eds), *Cleopatra of Egypt. From History to Myth*. London. 128–41.

Graefe E. and Belova G. (eds) 2010. *The Royal Cache TT 320: a re-examination*. Cairo.

Graves R. (trans.) 1957. *Gaius Suetonius Tranquillus THE TWELVE CAESARS*. London.

Griffith F. Ll. 1909. *Catalogue of the Demotic Papyri in the John Rylands Library* vol. III. London.

Grimal N. 1992. *A History of Egypt*. Trans. I. Shaw. Oxford and Cambridge, MA.

Gunn B. 1926. 'Inscriptions from the Step Pyramid Site' *ASAE* 26: 177–96.

Hardwick T. 2015. 'Is Nefertiti still buried in Tutankhamun's tomb? Archaeologists examine a new theory'. http://blog.hmns.org/2015/10/is-nefertiti-still-buried-in-tutankhamuns-tomb-archaeologists-examine-a-new-theory/; last accessed 18 May 2018.

Harris J. E., Wente E. F. *et al.* 1978. 'Mummy of the "Elder Lady" in the tomb of Amenhotep II: Egyptian museum catalog number 61070.' *Science* Jun 9 1978; 200(4346): 1149–51.

Hawass Z. 2010. 'The Search for the Tomb of Cleopatra' in Hawass Z. and Goddio F., *Cleopatra. The Search for the Last Queen of Egypt*. Washington. 200–203.

Hawass Z. 2016. 'The Egyptian Expedition to the Valley of the Kings. Excavation Season 2. 2008–2009 – Part 2: The Valley of the Monkeys' in van Dijk J. (ed.), *Another Mouthful of Dust. Egyptological Studies in Honour of Geoffrey Thorndike Martin*. Leuven. 233–49.

Hawass Z., Gad Y. *et al.* 2010. 'Ancestry and Pathology in King Tutankhamun's Family' *JAMA* 303(7): 638–647. http://jamanetwork.com/journals/jama/fullarticle/185393; last accessed 18 May 2018.

Hawass Z. and Martínez K. 2013. 'Preliminary Report on the Excavations at Taposiris Magna: 2005-2006' in Flossman-Schütze M., Goecke-Bauer M. *et al, Kleine Götter – Grosse Götter. Festschrift für Dieter Kessler zum 65. Geburtstag.* Vaterstetten. 235–51.

Hawass Z. and Saleem S. 2016. *Scanning the Pharaohs. CT Imaging of the New Kingdom Royal Mummies.* Cairo and New York.

Hessler P. 2015. 'Radar Scans in King Tut's Tomb Suggest Hidden Chambers'. http://news.nationalgeographic.com/2015/11/151128-tut-tomb-scans-hidden-chambers/; last accessed 18 May 2018.

Hessler P. 2016a. 'Exclusive Pictures From Inside the Scan of King Tut's Tomb'. http://news.nationalgeographic.com/2016/04/160401-king-tut-tomb-radar-scan-nefertiti-archaeology/; last accessed 18 May 2018.

Hessler P. 2016b. 'In Egypt, Debate Rages Over Scans of King Tut's Tomb' http://news.nationalgeographic.com/2016/05/160509-king-tut-tomb-chambers-radar-archaeology/; last accessed 18 May 2018.

Hölscher U. 1954. *The Excavation of Medinet Habu Volume V. Post-Ramessid Remains.* Chicago.

Holwerda E., van den Hoven C. and Weiss L. 'Summary of the Discussions During the Conference' in Broekman G. P. F., Demarée R. J. and Kaper O. E., *The Libyan Period in Egypt: Historical and cultural studies into the 21st–24th Dynasties.* Leiden. 441–45.

Hornung E., Krauss R. and Warburton D. 2006. *Ancient Egyptian Chronology.* Leiden.

James T. G. H. 1992. *Howard Carter: The Path to Tutankhamun.* London.

Jansen-Winkeln K. 1992. 'Das Ende des Neuen Reiches' *ZÄS* 119: 22–37.

Jansen-Winkeln K. 2006. 'The Chronology of the Third Intermediate Period: Dynasty 21' in Hornung E., Krauss R. and Warburton D. A. (eds), *Ancient Egyptian Chronology.* Handbook of Oriental Studies. Section 1 The Near and Middle East 83, Series

Editor-in-Chief W. H. van Soldt, eds G. Beckman, C. Leitz, B. A. Levine, P. Michalowski, P. Miglus. Leiden. 218–33.

Jones H. L. (trans.) 1932. *The Geography of Strabo* vol. VIII. Loeb Classical Library 267. Cambridge, MA.

Jones M. 1999. 'Saqqara, Serapeum and animal necropolis' in Bard K. A., *Encyclopedia of the Archaeology of Ancient Egypt.* Abingdon and New York. 712–16.

Kahn D. 2006. 'The Assyrian Invasions of Egypt (673-663 B.C.) and the Final Expulsion of the Kushites' *SAK* 34: 251–67.

Kawai N. 2012. 'Waseda University Excavations at Northwest Saqqara' *Friends of Saqqara Foundation Newsletter* 10: 38–46.

Kitchen K. A. 1986. *The Third Intermediate Period in Egypt (1100-650 BC)*, 2nd rev. ed. Warminster.

Kitchen K. A. 1996. *The Third Intermediate Period in Egypt (1100-650 BC)*, 3rd ed. Warminster.

Kitchen K. A. 2009. 'The Third Intermediate Period in Egypt: An Overview of Fact & Fiction' in Broekman G. P. F, Demarée R. J. and Kaper O. E. (eds), *The Libyan Period in Egypt. Historical and Cultural Studies into the 21st–24th Dynasties: Proceedings of a Conference at Leiden University, 25–27 October 2007.* Leiden. 161–202.

Lange E. 2010. 'King Shoshenqs at Bubastis' *EA* 37: 19–20.

Lauer J-P. 1996. 'Remarques concernant l'inscription d'Imhotep grave sur le socle de statue de l'Horus Neteri-khet (roi Djoser)' in Der Manuelian P. (ed.), *Studies in Honour of William Kelly Simpson.* Boston. 493–98.

Leahy A. 1985. 'The Libyan Period in Egypt: An Essay in Interpretation' *Libyan Studies* 16: 51–65.

Leahy A. 1990. 'Abydos in the Libyan Period' in Leahy A. (ed.), *Libya and Egypt c. 1300-750 BC.* London. 155–200.

Lichtheim M. 1973. *Ancient Egyptian Literature Volume I: The Old and Middle Kingdoms.* Berkeley, LA and London.

Lilyquist C. 2004. *The Tomb of Tuthmosis III's Foreign Wives*. New York.

Litherland P. 2014. *The Western Wadis of the Theban Necropolis*. London.

Malinine M. 1953. *Choix de textes juridiques en hiératique anormal et en démotique (XXVe–XXVIIe dynasties)*. Paris.

Martin G. T. 1974. *The Royal Tomb at El-Amarna vol. I. The Objects*. London.

Martin G. T. 1989. *The Royal Tomb at El-Amarna vol. II. The Reliefs, Inscriptions and Architecture*. London.

Mathieson I. 2006. 'On the Search for Imhotep' *Sokar* 16: 18–21.

Mathieson I. 2007a. 'Recent Results of a Geophysical Survey' in Schneider T. and Szpakowska K., *Egyptian Stories. A British Egyptological Tribute to Alan B. Lloyd on the occasion of his Retirement*. Münster. 155–67.

Mathieson I. 2007b. 'The Geophysical Survey of North Saqqara, 2001–7' *JEA* 93: 79–93.

McKenzie J. 2007. *The Architecture of Alexandria and Egypt: 300 BC–AD 700*. New Haven and London.

Meadows D. 2010. 'More Cleopatra Tomb Stuff'. https://rogueclassicism.com/2010/05/20/more-cleopatra-tomb-stuff/; last accessed 18 May 2018.

Mirsky S. 2010. 'Cleopatra's Alexandria Treasures' *Scientific American*. http://www.scientificamerican.com/podcast/episode/cleopatras-alexandria-treasures-10-01-31/; last accessed 18 May 2018.

Myśliwiec K. 2005. 'Saqqara: Archaeological Activities, 2005' *PAM Reports* XVII: 155–68.

Niwinski A. 2000. 'Deir el-Bahri: Cliff Mission, 2000' *PAM Reports* XII: 221–35.

Niwinski A. 2007. 'Archaeological Secrets of the Cliff Ledge above the Temples at Deir el-Bahari and the Problem of the Tomb of Amenhotep I' in Goyon J-Cl. and Cardin C. (eds), *Proceedings of the Ninth International Congress of Egyptologists – Actes du neuvième congrès international des égyptologues*. Leuven. 1391–99.

Niwinski A. 2015. 'A Mysterious Tomb at Deir el-Bahari. Revelations of the Excavations of the Polish-Egyptian Cliff Mission Above the Temples of Hateshepsut and Thutmosis III' in Kousoulis P. and Lazaridis N. (eds), *Proceedings of the Tenth International Congress of Egyptologists*. Leuven. 377–91.

Niwinski A. 2016. 'Amenhotep I, Herihor and the mysteries of Deir el-Bahari of the 21st Dynasty'. Lecture given at the Museo Arqueológico Nacional de España in Madrid in October 2016 and available via YouTube at https://youtu.be/i9y1SiRULXY; last accessed 18 May 2018.

O'Connor D. and Cline E. 1998. *Amenhotep III: Perspectives on His Reign*. Ann Arbor.

O'Connor L. 2009. 'The Remains of Alexander the Great: The God, The King, The Symbol' *Constructing the Past* vol. 10, iss. 1: 35–46.

Ohshiro M. Forthcoming. 'Searching for the tomb of a Theban King Osorkon III'.

Oldfather C. H. (trans.) 1952. *Diodorus Siculus Library of History*. Book XVI. Loeb Classical Library 340. Harvard.

Peden A. J. 1994a. *Egyptian Historical Inscriptions of the Twentieth Dynasty*. Uppsala.

Peden A. J. 1994b. *The Reign of Ramesses IV*. Warminster.

Peden A. J. 2001. *The Graffiti of Pharaonic Egypt. Scope and Roles of Informal Writings (c. 3100–32 BC)*. Leiden.

Peet T. E. 1930. *The Great Tomb-Robberies of the Twentieth Egyptian Dynasty*. Oxford.

Perrin B. (trans.) 1920. *Plutarch's Lives IX Demetrius and Antony. Pyrrhus and Gaius Marius*. Loeb Classical Library 101. London and Cambridge, MA.

Polz D. 1995. 'The Location of the Tomb of Amenhotep I: A Reconsideration' in Wilkinson R. (ed.), *Valley of the Sun Kings: New Explorations in the Tombs of the Pharaohs*. Tucson. 8–21.

Polz D. *et al.* 2012. 'Topographical Archaeology in Dra' Abu el-Naga.

Three Thousand Years of Cultural History' *MDAIK* 68: 115–34.

Porter B. and Moss R. B. 1960–64; 1972; 1974–81; 1934; 1937; 1939; 1952. *Topographical Bibliography of Ancient Egyptian Hieroglyphic Texts, Reliefs and Paintings*, I: *The Theban Necropolis*, 2nd ed. by J. Málek; vol. II: *Theban Temples*, 2nd edition by J. Málek; vol. III: *Memphis*, 2nd ed. by J. Málek; vol. IV: *Lower and Middle Egypt*; vol. V: *Upper Egypt: Sites*; vol. VI: *Upper Egypt: Chief Temples (excl. Thebes)*; vol. VII: *Nubia, Deserts, and Outside Egypt*. Oxford.

Rawlinson G. (trans.) 1909. *The History of Herodotus*. http://classics.mit.edu/Herodotus/history.mb.txt; last accessed 18 May 2018.

Reeves N. 1990. *Valley of the Kings. Decline of a royal necropolis*. London and New York.

Reeves N. 2000. *Ancient Egypt: The great discoveries*. London.

Reeves N. 2015a. 'The Burial of Nefertiti?' Amarna Royal Tombs, Project Valley of the Kings Occasional Paper No. 1. https://www.academia.edu/14406398/The_Burial_of_Nefertiti_2015_; last accessed 18 May 2018.

Reeves N. 2015b. 'The Gold Mask of Ankhkheperure Neferneferuaten' *Journal of Ancient Egyptian Interconnections* 74: 77–79.

Reeves N. 2015c. 'Tutankhamun's Mask Reconsidered' *BES* 19: 511–26.

Reeves N. and Wilkinson R. H. 1996. *The Complete Valley of the Kings*. London and New York.

Rice M. 1999. *Who's Who in Ancient Egypt*. London.

Ritner R. 2009. *The Libyan Anarchy. Inscriptions from Egypt's Third Intermediate Period*. Atlanta.

Rolfe J. C. (trans.) 1913. *Suetonius* I. Loeb Classical Library 31. London and Cambridge, MA.

Romer J. 1984. *Ancient Lives. The Story of the Pharaohs' Tombmakers*. London.

Rummel U. 2013. 'Ramesside tomb-temples at Dra Abu el-Naga' *EA* 42: 14–17.

Sagrillo T. 2009. 'The geographic origins of the "Bubastite" Dynasty and possible locations for the royal residence and burial place of Shoshenq I' in Broekman G. P. F., Demarée R. and Kaper O., *The Libyan period in Egypt: Historical and cultural studies into the 21st–24th Dynasties*. Leiden. 341–59.

Saunders N. J. 2006. *Alexander's Tomb: The Two Thousand Year Obsession to Find the Lost Conqueror*. New York.

Smith G. E. 1912. *The Royal Mummies. Catalogue General Des Antiquites Egyptiennes Du Musee Du Caire, Nos 61051–61100*. Cairo.

Smith H. S. 1971. 'Walter Bryan Emery' *JEA* 57: 190–201.

Smith H. S. 1974. *A Visit to Ancient Egypt. Life at Memphis & Saqqara (c. 500 30 BC)*. Warminster.

Spencer P. and Spencer A. J. 1986. 'Notes on Late Libyan Egypt' *JEA* 72: 198–201.

Taylor J. H. 1992. 'Aspects of the History of the Valley of Kings in the Third Intermediate Period' in Reeves N. (ed.), *After Tutankhamun. Research and excavation in the Royal Necropolis at Thebes*. London and New York.

Taylor J. H. 2016. 'Intrusive Burials and Caches' in Wilkinson R. and Weeks K. (eds), *The Oxford Handbook of the Valley of the Kings*. New York.

The Amarna Project, 'Guide book: Royal Tomb'. http://www.amarnaproject.com/downloadable_resources.shtml; last accessed 18 May 2018.

Theban Mapping Project. *Atlas of the Valley of the Kings*. http://www.thebanmappingproject.com/atlas/index_kv.asp; last accessed 18 May 2018.

Tzalas H. E. 2015. 'The Underwater Archaeological Survey conducted by the Greek Mission in Alexandria, Egypt (1998-2010)' in Tripati S. (ed.), *Shipwrecks Around the World: Revelations of the Past: Shipwrecks from 15th Century Onwards*. Available at http://honorfrostfoundation.org/wp/wp-content/uploads/2014/08/16-Harry-Tzalas.pdf; last accessed 18 May 2018.

Van der Perre A. 2012. 'Nefertiti's last documented reference (for now)' in Seyfried F. (ed.), *In the Light of Amarna. 100 Years of the Nefertiti Discovery*. Petersberg. 195–97.

Van Dijk J. 2000. 'The Amarna Period and the later New Kingdom (*c.* 1352-1069 BC)' in Shaw I. (ed.), *The Oxford History of Ancient Egypt*. Oxford. 265–307.

Vandersleyen C. 1967. 'Une tempête sous le règne d'Amosis' *RdE* 19: 123-59.

von Beckerath J. 1999. *Handbuch der Ägyptischen Königsnamen*. Mainz am Rhein.

Vörös G. 2001. *Taposiris Magna: Port of Osiris*. Budapest.

Vörös G. 2004. *Taposiris Magna 1998–2004*. Budapest.

Waddell W. G. 1940. *Manetho*. Loeb Classical Library. London and Cambridge, MA.

Wegner J. 2014. 'Kings of Abydos. Solving an Ancient Egyptian Mystery' *Current World Archaeology* 64: 20–27.

Wegner J. and Cahail K. 2015. 'Royal Funerary Equipment of a King Sobekhotep at South Abydos: Evidence for the Tombs of Sobekhotep IV and Neferhotep I?' *JARCE* 51: 123–64.

Weigall A. E. P. 1909. *A guide to the antiquities of Upper Egypt from Abydos to the Sudan Frontier*. London.

Weigall A. E. P. 1911. 'Miscellaneous Notes' *ASAE* 11: 170–76.

Wente E. F. and Van Siclen C. C. 1976. 'A Chronology of the New Kingdom' in Johnson J. and Wente E. F. (eds), *Studies in Honor of George R. Hughes*. Chicago. 217–62.

Whittaker C. R. (trans.) 1969. *Herodian. History of the Empire Books 1–4*. London and Cambridge, MA.

Wildung D. 1977. *Egyptian Saints: Deification in Pharaonic Egypt*. New York.

Wilkinson T. A. H. 1999. *Early Dynastic Egypt*. London and New York.

Willockx S. 2010. 'Three Tombs, attributed to Amenhotep I: K93.11, AN B and KV39'. http://www.egyptology.nl/3TA1.pdf; last accessed 18 May 2018.

Wilson P. 2016. 'A Psamtek ushabti and a granite block from Sais (Sa el-Hagar)' in Price C. *et al* (eds), *Mummies, magic and medicine in ancient Egypt. Multidisciplinary essays for Rosalie David*. Manchester. 75–92.

Wuyts A. 2010. 'Ptolemaic Statue and Temple Gate Discovered at Taposiris Magna'. http://www.independent.co.uk/life-style/history/ptolemaic-statue-and-temple-gate-discovered-at-taposiris-magna-5538736.html; last accessed 18 May 2018.

Wolohojian A. M. 1969. *The Romance of Alexander the Great by Pseudo-Callisthenes. Translated from the Armenian version with an introduction by Albert Mugrdich Wolohojian*. New York and London. Available at http://www.attalus.org/armenian/Tales_Alexander_Wolohojian_trans.pdf; last accessed 18 May 2018.

Yoyotte J. 1999. 'The Treasure of Tanis' in Tiradritti F. (ed.), *The Cairo Museum Masterpieces of Egyptian Art*. London. 302–30.

ACKNOWLEDGMENTS

If you're reading this book, then I did finally get round to writing it, *and* it got published, and I owe quite a few people a debt of thanks.

Colin Ridler at Thames & Hudson invited me to write something about Tutankhamun. I said that I didn't want to do that but that I had a few other ideas, and Colin could not have been more supportive and encouraging about the 'missing tombs' project, which would never have become a book without those initial conversations. He continued to be a source of help and encouragement throughout the first few months before retiring at the end of a long and distinguished career. I am grateful to him for his help and for all the books he commissioned from which I drew inspiration and facts while writing mine. Since Colin retired, Sarah Vernon-Hunt, Ben Hayes and, most of all, Jen Moore at Thames & Hudson have been supportive, helpful, encouraging and, above all, patient during periods of long silence from me, and I'm very thankful to all of them.

I have had numerous conversations with colleagues about various issues discussed in the book. In particular I'm enormously grateful to Kathleen Martínez and Andrzej Niwinski for discussing their ideas with me in person and inviting me to visit their sites – a joy and a great privilege. Professor Harry Smith, who worked with Emery during his Saqqara excavations and took on responsibility for publishing the results after the great excavator had died, was characteristically helpful and full of information when I asked about the Hasaballah photos of the Serapeum Way. Huub Pragt shared some fascinating ideas about the burial of Herihor; Steve Cross and Michinori Ohshiro were very generous in providing copies of articles they had written prior to publication. Joann Fletcher provided some much-needed support and advice at a very tricky moment when the book was close to going to press. Donald Winchester has been brilliant throughout. Very special thanks to George Hart, who read a draft of the book when I was hurtling towards what turned out to be the final deadline, when much of it was still in a rather scruffy and unfinished state. He never complained, found gentle ways to point out all my silly mistakes, and always had something positive to say about each of the chapters as he went along. There are few people with George's depth of knowledge, or his gift for communicating it to public audiences. This book is infinitely the better for both. Thanks George.

Friends and colleagues in two libraries have been unfailingly helpful in providing me with access to their collections: in particular I'd like to thank Susanne Woodhouse and Louise Ellis-Barrett of the Department of Ancient Egypt and Sudan at the British Museum, and Jan Geisbusch, Cédric Gobeil and in particular Carl Graves at the Egypt Exploration Society (EES).

Essam Nagy in the EES Cairo Office deserves a special mention for arranging, and accompanying me on, a series of visits to the sites discussed in this book. He facilitated access to many out-of-the-way places so that I could get a feel for the lie of the land, take a few photos and stand on the spot where some of the tombs in question might be found. I suspect he, and various Ministry of Antiquities inspectors at these sites, might have thought I was crazy (I am thinking in particular of a visit to North Saqqara to stand in the middle of the desert where there is nothing to see, but where my GPS device told me some very large mastaba tombs were buried. 'But there's nothing here ya Doctor…') but he – and they – never complained, and could not have been more helpful. Shukran gezeilan ya, Essam.

Too many friends and relatives for me to name individually have had to put up with me talking about this book for the last couple of years and have still found nothing but encouraging words to say. You know who you are – thank you.

Finally, special thanks to the special people in my life: Dad, Rachel and Suzanna.

Chris Naunton
London, November 2017

PICTURE CREDITS

2 Chris Naunton 11 Historica Graphic Collection/Heritage Images/Getty Images 13 Gianni Dagli Orti/REX/Shutterstock 14 © Associazione Culturale per lo Studio dell'Egitto e del Sudan ONLUS. Photo Alessio Corsi 25 dpa Picture Alliance Archive/Alamy 30 Sandro Vannini 35 from B. Gunn, *Annales du Service des Antiquités de l'Égypte* XXVI, 1926 (CSA) 37 Robert Burch/Alamy 39, 40, 42, 45 Courtesy of The Egypt Exploration Society 49 Chris Naunton 50 Courtesy of The Egypt Exploration Society 54 Courtesy Saqqara Geophysical Survey Project 61 Gurgen Bakhshetyam/shutterstock.com 68 Michael Johnson, Oxgarth Design 69, 70, 71a, 71b Chris Naunton 74 The Trustees of the British Museum 77 Image courtesy Richard Sellicks 79 The Metropolitan Museum of Art, New York. The Elisha Whittelsey Collection, The Elisha Whittelsey Fund, 1973 (1973.608.2.3) 82 Deutsches Archäologisches Institut Cairo. Photo Ute Rummel 85 Chris Naunton 89 Michael Johnson, Oxgarth Design 94 Chris Naunton 95 Werner Forman Archive/Diomedia 98 Chris Naunton 99 Michael Johnson, Oxgarth Design 104 Chris Naunton 109 from Theodore M. Davis, *The Tomb of Queen Tiyi*, 1910 (London) 111 Chris Naunton 116 © Griffith Institute, University of Oxford (Burton photograph po167) 117 Chris Naunton 118 Michael Johnson, Oxgarth Design 119, 121 Chris Naunton 125 Theban Mapping Project 126 Shawn Baldwin/Discovery Channel/Getty Images 139, 144, 145 Chris Naunton 153 © Griffith Institute, University of Oxford (Carter MSS i.D.176) 155 Chris Naunton 156 Courtesy New Kingdom Research Foundation 163 Image courtesy Margret Pirzer. Römer-Pelizaeus Museum, Hildesheim 169 Keystone/Hulton Archive/Getty Images 170 Photo Georges Goyon 171 DeAgostini/Getty Images 173 Keystone-France/Gamma/Getty Images 174 Michael Johnson, Oxgarth Design 175 Gianni Dagli Orti/REX/Shutterstock 177 Courtesy of the Tell Basta-Project (Dr E. Lange-Athinodorou) 179 Chris Naunton 183 from Uvo Hölscher, *The Excavation of Medinet Habu* Volume V, 1954 (The University of Chicago Press) 184, 188, 191 Chris Naunton 194, 195 Image courtesy Penelope Wilson, Durham University 207 Rizkallah Naguib Makramallah 208 Chris Naunton 211 Michael Johnson, Oxgarth Design 219 Chronicle/Alamy 220 Chris Naunton 222 from Mahmoud Bey El-Falaki, *Mémoire sur l'Antique Alexandrie*, 1872 (Copenhagen) 223 Chris Naunton 224 Daniel P. Diffendale (CC BY-SA 2.0) 230 Chris Naunton 238a Courtesy Hellenic Institute of Ancient and Mediaeval Alexandrian Studies, Athens 238b Michael Johnson, Oxgarth Design 240, 241, 242 Chris Naunton 244 National Geographic Creative/Alamy 250 Egyptian Museum, Cairo 251 © KU Leuven, Dayr al-Barsha Project. Photo Marleen De Meyer 256 Michael Johnson, Oxgarth Design

COLOUR PLATES

i Sabena Jane Blackbird/Alamy iia, iib, iiia Chris Naunton iiib Khaled Desouki/AFP/Getty Images iv Andrea Jemolo/akg-images v–xvi Chris Naunton

INDEX

Page numbers in *italics* indicate illustrations